Partnership and Participation

Partnership and Participation

Decision-making in the Multiagency Setting

Ann Taket and Leroy White
South Bank University, London

JOHN WILEY & SONS, LTD

Chichester • New York • Weinheim • Brisbane • Singapore • Toronto

Copyright © 2000 by John Wiley & Sons, Ltd,
Baffins Lane, Chichester,
West Sussex PO19 1UD, England

National 01243 779777
International (+44) 1243 779777
e-mail (for orders and customer service enquiries): cs-books@wiley.co.uk
Visit our Home Page on http://www.wiley.co.uk
or http://www.wiley.com

Other Wiley Editorial Offices

John Wiley & Sons, Inc., 605 Third Avenue,
New York, NY 10158-0012, USA

WILEY-VCH GmbH, Pappelallee 3,
D-69469 Weinheim, Germany

Jacaranda Wiley Ltd, 33 Park Road, Milton,
Queensland 4064, Australia

John Wiley & Sons (Asia) Pte Ltd, 2 Clementi Loop #02-01,
Jin Xing Distripark, Singapore 129809

John Wiley & Sons (Canada) Ltd, 22 Worcester Road,
Rexdale, Ontario M9W 1L1, Canada

HD
30.23
.T35
2000

British Library Cataloguing in Publication Data
A catalogue record for this book is available from the British Library

ISBN 0-471-72031-3

Typeset in 10.75/12pt Palatino by C.K.M. Typesetting, Salisbury, Wiltshire
Printed and bound in Great Britain by Bookcraft (Bath) Ltd, Midsomer Norton, Somerset
This book is printed on acid-free paper responsibly manufactured from sustainable
forestry, in which at least two trees are planted for each one used for paper production.

Dedication

In memory of John D. Smith
Foundation Professor of Computing and Head of Department
Central Queensland University
1973–1995

John was someone we are proud to call a friend and colleague, with whom we have shared many discussions about pragmatic pluralism and the need for its practice to be suffused with passion. He was steadfast in his encouragement that we should write this book, we are only sorry that he is not able to see the final result and to continue the discussions around the different issues involved – John died in August 1995, while we were en route to Australia to visit him and his colleagues.

Contents

Contents

Acknowledgements

We always enjoy reading the acknowledgement sections in books and tracing out the interconnections they add to the text itself. In writing this we are conscious that it is impossible to name all the individuals and groups who have shaped the work and the writing of this text – even though they may never have read a word of what is written here (and indeed some of them might wish to distance themselves from its content!).

We would like to thank first of all, all the individuals, groups and organisations that we have been privileged enough to work with in the diversity of multiagency settings where our practice has been based, in all the different sectors in which we have worked, in the UK and overseas, over the course of the many years that have elapsed since the mid 1970s. Without the opportunities this work has provided, we could not have written this book. These thanks also extend to our students, past and present, who have always asked challenging questions and provoked interesting debate.

Obviously, we cannot mention everyone by name, but we would like to provide particular thanks and acknowledgements to some individuals (in alphabetical order by first name): Alison West, Antoinette Ntuli, Anwara Ali, Bob Flood, Bui Dang Ha Doan, Charles Ritchie, Chrissie Bligh, Christine Sheppard, David Woodhead, Dawn Susan, Debbie Clayton, Dee Voce, Deirdre Babalola, Gerald Midgley, Gibson Burrell, Gillian Rose, Gordon Sturrock, Hugh Miser, Jahanara Loqueman, Jean-Paul Jardel, Joanne Barrie, John D. Smith, John Friend, Jola Scicinska, Judy Yewdale, Keith Barnard, Lindon Neil, Lisa Bateman, Liz Katis, Marion Gibbon, Mehul Kotecha, Michel Thuriaux, Mike Jackson, Mohammed K. Absar, Mosula Ntshona, Myra Garrett, Norma Romm, Red Collins, Richard Clark, Ron Draper, Rosie Gowing, Sarabajaya Kumar, Shaun Coffey, Sorrel Pindar, Trevor Jago, Vanilla Beer, Wendy Gregory and Yap Hi Chu. Whether they realise it or not, each of them has provided some very positive stimuli for this work.

Finally, but not least, many thanks to Nic Barnard and Catherine O'Donnell for moral and intellectual support, to the inter-library loan section at South Bank University library for tirelessly pursuing numerous references and to Diane Taylor at Wiley for contracting us to write the book.

Preface

This book is not:

- the provision of a grand theory
- the presentation of recipes to be slavishly followed
- comprehensive and all-embracing

This book is:

- informed by research, ours and others
- informed by practice and action, ours and others
- informed by theorising about practice
- intended to stimulate debate and practice

The book presents a framework that we have developed, called PANDA (participatory appraisal of needs and development of action), which we use as we plan and implement group working and group decision-making in the multiagency setting. We developed PANDA in the process of critically reflecting on our own practice and that of others. Underlying PANDA are a number of theoretical principles, which we label pragmatic pluralism. PANDA is based on a theoretical stance that we unashamedly label poststructuralist or postmodernist, and as such, makes no grand claims for being uniquely justifiable, or for guaranteeing success in application. PANDA represents one particular type of multimethodology.

This book describes how we have worked/work together with groups, it describes the methods and techniques we draw on, culled from a variety of sources and used sometimes whole, sometimes in part only, but always in response to what emerges as appropriate in the local context concerned. It reviews some of the research which supports the approach. It contains a number of case studies, which illustrate the points made and the methods of working described. It aims to be descriptive, not prescriptive.

It is explicitly offered not as a replacement for Rosenhead (*Rational analysis for a problematic world*, 1989, Wiley), Bryant (*Problem management*, 1989, Wiley), Flood and Jackson (*Creative problem solving*, 1991, Wiley), Eden and Radford (*Tackling strategic problems*, 1990, Sage), Huxham (*Creating collaborative advantage*, 1996, Sage) or Eden and Ackermann (*Making strategy: the journey of strategic management*, 1998, Sage). In our view it is a complement to them. What is distinctive about this book is that we ground our work in a postmodern, poststructuralist position. Everyone will have their own preference as to which they find most helpful, or perhaps it will be only bits from each and they might write their own version of pragmatic pluralism and produce their own book.

It is necessarily an unfinished product, or, if this sounds more positive, a work in progress.

It is a call to use diverse sources when planning and implementing work in the multiagency setting.

To emphasise, this is a book that offers no guarantees! No, rather to be playful, it does offer one paradoxical guarantee:

> A paradoxical guarantee: this book offers no guarantees

Furthermore, we wish to suggest that the possibility of any guarantee (even or especially the above one) should be questioned. We do not set out to prove that adopting method A in situation B is guaranteed to achieve an outcome desirable according to criteria C. From the perspective we adopt, we argue that such knowledge is unattainable (a version of Heisenberg's uncertainty principle in the social setting if you will). So, while for us the strong questions such as 'what methodology will guarantee improved decision-making in these circumstances?' are unanswerable and thus represent a diversion, this does not mean that we are left completely bereft of questions that we can ask and use to inform our practice. Instead we might focus on questions such as: 'which methods engage this group of people in the work?', 'were the results obtained satisfactory to the different participants?', 'was any particular group unable to participate?', 'were existing power relations challenged or reinforced?' Notice that we have shifted our focus to questions that are highly local in nature, are contingent and furthermore are dynamic. Note also that the answers will not necessarily all point in the same direction, choices will have to be made and a particular ethical/political standpoint adopted (either explicitly or implicitly). We note the diversity in the groups that we work with and argue that diversity in methods and process is needed to respond to this diversity, to allow equal access to participation in process (an ethical principle we wish to uphold).

Besides the highly local nature of these questions, there are also more general questions that we can ask, provided that we do not expect simple, deterministic/prescriptive answers to be possible. Such questions include:

- What is to be done?
- How shall we decide what to do?
- What can guide our actions?

This book presents a series of partial and personal answers to these questions. Some, we hope, will find it useful and stimulating. No one we hope, will find it provides all the answers they ever need.

Before commencing, a word about our use of the term 'multiagency setting'. This is intended to be read in multiple ways, based on different interpretations of the agent who exerts agency, or different levels of agency. The agent might be an individual, a group of individuals, a department or division in an organisation, an entire organisation or a 'community'. Whichever, as we indicate in our discussions later, we find it unhelpful to conceive of agents as homogeneous entities (at whichever level); multiple agendas and stances, values and principles need to be recognised within each agent (here we draw explicitly on postmodern/poststructuralist and social constructionist notions of identity as always contingent, multiple, dynamic and continually in the process of making and remaking themselves in interaction with the context in which they find themselves). Thus at the extreme, the situation of a single individual reflecting on a decision he or she is about to make (where to go on holiday, how to spend the vast royalties that will accrue from this book, etc.) can be regarded as a multiagency setting, given the diversity of jostling (and not necessarily complementary) agendas the individual will have associated with different facets of their lived material circumstances (social, cultural, religious, spiritual, work, demographic, etc.).

So we find our PANDA framework relevant in a multidimensional spectrum of multiagency settings:

- an individual making a decision
- a voluntary sector group planning and acting
- decision-making within a single organisation
- decision-making involving multiple organisations and individuals

In the context of what we have just said, two quotes seem particularly apposite. First, in the words of Roy Jacques (1989:708):

> A world of multiple knowledge frameworks is not valueless: it is a world of possibility and or responsibility. It is a world in which we refuse to use 'objectivity' as a reason for avoiding personal involvement in our knowledge productions.

Second, from Deleuze and Guatarri (1980:3)

> The two of us wrote Anti-Oedipus together. Since each of us was several, there was already quite a crowd. Here we have made use of everything that came within range, what was closest as well as farthest away. We have assigned clever pseudonyms to prevent recognition. Why have we kept our own names? Out of habit, purely out of habit. To make ourselves unrecognizable in turn. To render imperceptible, not

ourselves, but what makes us act, feel, and think. Also because it's nice to talk like everybody else, to say the sun rises, when everybody knows it's only a manner of speaking. To reach, not the point where one no longer says I, but the point where it is no longer of any importance whether one says I. We are no longer ourselves. Each will know his own. We have been aided, inspired, multiplied.

A WORD ON FORMAT

As we have indicated, the book is littered with examples from our practice. To aid cross-referencing and location of these, most of them are contained within 'Boxes' or Tables.

Finally, to repeat an adaptation from an early joint paper, as a kind of 'health warning' for what you are about to receive (may you be truly grateful): 'Hampered by the limitations of linear text — this book may seem bitty, fragmented, chaotic, incomplete. This is *not* a flaw, this is part of the point. There is not, will not be, should not be, a single possible reading of this text, the aim is to multiply possibility and choice, not to constrain it, the aim is to liberate' (adapted from Taket and White, 1993:880).

Multiagency working   I

Part I begins by introducing the context and various models for multiagency work in Chapter 1. This provides the necessary background to review the processes and methodologies that have been adopted in these settings as forms of organisation of multiagency work. In discussing the 'New Times' in which we find ourselves, our concern is to describe the context we find ourselves in and indicate why this implies a need for multiagency work. This is done in broad brush strokes, a bricolage of different pieces, rather than a detailed and comprehensive history of this present. We do not attempt to account for the arrival of the New Times, this would require an entirely different book!

Chapter 2 then goes on to deepen the discussion of models for multiagency working through the brief consideration of various empirical studies, drawing on the work of ourselves and others. The chapter will explore various views about the pros and cons of group working, and discuss different understandings of barriers and facilitating factors. These will include the diversity involved in the multiagency setting due to different individual and organisational characteristics, one of which is organisational culture. Chapter 2 concludes by summarising the discussion in the form of challenges which must be addressed if multiagency work is to be successful.

The final chapter in Part I, Chapter 3, then presents a critical review of a number of different approaches that purport to support multiagency working, in order to illustrate why we need to look at new ways of working with multiagencies. We look at methods from management science, systems science and development practice. Aspects of the implicit and explicit assumptions on which they are based are then explored using a deconstructive approach. In particular we identify how the use of unsupported binary assumptions and the unexamined role of experts/analysts within these methods lead to difficulties in dealing with diversity and enabling participation in an empowering way. In examining methods from development practice, we find that they are weak at developing action.

Introduction to the multiagency setting

1

INTRODUCTION

This chapter begins by introducing recent transformations in organisational life, including moves towards multiagency work, and more participatory, democratic and empowering forms of decision-making. The chapter will explicitly address the issue of relevance of multiagency work to the different sectors (private, public, voluntary, community) and demonstrate how recent changes in all of the sectors are bringing about a certain degree of convergence in organisational structure and processes. As we show, the multiagency setting often involves partners from two or more different sectors. Descriptions of the range of multiagency settings will be provided, and the range of models according to which multiagency work has been organised will be introduced.

The chapter describes the context for an interest in multiagency work, delineating the 'New Times' we find ourselves in. In what follows we discuss factors leading to the need for changes in organisational life and providing drivers for multiagency work along four different dimensions: the socio-economic; the cultural; the political; and the environmental. These are considered in turn and we note how many of the theorists discussed address the changes in accordance with two or more of these dimensions. Finally, the chapter will go on to introduce how and in what way organisations have responded to these changes, preparatory to deepening this discussion in Chapter 2.

THE CONTEXT – CHANGING TIMES: POSTMODERNITY – THE 'NEW TIMES'

In order to describe the 'New Times' in which we find ourselves, we begin by adopting the method of juxtaposing recent discourses with slightly older ones, from a number of fields in turn: government, organisation, operational research.

First from the field of government, the following quote illustrates some of the key terms which are used to describe the new forms of government:

> Entrepreneurial governments promote competition between service providers. They empower citizens by pushing control out of the bureaucracy, into the community. They measure the performance of their agencies, focusing not on inputs, but on outcomes. They are driven by their goals – their missions – not by their rules and regulations. They re-define their clients as customers and offer them choices between schools, between training programmes, between housing options. They prevent problems before they emerge, rather than simply offering services afterwards. ... They decentralise authority, embracing participatory management. ... They focus not simply on providing public services, but on catalysing all sectors – public, private and voluntary – into action to solve their community's problems (Osborne and Gaebler, 1992:19–20).

The features that Osborne and Gaebler describe are reflected in the changing forms of the civil service and local government bureaucracies, leading to the potential for reshaping governance in ways which support initiatives and action at local level. We can contrast this with Weber's earlier description of bureaucracy as a centralised, hierarchised, proceduralised structure, the 'old times', in the words of Reed (1992:6): 'rational bureaucracy, as exemplified in formal organizational structures characterized by extreme internal differentiation and rigid hierarchical control, constituted a universalizable solution to the problem of achieving operational efficiency and effectiveness in conditions of environmental uncertainty'. We can make this comparison explicit by contrasting some key terms of the old and new bureaucracies (see Table 1.1).

Moving on, we can see similar shifts observed in texts on organisation, for example: 'there appears to be much unspoken support for Heraclitus' contention that "no man steps in the same river twice" and a wide acceptance of such terms as

Table 1.1   Key Terms in the Discourses of the Old and New Times

The New	The Old
Competition	Rational comprehensive planning
Missions	Operational efficiency and effectiveness
Customers	Objects
Choices/flexibility	Universalisable solution
Decentralise	Centralise
Participatory	Hierarchical

"flux", "chaos" and "turbulent environment" as being meaningful descriptors of organizational life in the 1980s' (Burrell, 1992: 165).

In order to illustrate some of the different new forms of organisation we present some examples from the private sector, together with some parallels in the public sector. First the trend towards decentralisation and much flatter organizational forms, noted as an established trend by many including, for example, Drucker (1993). In terms of specific examples, Peters (in a seminar broadcast on *Arena*, BBC2, December 1993) describes a heavy engineering multinational with a work-force of 200 000, which has now been reorganised into 1300 separate organisations, with only four hierarchical levels. Within the public sector, the UK's NHS reforms enacted in 1991 have introduced organisational fragmentation, with the creation of health service trusts and GP fundholders, the separation of purchaser and provider functions and the creation of quasi-markets. The popular cartoonist Steve Bell summarises this graphically as the splitting of the NHS into 'individual bite-sized self-governing units' (Bell, 1990). Similar trends can be found within many other health systems in Europe. The growth of contracting out or outsourcing, found in both public and private sectors, provides a further example.

A second example given by Peters (in a seminar broadcast on *Arena*, BBC2, December 1993) illustrates the growth of new organisational forms; a Copenhagen-based hearing aid company has created what Peters refers to as a 'spaghetti organisation'. Individual members of staff each have a mobile desk which can be pushed around an open plan office to create the necessary (temporary) teams to work on particular projects, staff are expected to work at different jobs. The same company has also adopted the philosophy of the paperless office, with incoming mail scanned onto a computer and the originals destroyed. Within the public sector, again in the UK NHS, there are strong parallels to be found in the matrix management schemes adopted in some health authorities as well as in the collaborative working arrangements created between staff of health authorities and family health service authorities to allow for joint work prior to the existence of enabling legislation that permitted merger of the two types of authority. Another related example would be the case of the 'cyber' or 'virtual' office, a development of homeworking, utilising e-mail and the various global electronic networks like the Internet, etc. to facilitate remote working.

A final example quoted by Peters is the case of a London design firm, illustrating the operation of different motives than profit as the centrepiece of a company's mission. He quotes this firm as espousing a philosophy of employing 'wackos' and of 'diversifying for fun', on the basis that this will lead the firm into interesting new areas, ensuring change and growth.

All these shifts can be exemplified in the (sometimes apocalyptic) language of change adopted by the management gurus, for example:

> Every organization must prepare for the abandonment of everything it does (Drucker, quoted by Peters in a seminar broadcast on *Arena*, BBC2, December 1993)

> Crazy times require crazy organizations (Peters in a seminar broadcast on *Arena*, BBC2, December 1993)
> the New Times require 'perpetual revolution and reinvention' (Peters in a seminar broadcast on *Arena*, BBC2, December 1993)

Slightly less dramatically, we have Greg Parston noting:

> Re-engineering entails fundamental, radical and dramatic change in existing work processes, requiring a clear focus on customers and top management leadership. The results mean a shift from departmental hierarchies to process teams, from simple tasks to multi-dimensional work, and from a culture of supervisions and protectionism to one of coaching and productivity (Parston, 1994:19).

The shift has also been noticed within operational research (OR): 'Operational research is alive and well precisely because it is capable of evolving to meet the changing needs of the organisations it serves.... Moreover, OR takes different forms in different places and we should applaud the diversity' (Rapley, 1993:634). This has affected (and continues to affect) the way OR is practised, as discussed in Taket and White (1993) who contrast the old and new times in terms of OR practice.

Thus: 'We are living in a period of change that is qualitatively and quantitatively different from that typical of most of this century' (Pahl, 1988:4). This view is in keeping with the general one that describes the old order, characterised by hierarchy, centralisation and bureaucracy, as being swept away, and being replaced by non-hierarchical, decentralised and empowering forms of organisation(s). Organisational life is being transformed from above, below and from within (Lash and Urry, 1987). Lash and Urry present a theory of disorganised capitalism as a dynamic that encompasses processes as diverse as deindustrialisation, restructuring, changing patterns of organisational working and political and cultural change. The position has been summarised as one where current societal problems are varied and complex, and dealing with them is not easy.

Within this changing context, it has been claimed by a number of commentators that centralisation, hierarchy and bureaucracy no longer work. Lash and Urry (1987) argue that, in response to the changing situation, organisations have increasingly used subcontracting, outsourcing, licensing and franchising to externalise activities that have traditionally been managed internally.

At present there is a policy drive to build effective and sustainable partnerships and collaborations across organisations and sectors, in the belief that partnership working holds out the possibility of producing synergy or collaborative advantage in the solution of organisational issues. Making partnerships work is a major challenge, and only recently has there been an interest in this subject in the literature. However, signs of a need for understanding multiagency work have been around for the last 20 years. Many commentators have pointed out that our socio-economic, cultural and political environment is changing. Some have named the change as a move into the post-industrial, post-Fordism or postmodernity. There are key differences between these scenarios, yet they share the view that we are experiencing uncertainty in organisational life and that this uncertainty will continue in the foreseeable future. This chapter will summarise some of these views in order to describe the background to the demand for change. It will then go on to argue that much of the writings on organisational change indicate that the demand for change has outstripped the ability to respond to the changing environment. Finally, the chapter will go on to introduce how and in what way organisations have responded to these changes, preparatory to deepening this discussion in the next chapter.

In what follows we discuss the changes in organisational life along four different dimensions: the socio-economic; the cultural; the political; and the environmental. Many of the theorists address the change in accordance with two or more of these dimensions. We shall detail some of the major ideas below.

CONDITIONS GIVING RISE TO NEED FOR MULTIAGENCY WORKING – THE SOCIO-ECONOMIC DIMENSION

The socio-economic dimension to the conditions giving rise to the need for multi-agency working might be described as the coming of post-industrial society and the moves towards 'disorganised capital'. Bell has perhaps presented the best known analysis of the changes in organisational life (Bell, 1973). His analysis involves three interrelated components (conceived somewhat differently to the dimension we consider here):

- socio-economic system – that allocates scarce resources and symbolic resources on the basis of economic efficiency and profit maximisation
- political system – that mobilises and directs scarce resources according to utilitarian criteria of improving the general standards and quality of living for the population
- cultural framework – that facilitates conditions conducive to individual fulfilment and self-development

Through an analysis of these components, it is clear that a transformation is under way in the technological base and economic structure of industrial nations. This is pushing in the direction of a post-industrial society, and is generating a qualitatively different form of institutional framework from that envisaged by conventional social science. Thus, Bell argues that a different kind of interpretation is needed. Through his analytical framework, Bell suggests the transition from industrial to post-industrial can be described in terms of five interrelated dimensions:

1. Change from manufacturing to a service economy;
2. Increasing economic and political dominance of the professional/technical class;
3. Centrality of theoretical knowledge and knowledge-producing institutions in policy formulation;
4. Future orientation and development of information-based technology;
5. Creation of new intellectual technology that will guide and manage socioeconomic development.

For Bell, the primacy of knowledge and pre-eminence of professional/management expertise, as well as the technical class that produce and apply their expertise to direct the course and outcome of social change are particularly important. The post-industrial society is organised around generation and application of specialised knowledge geared to the realisation of social control and directing innovation and change.

In contrast to the above, but also in some ways an embellishment of Bell's analysis, Lash and Urry (1987) outline a set of broad interrelated changes that have been taking place within the industrialised nations. The key point of their argument is that industrial societies have changed from organised capital, characterised by the dominance of large national, economic and social institutions, to a disorganised capitalism in which the developments of organised capitalism have gone into reverse.

They argue that these changes have taken place through three parallel and interdependent processes, namely: the impact of globalisation of economic, social and political relationships; the emergence of decentralisation policies; the transformation of societies from within through the growth in size and effectiveness of the service (middle) class. These points clearly elide with Bell's. Taking the authors together, particularly their focus on the processes of change within industrial society, they clearly offer a range of insights into the developments of organisational life and an explanation for the possibility of the emergence of multiagency or intersectoral working to address or respond to working in a post-industrial society. However, equally clearly, there are a number of weaknesses in their espoused theories.

First, the premise for these authors is a need for a different form of analysis given that we are in a different era. However, although they claim that nothing novel can emerge from looking at the new era from the premise of traditional social science, their analysis still seems to be on the basis of traditional social science (e.g. periodisation). Thus the complexity of the change is captured on the basis of a dichotomy between industrial and post-industrial, or organised capitalism and disorganised capitalism. The categorisation into binaries is being asked to explain more than it can, it may appear to be too simplistic and obscure some quite separate and complex processes (both theories ignore Japan's or the Far East's industrial development for example). Although there probably is substance in the view that we are moving from industrial to post-industrial or from a society characterised by organised capitalism to a disorganised capitalism, a different interpretation is needed. We are not saying that the above theories are erroneous but that they only offer a partial view or interpretation. A much more pluralistic interpretation is needed which can take into account culture, politics and ecology as well as the socio-economic. Or perhaps these categories themselves are outmoded and a new set of categories is needed.

Other attempts at theorising the changes to organisational life have been characterised in terms of a transition from one mode of accumulation to another. That is, from one kind or form of economic organisation and regulation to another, usually more flexible form of accumulation, organisation and regulation. One popular label is post-Fordism (Harvey, 1989; Piore and Sabel, 1984; Hall and Jacques, 1990). Fordism took shape at the turn of the century but did not fully develop until after the Second World War. However, by the 1970s this structure of accumulation and regulation was beginning to experience difficulties and the foundations upon which this model was based were beginning to fracture. Among these difficulties were tensions due to the rigidity of mass production, growing problems of workers' morale, rising production costs, patterns of consumption and improvements in technology. These have given rise to innovations within production that emphasise flexible specialisation and flexible integration giving rise to a new system of labour, management and organisation. These changes are not confined to manufacturing but have also affected the service industry.

The weaknesses of this view are very similar to the ones described above for post-industrialism. But post-Fordism raises an important question in terms of an overarching theory accounting for changes more broadly. The characteristics of the analysis, i.e. Fordism to post-Fordism, may be assumed to be elastic enough to show a wide range of developments, but the analysis may serve to stretch to a point which can hinder rather than expand an explanation. It is questionable whether any of the above theories taken individually or together can provide a satisfactory framework for understanding the changes in organisational life. They jump from basic production systems to the basic structures of economies, organisational life and even societies and vice versa. It ought to be possible to admit the importance of many different theories or analyses without drawing broad, sweeping conclusions.

In relation to the public sector perhaps the best known analysis is provided by Osborne and Gaebler (1992), which we have already alluded to above. Parts of their analysis have, however, been disputed. Young (1996) examines the evidence regarding UK local government to see how far the conclusion of Osborne and Gaebler that government is undergoing radical change is borne out in practice. He identifies four different areas where considerable data are available from the 1992 and 1994 Local Government Management Board surveys, namely: the question of a catalytic role for central government (steering not rowing); moves towards competitive local authorities and internal market development; moves towards mission-driven local government; and the introduction of more flexible informal decision structures. In terms of the last of these in particular he does find evidence of extension of the decision-making process into small deliberative groups and development of new ways for members and officers to work together – e.g. joint working groups of various types. While not questioning the power of Osborne and Gaebler's analysis as a description of the 'New Times', Young concludes that their analysis of the drivers for this change is flawed. He concludes that, in the case of the UK at least, changes in local government are driven not by entrepreneurial spirit, but by central government's own purposes.

Within the social sphere there have also been widespread social changes, including in family forms, and in patterns of participation in the workforce (Duncan and Edwards, 1997; Duncan and Edwards, 1999; Silva and Smart, 1999; Weeks, 1999). There is an increased adoption of multiple roles, not just the working mother (who arguably has been with us for quite some time), but also the active father, in the shape of 'new man' who recognises a role in parenting as well as in the workforce. These changes all have implications for organisational life.

In summary, all of these above indicate that there is, or has been, a transformation in structure of organisational life towards fragmentation, decentralisation and networks, and further that this offers a (partial) explanation for organisational moves towards joint working or alliances. However, we have not so far discussed changes in organisational culture, which we move on to next.

CONDITIONS GIVING RISE TO NEED FOR MULTIAGENCY WORKING – THE CULTURAL DIMENSION

In our view, postmodernism has not been well articulated in the field of organisational analysis or development, although this situation has been changing during the time we have spent writing this book and treatments of postmodernism are now becoming rather more widespread. Hatch (1997) provides just one example that the concern with postmodernism, heralded as a 'new direction' in the subtitle of Reed and Hughes' (1992) edited collection on rethinking organisation, has now become more mainstream within organisation theory. There has been a series of developments in our understanding of the transformation of organisational context which can be better understood with reference to postmodernism as it has been articulated in other contexts. Our approach is not to see postmodernism in light of some theory that assumes a rejection of modernism. Below, we explore more closely the literature that deals with the cultural context and how some ideas from postmodernist thinkers have helped to articulate the transformation of organisational life by paying attention to organisational culture.

The postmodernism we will discuss here is that which is concerned with pluralism. We recognise that the issue might be confusing since pluralism means different things at different levels. Our pluralism which we will discuss in more detail later can be broadly defined as an openness to a range of methodologies, disciplines, influences and approaches, accepting that no theory can be regarded as true in any absolute sense. This viewpoint is usually open to criticism by those advocating a modernist perspective on the grounds that postmodernism either lacks coherence and is vague or that it is ultimately lost in nihilism. Some writers have even tried to claim that they can see a path through this criticism (Flood and Romm, 1996); we return to their work later on in Chapter 3.

In relation to understanding the transformation in organisational life, it is useful to explore postmodern theorising which concentrates on organisational culture. In particular, the focus on describing how organisations are moving towards multi-perspectivism, multiculturism and multiprofessionalism (Toffler 1980). A postmodern organisation, according to these views, encourages the understanding of the culture and attempts to enhance it rather than changing it especially if it is working in a positive manner.

In relation to culture, Jameson (1984:15) conceives postmodernism as follows: 'a periodising concept whose function is to correlate the emergence of new formal features in culture with the emergence of a new type of social life and a new economic order – what is euphemistically called modernisation, postindustrial or consumer society'. This conception concurs with many theorists who subscribe to the periodising view of postmodernism. Much of this ground has been covered elsewhere (Harvey, 1989; Lyotard, 1984; Rosenau, 1992). This has led a number of researchers interested in organisations and postmodernism to, in their own way, claim that a more promising alternative for understanding organisations is to be found in the discursive context. Here, we place discourse(s) into a relational space and make no mention of knowing minds or reasoning powers. It has been proposed that self-reflexivity or critical suspicion of one's own assumptions (see Rosenau) is a prevailing tool used by many theorists. Lyotard refers to it as being incredulous to 'grand narratives'. Grand narratives can be seen as stories we repeat to ourselves to justify what we do. Such stories say that with a combination of rigorous rationality and method we can move ever closer to the knowledge of the object. It is this that Lyotard suggests needs to be challenged, and we agree. Derrida, Rorty and Kristeva in their own way offer similar tactics (e.g. deconstruction) for self-reflexivity. As a social or cultural practice, reflexivity becomes increasingly important. As Giddens puts it: 'the reflexivity of modern society consists in the fact that social practices are constantly examined and reformed in the light of incoming information about those very practices ... a world which is thoroughly constituted through reflexively applied knowledge' (Giddens, 1990:72).

In relation to organisational culture, the focus is on studying values or interpretations, focusing on stories, myths, ceremonies and ritual. Postmodern writings on organisations focus on the assumption that organisations do not have a unitary culture but are assumed or found to have multiple cultures, perspectives and so on.

CONDITIONS GIVING RISE TO NEED FOR MULTIAGENCY WORKING – THE POLITICAL DIMENSION: NEW LIBERALISM

There are different strands to new liberalism, though a common theme is the criticism of the unquestioned growth of the modern service state and its involvement in all aspects of social and economic life, coupled with a transformation in notions and mechanisms of governance. Friedman and Friedman (1985) and others see this as the primary cause of the distortion of the role of the state in the operation of the pluralistic democratic process. That is, the increase in the volume of state activity while politicians struggle to accommodate various demands of the growing number of interest groups.

From a new liberalist perspective, size and cost of state activity are further extended by activities of two sectional interest groups (the public servants – who wish to maximise their own budgets, and the 'experts' of various types); this presents issues to be resolved. It is argued that there is a need to analyse dependency on the state and to encourage greater individual self-reliance, and further that in order to do this, there must be an end to the monopoly of state provision. Friedman and Friedman argue that monopoly inhibits choice and increases dependency. It must be replaced by arrangements that empower individuals to provide for themselves and their families. For new liberalists, only the unfettered operation of the market can achieve this.

While it is possible to identify common themes and interpretations in the critique of 'big government', this does not imply unanimity in terms of the nature of the solution. New liberalism, operationalised as new public management, exaggerates the universality of the changing forms of public services in different states. The specific nature of new ways of organising and delivery of public services, and the extent to which traditional forms have disappeared, is likely to vary from country to country and even within society from sector to sector. What is agreed is that there appears to be two common strands: a new institutional economics with competition and choice on the one hand, and managerialist concerns with professionalism, expertise and freedom to manage on the other. The balance between the two varies from country to country and society to society.

The new public management (NPM) is usually associated with new right administrations. NPM has varied from country to country in terms of the extent to which it has been accompanied by an explicit ideological commitment to privatisation. Australia and Sweden, for example, explain change in terms of modernising and improving quality, whereas in the UK there was a political imperative to drive towards privatisation. In the UK, many state services transferred where possible to the commercial and voluntary sectors. If it was not possible to transfer, then the imperative was that the service must improve. This was achieved by subjecting them to the discipline of the practices of the private sector. Thus, contracting out and privatisation become the cornerstone of policy. For example in the health service in the UK, there was a development towards management by contract with simulated market conditions. There was also a shift in the public sector towards more post-Fordist methods, i.e. to more flexible models of management based on primacy of market-based conditions (Walsh, 1991; Harden, 1992).

Looking at this in a slightly different frame, Giddens' concept of generative politics is of relevance: 'Generative politics exists in the space that links the state to reflexive mobilization in the society at large ... generative politics is a politics which seeks to allow individuals and groups to make things happen, rather than have things happen to them' (Giddens, 1994:15). Kickert et al. (1997) point to the emergence of complex policy networks involving interdependent governmental and non-governmental organisations as well as the private sector. They argue that such policy networks represent an emerging form of governance. All of this points directly to the need to conceptualise and enact new forms of multiagency work in all spheres of life.

CONDITIONS GIVING RISE TO NEED FOR MULTIAGENCY WORKING – THE TURBULENT ENVIRONMENT

Much of the writing on management of organisations tends to assume that the environment is given, and that the purpose of management is to concentrate on organising internally in the most efficient way in response to this, i.e. there is a tendency to overlook the dynamic nature of the environment. Lately, this has been viewed as pursuing a dangerous course. A number of systems thinkers have been, for many years now, advocating that managing organisation(s) as a whole should relate the whole system to its environment through exploring the boundary interchanges rather than internal regulation (Churchman, 1968). Emery and Trist (1965) go on to argue that management should not just be concerned with internal problems but that such concerns must also be oriented to the environment. They say that the main issue is that the environments are changing rapidly and towards increasing complexity. Small factors in the environment may cause significant changes. Their analysis does not look out of place with current interest in chaos and complex adaptive systems (e.g. Gleick, 1987; Waldrop, 1992) and its relations to management (see e.g. Stacey, 1993). Emery and Trist have classified environments according to their degree of complexity from simple to that of a 'turbulent field', in which significant effects not only arise from competitive organisations involved but also from the field itself (e.g. the market). They argue from an analysis of a case study that many organisations are designing structures to be appropriate to simpler environments rather than the complex turbulent ones which they are actually facing. More recently in light of today's organisational order, collaborative alliances have been identified as a logical and necessary response to such turbulent conditions (see Gray, 1996:58). It is claimed that under turbulent conditions organisations become highly interdependent with others in unexpected and significant ways. Turbulence occurs when organisations acting independently in diverse directions, create unanticipated consequences for themselves and others (Emery and Trist, 1965). Turbulence cannot be adequately anticipated or averted by unilateral action. In the face of turbulence, the ability of any single organisation to plan accurately for its future is limited by the unpredictable consequences of actions taken by seemingly unrelated organisations. Designs to cope with this are based on variety-increasing systems rather than variety-reducing as seen in the traditional means of control in organisations (Emery and Trist, 1965, following Ashby, 1965).

Emery and Trist (1973) heralded an era of collaboration and called for collaboration theory to be applied to societal problems. They thought that multiagency working in its many forms offers an antidote to turbulence by building a collective capacity to respond to turbulent conditions. Through collaboration efforts the stakeholders can gain appreciation of their interdependence, pool their insights, increase the variety of their repertoire of responses to problems, and achieve increased reciprocity, efficiency and stability among themselves.

From our discussion above we can discern many factors which have contributed to the need for multiagency working. However, each of the perspectives focused on a limited set of factors. Most theories take as their focus a single organisation or single sector and ignore the domain dynamics. There is clearly a need for a more multifocus approach.

PARTICIPATORY DECISION-MAKING AND MULTIAGENCY WORK: A RANGE OF MULTIAGENCY SETTINGS AND MODELS OF ORGANISATION FOR MULTIAGENCY WORK

The 'New Times' delineated above are held to herald the need for increased multiagency work, to respond to the challenges they pose. What is implied here is a 'double movement' of reflexivity (Balbo, 1995), from individual actors to the level of social practices, networks, organisations, and from social institutions and contexts to social actors in their daily lives, producing a series of generative processes, generative of knowledge, resources and skills, new models of social organisation and the organisation of multiagency work, and last, but not least, social change at all levels.

In talking about multiagency work, since it is concerned with the task of collaboration, let us borrow the definition of Feighery and Rodgers (1992:3) as a starting point: 'an organization of individuals representing diverse organizations, factions or constituencies who agree to work together in order to achieve a common goal'. We note that they use this as a definition of a coalition, and we are not using it in the same fashion. The move to multiagency work is often strongly linked to moves towards participatory decision-making, and we consider both here as we discuss the range of different models of organisation for collaboration in multiagency work.

As Heller et al. (1998) observe in their book which sets out to describe and evaluate nearly half a century of research and experimentation with the democratisation of organisational life, factors such as growing international competition and financial adversity have led many companies to experiment with new forms of organisation, including participation. They note a variety of different reasons why participation has been introduced (including technological change, management strategy and philosophy, fads and laws) and delineate a number of different forms of participation. They also note a variety of different forms that organisational participation has taken, including: works councils; autonomous or semi-autonomous work teams or groups; quality circles; co-operatives; consultative councils/committees. They note that the names used vary, with little consistency emerging. Their discussion focuses only within companies, albeit distinguishing different levels within the company (from the individual, through small group, department and plant, to the whole company). As the definition with which we started this section implies, our understanding of the multiagency setting is much wider, including also situations which involve more than one organisation (or group or faction or constituency). Most of the forms of organisational participation Heller et al. (1998) identify have some parallel in the multiorganisational setting, and it should come as no surprise that additional forms can be found once organisational boundaries are crossed, so that we can identify various forms of networks (discussed frequently in the form of inter-firm collaboration), strategic alliances, joint working groups, advisory groups, steering groups, consultative groups, coalitions, partnerships, joint ventures, joint planning, joint agency, intersectoral collaboration, multisectoral collaboration, outsourcing, contracting out, etc.

This plethora of terms is not used consistently across the literature. Some writers make very clear distinctions, for example Chavis (1995) reserves the use of the term 'partnership' to refer to multisectoral coalitions. Heller et al. (1998), who also note the lack of consistency, distinguish in their discussion the different subtypes corresponding to consultative committees and works councils, noting in their discussion of the latter, that the term carries very specific rights and responsibilities enshrined in law in certain countries (for example Portugal and Germany) or by company policy (the example of Toyota in the UK is one they discuss). We do not wish to attempt to impose any discipline of categorisation; we will adopt the convention that when we discuss a case study drawn from the literature we will use the term offered by the authors.

It is useful to distinguish different multiagency settings in terms of some distinct dimensions, accepting that any use of these to categorise case studies must be wary of the dynamic and contingent nature of the categories assigned. We present here two different classifications: the first by Friend (1990) in terms of the different types of accountability operating in the multiagency setting which is presented in Table 1.2. The second is a classification offered by Taket (1998b) in her discussion of partnership, shown in Figure 1.1.

We note that Friend's discussion (Friend, 1990) was of the multiorganisational setting, but we believe it is equally useful in the wider multiagency context that we are concerned with. From our experiences, these different types of accountability are often found to be coexistent to varying extents in multiagency work, and only rarely does a case display a pure form of only one type of accountability.

Table 1.2   Different Types of Accountability in the Multiorganisational Setting

1. Teamlike – individuals within the team differ in skills and ability but are assumed to be identical in terms of accountability to outside interests, consensus is sought in decision-making; if different value judgements exist or arise, it is usually assumed that they can be ironed out by allowing them to surface and be negotiated towards consensus
2. Partnership – i.e. two or more organisations with separate structures of account-ability acting together as partners in some common task/area. It is usually assumed that partners are equal, however it is recognised that in the earlier stages of the work there may be some inequality
3. Inclusive group – i.e. representatives from all organisations to search for resolution to some issue or problem, usually seen as joint endeavour
4. Multiorganisational – task usually of conflict resolution, usually by an outside facilitator who not only facilitates but also acts as conciliator or arbitrator

Source: Friend (1990).

Taket (1998b) argues that in any discussion of partnerships, it is important to distinguish that this may involve interaction at any of a number of different levels: international, national, regional, local; and for a number of different purposes (see Figure 1.1). Figure 1.1 also distinguishes three different types of partnerships (these perhaps should be referred to as components, since more than one may be mixed together in any situation). The strategic component is concerned with things like: developing policy with respect to some topic; improving perception and under-standing of relevant problems/issues; development of political will; and target setting. The tactical component on the other hand involves: establishment of bodies to carry out necessary work; development of instruments (budgets, expertise, legislation etc.); setting of operational targets; and resource allocation. Finally, the operational component encompasses: use of instruments; service delivery; implementation; and monitoring/evaluation; and so can be summarised as being primarily concerned with taking action.

The calls for multiagency collaboration of various forms found in the literature discussed earlier in this chapter are also echoed in smaller-scale studies of particular

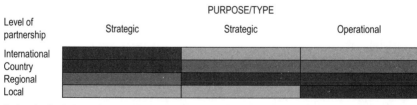

Darker shading indicates increased frequency/importance of partnerships at level shown for purpose shown

Figure 1.1   Partnership – Different Levels and Different Purposes/Types

situations reported in the literature. We review just a few of these here to demonstrate the diversity of settings involved, across private, public, voluntary and community sectors.

There has been a rapid growth in outsourcing, from a global market share of US$50 billion in 1994 to US$70 billion in 1998 (estimate) and US$121 billion in 2000 (estimate) (estimates quoted in Willcocks and Kern (1998) from multiple sources). As Willcocks and Kern (1998) observe, in the case of IT, outsourcing agreements result in interorganisational relationships due to dependency that arises. Organisations have begun to consider vendors as their partners, causing many companies to enter into more intricate deals that include both contractual and informal issues. One of their conclusions from a case study of the UK Inland Revenue is that 'in strategic partnering for IT outsourcing, getting the "contractual" level right is central to success but falls into the "necessary but not sufficient" category. [There is also] a complementary additional set of levels at which the vendor(s) and client organizations need to interact' (Willcocks and Kern, 1998:43).

Gronstedt (1996) presents a study of communications professionals in eight leading total quality management corporations in the USA (AT&T, Allen-Bradley, Eastman Chemicals, Federal Express, Hewlett-Packard, Motorola, Saturn and Xerox). The study examined features of organisation and work processes, and noted the use of fixed and ad hoc teams, the adherence to shared vision, and the use of a variety of participative fora.

Stein et al. (1992) report a study of multiagency collaborative strategies between agencies involved in addressing juvenile justice and substance abuse in Colorado, USA. The agencies involved spanned the public and private sectors and their analysis demonstrates clearly the need for multiagency work. Moran-Ellis and Fielding (1996) report a national survey of the investigation of child sexual abuse carried out in 1990–91, which reveals that police and social services arrangements for the investigation of child sexual abuse cases provide for joint working in 94% of police forces and social services departments.

Chavis (1995), writing on the US situation, identifies a growing need for multiagency work to tackle the issue of preventing violence; again this is argued as requiring involvement from community, public, private and non-governmental sectors. Also involving all sectors, responses to the international policy agenda of intersectoral and multisectoral collaboration, promulgated by the World Health Organisation, provide good examples of multiagency work at all the different levels distinguished above. We consider this example further in the next chapter.

Models of multiagency working   2

INTRODUCTION

Moving on from the introduction to the different models that have been used within a multiagency setting to organise multiagency work given towards the end of Chapter 1, we now deepen our understanding of these through the discussion of various empirical studies, drawing on the work of ourselves and others. The chapter will discuss the pros and cons of collaboration, in particular discussing different barriers and facilitating factors. These will include the diversity involved in the multiagency setting due to different individual and organisational characteristics, one of which is organisational culture. The chapter concludes by summarising the discussion in the form of challenges which must be addressed if multiagency work is to be successful.

To summarise the discussion from Chapter 1, the changing context we delineate there may be described as involving, drawing on Gray (1996), the following seven factors that have proved to be drivers for alliances and multiagency work in diverse forms:

- rapid economic and technical change
- a declining growth rate and increasing competition pressures
- global interdependence
- blurred boundaries between business and government
- shrinking finance for social programmes
- dissatisfaction with legal processes for solving complex problems
- differing perceptions of environmental risk

The responses to changing conditions have been diverse. In the private sector we have seen inter-firm collaboration in the forms of strategic alliances, integrated supply chains, joint ventures and various forms of networks. Perhaps the weakest forms of collaboration have been where the concern is only to share resources through some form of mutual service consortium, the resources concerned may include, and sometimes be limited to, information. These are of less interest to us than collaborations which include at least some joint decision-making or action, the focus of this book. We then encounter various forms of joint venture, with variations along a spectrum in terms of how closely the organisations concerned are bound together, from informal agreements only, through to legally enforceable contracts. These forms have been mirrored in public sector developments, and also in collaborations that involve the private, public, voluntary and community sectors, including non-governmental organisations. In intersectoral or multisectoral collaborations it is rare to find legally enforceable contracts.

As we have indicated in Chapter 1, the plethora of terms used to describe the different forms of organisation of multiagency work is not used consistently across the literature. Furthermore, we do not wish to attempt to impose any discipline of categorisation; we will adopt the convention that when we discuss a case study drawn from the literature we will use the term offered by the authors.

In the remainder of this chapter, we consider various empirical studies of multiagency work in different forms, identifying where possible the pros and cons of each model of multiagency work and barriers and facilitating factors for multiagency work. We discuss these in the following nine sections:

- matrix management
- joint planning
- joint working/co-ordinated working/collaboration/coalition/partnership/ alliance
- co-management/joint agency
- outsourcing/contracting out
- networks
- task forces/advisory groups
- intersectoral collaboration
- rhizomatic networks

It is tempting to say that these have been ordered strictly and carefully along a single dimension, but that would be oversimplifying. The sections do have a rough ordering in terms of complexity, conceived of as a mixture of the involvement of different organisations, sectors and issues, as well as the complexity of connections between them, but in terms of the case studies to be considered under each heading, there are some exceptions to this. As with all attempts at nice tidy linear ordering, this one is highly subjective, contains within it contradictions and tensions and is ripe for deconstruction! Although we begin each section with a summary of our understanding of the relevant label, these are *not* intended as precise definitions; as noted earlier, the literature is not consistent in this regard, not least because clear boundaries are actually very hard to delineate, especially when there may be a considerable distance between ostensible and actual purposes of any multiagency work.

The chapter then concludes with a further section, summarising what can be said regarding barriers and facilitating factors to multiagency work, and discussing the challenges to multiagency work.

MATRIX MANAGEMENT

We interpret matrix management as a form of multiagency working which is typically only found within a single organisation; the multiagency nature arises from the involvement of different agendas arising from different functions, tasks or roles. As an example, Handyside and Light (1998) report a private sector case study of the introduction of matrix management in Courtaulds. This involved a change in the structure of the internal R&D group in Courtaulds (size 60), from a traditional hierarchical structure based on scientific disciplines to four-dimensional matrix management, based on four new roles: business market manager; project manager; technology champion; and people manager. This was accompanied by a growth in teamworking. There was an increased emphasis on development of hybrid skills (deliberate highly selective matching of two or three specialist skill areas) in individuals so they could cross disciplinary boundaries. Handyside and Light (1998:166) observe that there were casualties along the way: 'Some have left the group, finding it too uncomfortable'.

JOINT PLANNING

We will take joint planning to refer to the situation where multiple parties are involved in planning or strategy generation, but where the implementation is essentially a task for each party acting independently. In the health and social care sector, Higgins et al. (1994) and Leathard (1994) conclude that joint planning has proved notoriously difficult to implement because of different organisational philosophies, objectives and management cultures across the agencies involved.

JOINT WORKING/CO-ORDINATED WORKING/ COLLABORATION/COALITION/PARTNERSHIP/ALLIANCE

We will take joint working, etc. to refer to the situation where multiple parties are involved not only in planning or strategy generation, but where the implementation or action that follows a decision is essentially a task for the parties acting jointly.

There is quite a literature in the field of health and social care, particularly in the UK, where historically provision has been divided between a number of different statutory agencies (health and local authorities), the voluntary sector and the private sector (e.g. residential care homes and general practitioners, who are essentially independent small businesses operating under contract to the Secretary of State). Ross and Tissier (1997) present an evaluation of a one-year pilot study of the care management interface with general practice in inner London involving two general practices, the local authority and the health authority, supernumerary social worker and district nurse. This operated through a steering group that met monthly, plus close operational contact between the district nurse and social worker. The district nurse and social worker found the operational contact particularly valuable. Taking the interface as a whole, there were problems in communication due to different organisational objectives, priorities and working systems.

Onyett et al. (1997), in a study of community mental health teams in the UK, find that many of them fall foul of one or more of Hackman's (1990) trip wires to be avoided when establishing productive work groups:

1. Describing the performing unit as a team, but continuing to manage members as individuals;
2. Failing to exercise appropriate authority over the team, leaving it to clarify its own aims and objectives;
3. Providing inadequate internal structures for operational management – leaving the team to 'work out the details';
4. Failing to provide organisational supports in the form of rewards, training, information and the material resources required to get the job done;
5. Assuming that team members already have all the competence they need to work well in teams.

Lang's (1982) participant observation study of a community mental health team (also in the UK) found concealed power relations which were all the more oppressive by being implicit and difficult to challenge owing to the supposed consensus operation of the team (re trip wire number 2 above), and noted hierarchies based on gender and a team member's facility with jokes based on psychoanalytical principles (re trip wire number 3 above). As we will show in Chapter 10, we would not elevate Hackman's trip wires to the status of a general law, nor infer that the presence of these in any situation impedes any productive teamworking (see the discussion of case E in Chapter 10 for example). Other case studies falling broadly within this model include: Stein et al. (1992), who report a collaborative project between agencies involved in addressing juvenile justice and substance abuse in Colorado, USA, the agencies involved spanning the public and private sectors; and Chavis (1995), who documents several coalitions tackling the issue of preventing violence, the agencies involved including private, public and non-governmental.

Higgins et al. (1994) and Leathard (1994), writing in the context of health and social care, both point out that joint working, like joint planning, is notoriously difficult because of different organisational philosophies, objectives and management and professional cultures. Higgins et al. (1994) go on to identify factors facilitating inter-agency collaboration as: a single organisational framework; a dedicated project leader; decentralised control of resources; and a common budget.

This seems to amount to a call for the creation of a joint agency. We note also that culture is implicit or absent rather than explicit in their factors.

Graver (2000), in a detailed study of multiagency work carried out in Liverpool to facilitate the development of primary health care teams, notes the importance of attention to process and facilitation; the approach used in her study was one based on a participatory action research/action learning framework. The system they set in place though was more than developing joint working in each team, there was also networking between the facilitators and the teams, so this example at once becomes a hybrid between joint working, and the type we shall discuss shortly in terms of networks.

Partnership in the UK has come about in the field of public and voluntary sector housing, e.g. tenant–management co-operatives, facilitated by a requirement for full participation being built into UK housing legislation, along with sufficient funds and timescale, particularly for training (Cadbury, 1993). Many specific policy initiatives, for example City Challenge funds for redevelopment in urban areas in the UK, do not have the same legislative requirement for partnership with the community, and given the precariousness of voluntary sector funding, this makes it difficult for the voluntary and community sector to be 'equal partners' (Cadbury, 1993).

There have also been some interesting investigations of the question of multi-agency work in the context of cross-cultural collaborative research. Easterby-Smith and Malina (1999) report their experience of cross-cultural management research, arguing that it requires considerable flexibility and provides insight into the cross-cultural research process and each researcher's own assumptions through the exercise of reflexivity. The insights they report were obtained, in the main, after the event. The authors conclude that they might have been reached in the course of the research had some process like Bohm's reflexive dialogue (Bohm, 1994; this is discussed further in Chapter 8) been adopted.

As a final contrasting example in this section, there is also Kanter's work on alliances (Kanter, 1994), based around work in the private sector. Her conception of an alliance is joint working for any combination of the following three purposes: to acquire knowledge and expertise in a new field (she refers to these as opportunistic alliances); to share services or products; and finally as a mechanism for joint work to improve quality and effectiveness of goods or services. We note that her concept of an alliance straddles what we discuss in this section and what we cover later in the section on networks.

CO-MANAGEMENT/JOINT AGENCY

We will regard co-management, or joint agency, as a special case of joint working, where the parties concerned form a special organisation or agency as a part of the working arrangement. This can create particularly complex arrangements, whereby some parties have responsibilities to two different organisations. Prystupa (1998) presents a case study of strategies used to overcome resistance to co-management in the case of natural resource management in New Zealand. A variety of strategies were used by indigenous groups to overcome resistance of conservation agencies and the study provides an interesting example of how entrenched power relations can be overcome.

Health Action Zones, created in 1998 in the UK, provide an interesting example of joint agency. There is considerable variation in their different organisational forms, although most involve some form of Partnership Board, containing parties from the different organisations and agencies involved (the precise configuration differs from zone to zone). Employees of the agency created are sometimes on secondment from another organisation, while others owe allegiance only to the joint agency.

Yet another example is presented in case C in Chapter 10, which is described as a voluntary sector 'umbrella organisation', a term also applied to the case of Nucleus Housing (Taket and White, 1994; Rosenhead and White, 1996).

Also relevant here (and drawn from a very different situation) is some literature that has looked at acquisitions of one enterprise by another; these can be regarded as a special case involving the creation of a joint agency. Kanter and Corn (1994) study eight instances of foreign acquisitions of mid-sized New England-based US companies, the acquisitions took place in a variety of different circumstances over the period 1984–90. They found very few difficulties attributed to national cultural differences, the origins of the acquiring firms ranging across S. America, Japan and Europe. They identified six facilitating factors accounting for the ease with which the mergers took place:

- desirability of relationship, especially in contrast to recent experiences of acquired companies
- business compatibility
- willingness of acquirer to invest in acquiree and allow operational autonomy
- mutual respect and communication based on it
- business success
- the passage of time

They argue that their findings suggest that contextual factors act either to fan the flames of intergroup conflict and cross-cultural polarisation or encourage organisational members to accept these differences. Cultural differences do not automatically cause tensions, although they may be blamed for difficulties which actually arise from other contextual factors. They note that this view is consistent with Argyris's perspective on defensive routines in organisations (Argyris, 1990).

OUTSOURCING/CONTRACTING OUT

Outsourcing or contracting out is understood as a form of multiagency working where a particular set of functions or tasks required by one organisation is performed by a separate organisation working under some form of contract, licence or franchise. As noted in Chapter 1, there has been considerable use of outsourcing in both private and public sectors.

The case study presented by Willcocks and Kern (1998) of the UK Inland Revenue, which we have already mentioned in Chapter 1, identifies that getting the contractual level right is central to success, but also points out that this falls into the 'necessary but not sufficient' category. They identify a complementary additional set of levels at which the vendor(s) and client organisations need to interact, besides that of the contract.

The UK's health service reforms introduced in 1991 by the then Conservative government, resulted in the introduction of the purchaser/provider split, also known as the introduction of the internal market. This was just one of the reforms affecting the public sector, collectively often referred to as the features of the new public management (NPM). Initially this was seen as the introduction of competition, and argued for in a rhetoric of reducing bureaucracy and inefficiency (something not entirely borne out by the research evidence); later, contracts were seen as providing a mechanism for collaboration. Contracting has been introduced on a fairly widespread basis in the public sector throughout Europe, North America and Australia. Walsh et al. (1997) provide a detailed study of contracting in the UK public sector, together with an examination of the experience of other countries. Reviewing the international experience, they conclude that 'contracting does not appear to be a precise solution to the problem of managing public services in a uncertain environment but is rather the key to the door to a whole new set of problems to be managed' (Walsh et al., 1997:201). They note considerable variation in the meaning of the term 'contract' across different cultures, and a lack of consistent evidence on effectiveness, finding that the introduction of contracts into different cultural, political and organisational contexts has led to a wide range of outcomes. 'Market imperatives' are found to be only one of a complex set of determining factors.

NETWORKS

The term 'network' is used to cover a variety of different circumstances, ranging from fairly loosely coupled organisations to more closely tied but diverse organisations. Networks are usually (but not always) understood *not* to include specific joint working. We have already mentioned Kanter's work on alliances, her concept of an opportunistic alliance (Kanter 1994) has resonance with our use of the term network. Elg and Johansson (1997) examine decision-making in inter-firm networks as a political process. Their study is carried out within the framework of the resource dependency approach, which sees resource interdependencies as the prime motivator of inter-firm exchange. They present a case study of the (failure of) introduction of a computer-based decision aid in the Swedish food industry, which 'demonstrates how powerful firms can utilize their position in controlling which aspect will be highlighted and in what forums discussions will take place' (Elg and Johansson, 1997:378). They found actual inter-firm decision-making generated by the process was not supported by any overall investigation of potential overall efficiency gains. The more (resource-)dependent firms do not necessarily give priority to balancing dependencies, since they may actually jeopardise privileges which would not be attainable within a less asymmetric structure, i.e. they have a vested interest in maintaining an asymmetric structure. Chisholm (1996) examines a case study of a network organisation, which utilised a strategic planning meeting based on a (substantially) modified search conference design. This is documented in more detail in Chapter 10, where it is contrasted with case study E presented there.

Kickert et al. (1997) explore the possibilities and strategies for managing the complex policy networks that they find taking shape around policy problems or programmes. Their analysis suggests a number of strategies to be important in working successfully under this new form of governance, characterised by a shift in the role of government from directing to enabling. These strategies include: accepting multiple goals; influencing perceptions; developing common language; and using instruments such as covenants, contracts and incentives, instead of regulation and central planning.

TASK FORCES/ADVISORY GROUPS

Task forces or advisory groups will be taken to relate to the situation where parties come together around a particular issue. They may be planning or strategy generating alone, or they may also be charged with implementation. The number of different parties involved is typically large and typically their life is a limited one. Aronoff and Gunter (1994) examine seven US case studies of local technological hazard disputes to clarify factors contributing to more effective public involvement strategies. They set out a seven-step participation process based on Guba and Lincoln's fourth-generation evaluation. Contributory factors include:

- agency/community relationship, and agencies' willingness to negotiate collaboratively
- community characteristics including background experience in problem solving and negotiation and representativeness of local organisations and institutions
- broader opportunities and constraints outside the local (in particular one case failed due to action not implemented at state/regional level – by those who had not been involved)

Aronoff and Gunter note that 'formalized collaborative participatory processes are not, themselves, sufficient to guarantee successful resolutions of community risk concerns' (p. 236) – surely they were not expecting that they would be!

Lober (1997) describes a study of the formation of a business–environmentalist collaboration, the Paper Task Force, based in the USA. According to his analysis, multistakeholder collaborations require the opening of a 'collaborative window' for their formation – such windows occur when four process streams (problem, policy, organisational and social/political/economic) converge. A 'collaborative entrepreneur' plays a critical role in defining and joining solutions to the problem.

INTERSECTORAL COLLABORATION

Intersectoral collaboration is a term which has found widespread use to describe the situation where the parties in multiagency work are drawn from several different sectors. In some places this is used to refer to the sectoral division by ownership/control: private, public, community, voluntary (or variants thereof); in other places it is used to refer to different policy sectors: health, transport, industry (and its various subdivisions), education, environment, housing, etc.

As an example, Taket (1998b) analyses the case of various health policy initiatives which have as their base a desire to stimulate partnerships across sectors in taking action to improve health and the ways they have been taken up in the UK. Figure 2.1 shows a selected number of policy initiatives involving partnership from the 1980s on. It is a mixture of UK initiatives and WHO initiatives which have been taken up in various ways within the UK. First, the WHO European Health for All (HFA) strategy, published in 1980 and containing a focus on ISA – intersectoral action – had a strong emphasis on the notion of creating partners for health. Second, 1984 saw the start of the WHO Healthy Cities programmes, the first of

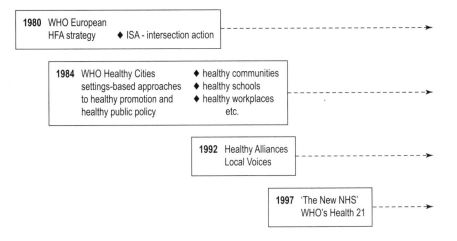

Figure 2.1   Selected Health Policy Initiatives, 1980s on

a number of settings-based approaches to health promotion and healthy public policy, later to be joined by healthy communities, healthy schools, healthy workplaces and so on. Third, turning to specific UK initiatives, 1992 saw policy initiatives in terms of Healthy Alliances and Local Voices. Each of these initiatives involved the notion of partnership, and all of them have been the subject of research which has examined the effectiveness in implementation of these various policies. There is not sufficient space here to examine all of these in detail, but some general messages can be drawn out.

Here we consider only the specific example of intersectoral action (ISA), which has been widely acknowledged as an essential component in the WHO's Health for All policy, and as such forms an integral part of the strategies adopted for its achievement. WHO has led considerable programmes of work on ISA, and at a major meeting in 1988, explored the state of the art on the achievement of ISA after almost 10 years of work in this area (Taket, 1990). This analysed strategies and tactics/mechanisms for achieving successful ISA, identifying a number of important factors.

First comes flexibility and opportunism, i.e. learning to be flexible in response to changing situations, building strategies for action that can adapt quickly to what are observed to be successful tactics, building on past success. Although requiring a systematic approach, mechanisms for ISA must not be rigid or unresponsive. Capability needs to be maintained to seize opportunities brought about by changes in external circumstances, to use instability and the results of crises or even disasters to work in support of long-term goals. Flexibility in willingness to enter negotiation with potential partners on an equal basis and to compromise (where appropriate) is also important.

The organisational structures set up to carry out ISA must support this achievement of flexibility and the use of opportunities. Extremely hierarchical and centralised structures may not always be the most helpful, although they can be particularly appropriate for the dissemination of information. The use of an alternative model, based on the fostering of networks, is often more productive for the achievement of successful ISA.

Differences in organisational/group culture is another important factor which affects appropriate ways of working in any particular situation. Closely connected to this is the need to pay careful attention to the use of language and metaphor. Common and easily understood language should be used, avoiding professional jargon. ISA requires clear communication — pictures and metaphors can be particularly valuable. Choosing an appropriate metaphor to use is something that can only be done with regard to a specific situation. While it might be considered ideal to use always co-operative, collaborative metaphors, e.g. husbandry, and to ensure that all parties gain from the results of the action, in some situations it is extremely hard to avoid shifting into confrontational metaphors like those of war or battle.

Mechanisms, strategy and tactics need to draw out the positive aspects of ISA; these may include: economic benefits, either for collaborating partners or for the economy as a whole; its contribution to the attainment of the goals of other sectors or groups, and the identification of common goals; any focus on issues which already have wide public support; the possibilities for true negotiation and equal partnership.

Finally, equal partnership, the ideal of ISA, requires the health sector to enter into equal partnership with other sectors, organisations and groups in the community at all levels. The most successful ISA requires this to be a partnership of equals, where the goals of others are accepted as equally valid as our own, where power and responsibility are shared — the achievement of this remains one of the largest challenges to future successful ISA. One particular challenge is that posed by adversaries: where divisions within the health sector exist or there are strong industrial adversaries. Here, possibilities for ISA may be more limited, and require careful planning and execution for success. In situations where 'opponents' to ISA exist, it is particularly important to devote attention to ensuring the selection of the 'game' to be played, rather than being forced into a game of our opponent's choice. Effective ISA requires not compromising core values, and also acting from a basis of realism, not naivety, particularly in recognising that some potential partners may not share your core values.

Case studies of ISA (Taket, 1990; van der Vorm, 1990; Boonekamp et al., 1996; Vaandrager and Koelen, 1997; O'Neill et al., 1997) emphasise the conclusion that although much has been achieved, the understanding of appropriate strategy, mechanisms and tactics gained does not guarantee a recipe for successful ISA. Each intersectoral partnership created requires specific designing to fit the demands of the particular issue concerned and the contours of the social–political–economic context concerned. These case studies, along with that of Costongs and Springett (1997), conclude that emphasis on the process(es) of people working together is more important than formal interorganisational structures.

Huxham (1991), drawing on multiagency work carried out in connection with the designation of the city of Glasgow in Scotland as European City of Culture 1990, identifies four conditions which are important for successful work to take place: participants must believe in the importance of collaboration; they must agree that the issue is both important to themselves and worth collaborating over; they must recognise the right of others to be a part of the collaboration; and they must have appropriate expectations about what can be achieved. She explicitly links the first three of these to the conditions identified by Gray (1985) as facilitating interorganisational collaboration. It should per-haps be pointed out here as well that these conditions should not be inter-preted as either necessary or sufficient for successful multiagency work to take place (no guarantees!); in particular we might expect some or all of these to change over the course of any engagement. Huxham (1991) goes on to point out the tension that can occur over selection of participants for multiagency work in terms of seeking a group of manageable size versus attempting to involve all stakeholders.

RHIZOMATIC NETWORKS

The final model of organising multiagency work we refer to as rhizomatic networks, to be understood to refer to a complex level of connectivity. This has parallels to Peters' spaghetti organisation mentioned in Chapter 1. We do not introduce the rhizome in detail here, as we will cover it in Chapter 4. Here we restrict ourselves to some examples of case studies. For the moment it will be sufficient to understand a rhizomatic network to be a network with a complex set of dynamic and contingent cross-connections, many of which are unseen or unnoticed (or underground) according to the perceptions of parties involved.

To give first a detailed example of what we mean, as we finalise the text for this chapter, in late June 1999, we have just seen the extensive results of such a networked form of organisation in the protests/carnivals that took place in cities across the globe on 18 June 1999, timed to coincide with the opening of the G8 summit in Cologne. A campaign to cancel Third World debt was the touchstone but the aims of the day were far wider. Organised by loose networks of small groups and individuals, with internet-based communication of information, a wide variety of action took place – electronic forms of protest (a virtual sit-in), as well as actions requiring physical presence; central co-ordination or direction were not apparent. Web sites contained links to 43 different country sites, and alternative sites were made available for when the traffic on others became too great. This form of organising was heralded in some quarters as posing a unique challenge to the authorities in terms of attempting to respond. Reports presented a mixture of predominantly carnivals, with some violence against property (on the part of the demonstrators) and against people and property (on the part of the police and authorities) (see Box 2.1).

BOX 2.1   NEW FORMS OF ORGANISATION FOR MULTIAGENCY – RHIZOMATIC NETWORKS

Des Kelly of the Save the World club who had a bicycle with the slogan 'Free the Spirit', said: 'we don't want to overthrow the system, we want to caress it', and praised the police for their low-key presence ... some workers left their offices to join in the wild pagan dance being led around Liverpool Street to a military drum tattoo. Commuters on the station platform were handed a spoof evening newspaper entitled *Evading Standards* with the screaming headline: 'Global Market Meltdown'. ...
The Times, Saturday 19 June, 1999, p. 4, Adam Sherwin

'The chaos yesterday on the streets of London was fomented by a previously unknown anarchist umbrella group called J18 which used cyberspace to galvanise anti-capitalism protesters around the globe. ... J18 group claims no leaders. ... Through the Internet, it maintains a network of anarchist groups.'
The Times, Saturday 19 June, 1999, p. 4, Adam Sherwin and Tracey Connor

'Autonomously organised events ranging from education forums, pickets, protests, discussions, blockades and street parties will disrupt business as usual and show the world that things could be very different.'
J18 web site

'J18 appears to be an umbrella network for other activist groups which came together for yesterday's protests.' *Daily Telegraph*, Saturday 19 June, 1999, p. 5, Tom Sykes

Sections of the media presented what was criticised on the J18-linked web-sites as misleading information, for example:

'Several of the articles covering events in London published in the UK daily papers on Saturday June 19th included references to the use of the Internet. It is important to take a closer look at some of what was said:

THE EXPRESS: 'They (the campaigners) used the latest computer codes to try and ensure secrecy while communicating over the Internet.'

THE DAILY TELEGRAPH: 'The 'Carnival Against Capitalism' posed particular problems to the authorities because it was co-ordinated via the Internet.'

These reports give an incorrect impression, they imply that there was something sinister about the use of the Internet. Full and extensive J18 information was placed on the Internet to ensure that information was freely available. The general approach was to be as open as possible, and to set up a website which would reflect the diversity and wide reach of the current campaign against globalisation.

In line with this transparent approach the campaigners did not use encryption, or as *The Express* put it 'computer codes'. Anyone visiting the website was invited to join the 'organising' discussion mailing list, an open email list that anyone in the world could join or post their own messages to. While the Internet was an important communication channel between the 40 or so countries, it must be realised that the number of people connected to the Internet, while being roughly 170 000 000 – still only accounts for 5% of the world population. Many many countries with limited Internet access took part in the J18 protests – their reports will take longer to come in.

The website was always intended to be used as a reporting tool to provide a space for all of the news from the different actions. Reports are still coming in and the site will continue to be updated as and when updates are received.'
Source: J18 Web site

Extracts from various web sites on country-specific reports

'JUNE 18: THE VIRTUAL AND THE REAL **ACTION ON THE INTERNET AND IN AUSTIN, TEXAS** ZAPATISTA FLOODNET AND RECLAIM THE STREETS by Stefan Wray, June 19, 1999, 6:00 CDT

'The resistance will be as transnational as capital.'

On June 18, 1999, simultaneous with the G8 meeting in Koln, Germany, people all over the world participated in actions and events under the banner 'Reclaim The Streets.' Email reports coming in today indicate that 10 000 people gathered in Nigeria and that San Francisco drew crowds of around 500. More news and reports of events will surely be posted in the coming days. What follows is a contribution to this emerging body of material.

Reclaim the Streets European Headquarters http://www.gn.apc.org/rts/ Below are two separate and very different reports. The first describes the results of the virtual sit-in called by the Electronic Disturbance Theater opposing the Mexican government that involved thousands of people from 46 countries. The second is a longer narrative account describing events as they unfolded in Austin, Texas, an action that involved about 50 people and resulted in three arrests. It ends with some comments on hybridity, meshing the virtual and the real.'

'**Toronto:** Reclaim the Streets Toronto has just concluded peacefully, with over 2 thousand cyclists, dancers, pedestrians and protesters participating, presided over by a giant goddess. Police presence was extremely heavy with riot police, horses, bullet-proof vest wearing Emergency Task Force cops and bike fuzz, but despite the burning effigies in the streets (a television/VCR, Mercedes symbol, and a giant asshole) there were no arrests. Viva sans temps mort!'

'18th of June – **URUGUAY (English Translation):** The Montevideo June 18th Network occupied the main square of the Old Town (the financial centre); at about 12:30 a type of trade fair was set up.

Participating groups in the trade fair had stalls on various themes:

- Work, selling cheap labour and focusing on the theme of child labour
- Education, where public education could be acquired for a modest price and the education reform was questioned
- Plastic, with a PVC jockey riding the Pollution Plastisaurus, spotlighting non-returnable bottles and packaging (we're experiencing an invasion of these) and rejecting PVC
- Local Culture, with a test to see how globalised and how Uruguayan we are. TV as the manipulator of our lives
- Consumption, showing us how to be perfect consumers and have a clear conscience
- Communication, criticising the prohibition of community and free radio stations

Also participating were some trade unions involved in disputes such as Cristaleri'as del Uruguay, which locked out its employees, leaving them in the street and Uruguay without its only glass factory. They brought along a cardboard factory with an exhibition about glass. The fishworkers' union also attended with placards protesting about their situation. Also present were the workers of the 'El Cine' supermarket who have been in occupation of the supermarket for the last two months.

The square was decorated with balloons and posters. A lot of noise was made which attracted the attention of passers-by who had a look at our trade fair. There was music, candombe, musicians playing live. It's worth emphasising that the majority of stalls were made of materials skipped and recycled from the streets and with posters taken from this year's elections. The second action of the day was a parade along the main streets, a really lively parade with singing, stilt walkers, jugglers, puppets, the Plastisaurus and the glass factory occupying the streets and entering into the Stock Exchange, the Banco de Montevideo (to the surprise of the staff) and passing in front of the Ministry of Housing and the Environment and McDonald's, where we stayed for a while singing and getting in the way. The day finished with a puppet show about the media, which ended up with the burning of a cardboard television. The activities were filmed and photographed. We'll upload the photos onto the web-page but the video is more difficult because we don't know anyone who can upload it onto the computer. Greetings and well done to everyone!'

'**Gujrat Pakistan**: On June 18, 1999 our organization demonstrated against nuclear weapons and against the explosion of atom bombs by Pakistan and India. In the meanwhile a necessary report was transmitted to you by our acting secretary for information Mr. Asghar Ali on June 19, 1999. However the same is recapitulated here with some additional information. The rally was started early in the morning from the gts chowk and the enthusiasm of the workers and schoolchildren was a sight to behold. No doubt it was the movement of APFUTU (all Pakistan Federation of United Trade Unions). The leadership of APFUTU already had gone underground on 14.06.99. Suddenly the said leadership came out on 18 June wearing masks and veils and joined the rally, in spite of the fact the local administration had blocked off access and were even ready to arrest them. The police had been making raids for two nights. The police entered the union house as well as Imtiaz Labour Hall at midnight of 17 & 18 June and tried to find clues about the leadership. When the police failed to achieve their object they became revengeful and destroyed the office records. While leaving the union house they carried away with them the office computer with accessories, movie camera, electric typewriter, panasonic fx-f 90 fax machine, banners inscribed, with slogans, 26 inch tv (colour), two carpets and crockery, etc. They also burnt the office records.

When the underground leadership appeared in the demonstration the protesters became agitated and started their march by breaking through the police cordon. The demonstrators passed through chowk fawara, kabuli gate, shahfasil gate, chowk pakistan, prince cinema chowk, jail chowk and they reached district courts chowk; chanting slogans against the government as well as nuclear arms. In front of the deputy commissioner's office the APFUTU (women's wing) leadership had been sitting on hunger strike since the morning as a protest against the nuclear explosion.'

Another empirical study that documents a rhizomatic form of the organisation of multiagency work is provided by Opie (1997). Opie's case study is of multi-disciplinary teams in New Zealand in two different settings: a rehabilitation unit; and a medium secure unit for psychiatric patients; this example is thus on an entirely different scale from the discussion of the J18 action above. The organisational conditions which facilitate the work are analysed, following Nonaka and Takeuchi's work on organisations and knowledge creation carried out in the context of Japanese companies (Nonaka and Takeuchi, 1995). Summarising considerably, and drawing on Opie's own summary, Nonaka and Takeuchi argue that first, knowledge is not just a significant organisational resource, instead, it needs to be regarded as something subject to active creation, through the development of processes and structure. This involves regarding knowledge as other than formal and easily transmitted. The reworking of diverse knowledges requires: the (difficult) articulation of tacit knowledge (on both its craft and cognitive dimensions); the questioning of one's own knowledge; the presence of productive, because unsettling, ambiguity; the presence of redundancy which enables the identification of shared ground and of difference; and the arrival at a different mode of sense making. Second, they argue that 'knowledge' should not be regarded as synonymous with 'information', instead it is: 'the function of a particular stance, perspective, or intention ... knowledge, unlike information, is about action. It is always knowledge "to some end". And ... knowledge, like information, is about meaning. It is context specific and relational' (Nonaka and Takeuchi, 1995:58). Information is the material enabling the creation of knowledge; knowledge enables the development of new positions, the achievement of new dynamic and contingent truths. Third, Nonaka and Takeuchi draw our attention to knowledge as the interaction between explicit or formal knowledge(s) and tacit knowledge(s). This interaction depends on several processes: socialisation, i.e. the sharing of experiences informing tacit knowledge; externalisation, i.e. the articula-tion of tacit knowledge into explicit concepts, a process involving dialogue and reflection; the development of combinations, i.e. the combining of different modes of explicit knowledge; and internalisation, i.e. the translation of newly acquired explicit knowledge into tacit knowledge bases to inform work (drawn from Nonaka and Takeuchi, 1995:61–72).

Looking at conditions for productive multiagency work, it therefore seems axio-matic that we must look for suitably facilitative environments, understood as environments where the parties concerned can achieve their potential to voice and then work conceptually with the different narratives circulating within and between the parties involved. A useful first step is a move to conceptualising multiagency work as engaged necessarily in knowledge creation. Nonaka and Takeuchi (1995) have set out five organisational conditions which promote this, which we have recast here for the multiagency situation as:

1. Intention, i.e. the parties involved need to develop a strategy 'acquire, create, accumulate' (p. 74) and use knowledge, so conceptualising what kind of

knowledge it requires and how this knowledge can best be utilised. This, then, involves problematising the notion of multiagency work, rather than regarding it as something to be taken for granted, and addressing processes and organisational structures which could facilitate its development;

2. The presence of autonomy, which enables the development of new knowledge and permits individuals to work creatively;

3. The presence of fluctuation and creative chaos. These terms refer to modes of dialogue and discussion which allow for the questioning of one's own and others' premises, and encourage disciplinary overlap in order for the parties involved to push the boundaries of their own knowledge;

4. The utilisation of redundancy, i.e. 'existence of information that goes beyond the immediate operational requirements of organizational members', and assists in 'intentional overlapping' (p. 80). 'Sharing redundant information promotes the sharing of tacit knowledge because individuals can sense what others are trying to articulate. Redundancy encourages concept development and 'enables individuals to invade each other's functional boundaries and offer advice or provide new information from different perspectives' (p. 81);

5. The presence of requisite variety, i.e. the organisation's or team's 'internal diversity must match the variety and complexity of the environment in order to deal with the challenges posed by the environment' (p. 82).

Multiagency work, then, is about 'making things happen' in a complex world. It occurs in an environment productive of different narratives because of the heterogeneity of representations available to the parties involved. The narratives produced are the result of recursive and interactive processes which enable the parties involved to explore the possibilities and constraints made available to them through their different constituent knowledge bases (hence drawing on and working with tacit and explicit knowledges) in order to develop a plan which allows the work to move on. It is also important that the plan is regarded as provisional, as open to change as circumstances change. The outcome of the multiagency work cannot, therefore, be a single, authoritative narrative defined largely by knowledge deriving from one discipline.

Two other case studies of multiagency work described in White and Taket (1995b) provide further examples of this diversity. The first of these dealt with the London Borough Grants Unit which is responsible for the management of decisions for the allocation of grants to voluntary organisations in London. The decisions made as to which group gets funded and how much, are based on the information collated by the unit from the application forms and other means. The final decision is left with the London Borough Grant Committee, which comprise representatives from each of the boroughs in London and Greater London (who each allocate money to the overall fund). Once the decision is made as to funding, the unit then manages the funding with the voluntary group. The London Borough Grants Unit administers and monitors the grants awarded. The unit has senior managers and staff arranged in teams responsible for sectors such as housing, ethnic minorities and community arts. The unit's activities are to collate information, assess funding applications and inform the committee with interim reports about the voluntary sector.

The setting for the second case study was the context for work carried out in Lahore, Pakistan. This involved different organisations in both Lahore and London, in both public and private sectors. There were also a number of different specific projects. The situation was viewed in systemic terms by many of the participants, however there was no common view. To some extent this was facilitated by the involvement of different individuals in some of the organisations with the different projects, and it was common to find a view that treated the projects as unconnected, and also on the part of many organisational representatives, to neglect the connections into the community sector. In both these cases, the use of the metaphor or model of the rhizomatic network, with a high degree of cross-connectivity, that was both dynamic and contingent, provided a useful descriptor of the context, so that progress could be made. In both cases there were a variety of issues being dealt with and an important part of this was to recognise that the connectivity depended heavily on the particular issue under consideration at the time (these changed over the course of the work in both cases). A second shift was also necessary to facilitate progress, this time in the nature of the connectivity, distinguishing different connections for financing, managerial accountability, information provision, consultation and service provision. Thus the nature of the context, complexly interconnected, with dynamically evolving links, was hard to match with other systemic metaphors (indeed progress was impeded when these were being drawn on). It is also important to avoid a pessimistic view of the situation as just a chaotic mess, the metaphor of the rhizome with shifting boundaries, multiple entryways and exits, rather than singular static structure, proved helpful. Once a more rhizomatic view could be adopted, and participants felt comfortable with the complexity of the situation, discussion and prioritisation were able to proceed.

BARRIERS AND FACILITATING FACTORS – CHALLENGES TO MULTIAGENCY WORKING

The brief review contained in the sections above indicates the complexity of factors that affect the outcomes of multiagency work. While it is possible to point to barriers and facilitating factors, generally these are found to be neither necessary nor sufficient for successful outcomes (however defined) to occur. They do, however, enable some general points to be raised.

A number of studies point out the value to multiagency work of paying explicit attention to designing appropriate processes. In addition to those discussed above in the section on intersectoral collaboration, Effken and Stetler (1997) present a study of the redesign of a hospital health care delivery system in the USA, showing also the positive effects of the improved collaboration achieved on a range of intermediate outcomes, as well as cost and quality outcomes. Bain (1998) reports on three case studies: a UK computing bureau; a day care nursery (also in the UK); and a maximum security prison (Australia). His studies demonstrated links between individual, group and organisational learning and in each 'social defenses' were successfully overcome. The studies also showed the importance of a number of factors including: high level support; creation of high level of ownership through processes used; construction of space for common reflection, with three 'essential' features (agenda derived from those involved, not filled by CEO or equivalent, acceptance of silence at appropriate times); and finally development of organisational awareness. Some studies argue that they have demonstrated the specific value of facilitation (Offner et al., 1996; Vennix, 1995).

Participation and ownership are important. Harrington et al. (1998) present a study of the introduction of business process re-engineering (BPR) in the Contributions Agency (a UK public sector organisation). This did not lead to radical change, empowerment, or new ways of working, and his analysis points to the top-down nature of BPR as a key reason, together with its lack of attention to the human dimension of organisational change, to organisational culture, and organisational politics. However, as mentioned earlier, the study by Huxham (1991) points out the tension that can occur over selection of participants for multiagency work in terms of seeking a group of manageable size versus attempting to involve all stakeholders. Here we should point out that what is manageable will depend on the nature of the organisation/structure envisaged for the multiagency work. Where it is an essentially one-off event/meeting, large numbers can be fully involved with appropriate choice of processes for use. Where the work will be ongoing over a considerable time, a manageable number will be much smaller, given especially the constraints of trying to match diary slots.

If it has done nothing else, the *bricolage* from diverse literatures presented in this chapter should have convinced the reader of the existence of tremendous diversity in multiagency work, diversity in terms of: purpose; type of issue; situation/context; model of organisation of work; time span of the work; varying levels of commitment; varying levels of resources; varying levels of authority to commit their own organisation, faction or constituency (to hark back to the definition of multiagency work we outlined in Chapter 1); etc. For those concerned with working in multiagency setting, and perhaps most especially for those who take on, or are given, responsibilities for facilitating such work, we argue that it is vitally important to acknowledge the challenge posed by this diversity and to find ways of working with, and not against, it. Doing this will necessarily throw up specific challenges in terms of issues like: selecting/negotiating participation; enabling 'good enough' communication; securing adequate resourcing; achieving necessary information sharing; negotiating/designing appropriate processes; appropriate attention to the task of facilitation. PANDA is our answer to these challenges for ourselves.

Methods used in multiagency settings

3

'Adso: But how does it happen ... that you were able to solve the mystery of the library looking at it from the outside and you were unable to solve it when you were inside?'
William de Baskerville: the world ... [is] conceived as if from the outside ... and we do not know its rule, because we are inside it, having found it already made.' (Eco, 1984:218)

INTRODUCTION

In this chapter we present a critical review of a number of different approaches that purport to support multiagency working, in order to illustrate why we need to look at new ways of working with multiagencies. We will look at methods from management science, systems science and development practice. The use of decision conferencing, strategic options development and analysis (SODA), the strategic choice approach (SCA), team syntegrity, soft systems methodology (SSM) and total systems intervention (TSI) are first introduced. Aspects of the implicit and explicit assumptions on which they are based are then explored using a broadly deconstructive approach. In particular we identify how the use of unsupported binary assumptions and the unexamined role of the expert/analyst within these methods lead to difficulties in dealing with diversity and enabling participation in an empowering way.

Methods from development practice, e.g. participatory rapid appraisal (PRA), will then be explored and critiqued. In particular, we will show that the methods are weak at developing action.

Within operational research and the management sciences a number of different approaches to methods for group decision-making and group decision support have been developed. One group are the so-called soft operational research methods, including SCA, SODA, hypergame and metagame analysis; see Rosenhead (1989) for coverage of all of these. A second group can be associated with systems science, including SSM, strategic assumption surfacing and testing (SAST) and critical systems heuristics (CSH); see Flood and Jackson (1991) for an overview of these. A third group is provided by the various group decision support systems (GDSS), oriented around the use of particular group decision computer software and remote conferencing technology; see Bryant (1993a) for an overview of these. (This is not to say that earlier methods do not involve computer software, many can do, but this is not necessarily the central part of their use.) Within this last group are included the various approaches to multi criteria decision analysis (MCDA); see Belton (1990) and Elder (1991) for a review of these. Later we provide our own introduction to some of these. We concentrate less on those approaches that are dependent upon a particular technological system (such as software packages and remote conferencing), since they are less commonly used in the multiagency setting, something that is perhaps unsurprising given the investment required. They can also be regarded as less feasible, given that they are not widely available.

SYSTEM DYNAMICS MODELS

Vennix (1996) believes that group model-building is an approach which involves the individuals deeply in the process of model-building in order to enhance group learning, build consensus and create commitment. He provides a framework for designing a group model-building project. The first issue to explore is whether systems dynamics is suitable for the problem in question. If the answer is yes then a number of questions relating to design need to be asked. The diagram in Figure 3.1 is a flow chart of the framework.

The most important question is related to who, and how many, should participate. Vennix claims this is important because it helps to determine what group processes it will be necessary to use. The most difficult question to be asked is when to use system dynamics. The problem needs to be dynamically complex with underlying feedback processes. He uses system dynamics as a diagnostic and impact assessment tool for finding out what the problem is and what causes are responsible for it.

Causal diagrams can be built up within a group setting, or from individual interviews followed by working in the group setting with the members of the team. From these diagrams (see Chapter 7 for details) a system dynamics model can be produced and the dynamics of the relationships can be explored.

Senge also suggests that causal diagrams and system dynamics modelling are useful to enhance group learning and to tackle complex problems. Model-building in teams using devices to generate dialogue then analysis follow a similar pattern to Vennix's framework.

Vennix (1996), Vennix et al. (1996) and Andersen and Richardson (1997) illustrate how the process of constructing a system dynamics model can be carried out within a group context. Wolstenholme (1999) concludes that both quantitative and qualitative system dynamics are important to management problem solving (his term), and suggests a process (intertwined project learning) whereby both can

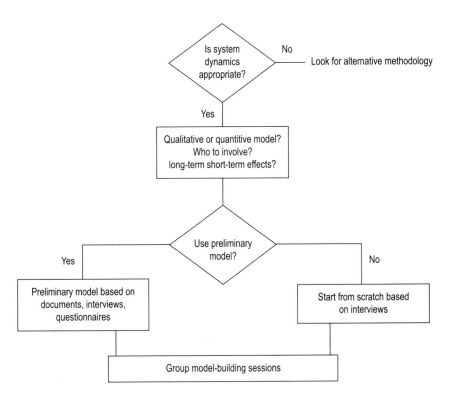

Figure 3.1   Vennix's Framework for Model-building Projects

be harnessed within a particular study/project, as well as a wider process (accelerated business learning) which he argues is necessary to link qualitative system dynamics in management development programmes and quantitative system dynamics modelling projects into an integrated organisational learning activity.

DECISION CONFERENCING

Decision conferencing was developed because of the failure of the traditional decision theory in dealing with conflict and diversity (Phillips, 1984). The developers thought there may be a place for an improved approach to decision-making, so that people can arrive at a common understanding of the issues, develop a sense of common purpose and achieve commitment to action.

The process for decision conferencing has many variants, but mainly it is understood as an intensive two- or three-day workshop attended by a group of people who are concerned about some complex issues facing an organisation. There are no prepared presentations or fixed agenda; the meeting is conducted as an ongoing session. A key feature is the use of a computer-based model which incorporates data and the judgements of the participants in the group as they are learning about the issues at hand (Eden and Radford, 1990). The model is a 'thinking tool' which enables participants to see the consequences of differing viewpoints, and to develop a higher-level perspective on the issues. By examining the implications of the model, then changing it and trying out different assumptions, participants develop a shared understanding and reach agreement about the way forward.

Proponents of this process suggest that there are four stages which typify most decision conferences, though every event is different (Phillips, 1988). The first phase is a broad exploration of the issues. In the second stage, a model is constructed of participants' judgements about the issues, with data used where available. An attempt is made to represent all perspectives in the model. In the third stage, the model combines these perspectives, reveals the collective consequences of individual views, and provides a basis for extensive exploration of the issues. Discrepancies between model results and members' intuitive judgements are examined, causing new intuitions to emerge, new insights to be generated and new perspectives to be revealed. When this revision process, which is highly iterative, has been completed, the group moves on to the fourth stage in which key issues and conclusions are summarised, a commitment package is created and an action plan or set of recommendations is agreed. A report of the event's products is prepared by the facilitator after the meeting and circulated to all participants. A follow-through meeting is often held to deal with afterthoughts, additional data and new ideas.

Facilitators who are experienced in working with groups aid the group. The main tasks of the facilitators are to see and understand the group life, and to intervene, when appropriate, to help the group stay in the present and maintain a task orientation to its work (Phillips and Phillips, 1993). The facilitators attend to the processes occurring in the group, provide structure for the group's task, but refrain from contributing to content. They structure the discussions, helping participants to identify the issues and think creatively and imaginatively. Models are developed using proprietary software packages such as HIVIEW and Equity.

Decision conferencing combines information technology, group processes and modelling of issues. The proponents claim that the process is appropriate for organisations in both the private and public sectors, and that it helps them to arrive at better and more acceptable solutions than can be achieved using orthodox procedures, and agreement is reached more quickly. Decision conferencing can be effective in multiorganisational situations for several reasons. First, it can work with participants who are selected to represent all key different organisational perspectives on the issues. Second, the group works in the 'here and now', and participants get to grips with the real issues that help to build agreement about the way forward. Third, the model plays a crucial role in generating commitment. All model inputs are generated by the participants and nothing is imposed, so that the final model is the creation of the group, thus 'owned' by participants. Fourth, computer modelling helps to manage conflict. The model allows participants to try different judgements without commitment, to see the results and then to change their views. According to the proponents decision conferencing works best in organisations when these four conditions just discussed are met reasonably well.

STRATEGIC OPTIONS DEVELOPMENT AND ANALYSIS (SODA)

SODA is a method developed for use on complex organisational problems. It is used to structure the perceptions of each individual within the issue-owning group. This is initially done through a series of interviews in which the interviewer builds a cognitive map of the interviewee's responses. When all problem-owners have thus been interviewed, the facilitator undertakes an analysis of all individual cognitive maps with a view to identifying clusters of similar perceptions between them. The maps (for more detail see Chapter 7 'Modes of representation') are combined in this way and presented to the group as a whole so that each member may gain an appreciation of the others' perspectives. In SODA cognitive maps are first produced for each individual by interviewing them in a relatively unstructured 'free-flowing' way to try to elicit their thought processes about the problem under discussion and what they think is important about the problem. Such maps often contain 40–100 concepts and may also help each individual to refine their thinking. With the assistance of the maps, the facilitator is able to promote discussion and negotiation towards a resolution to the problematic situation. Thus, the process brings together two specific skills: the skills of the facilitator in managing the process to get the group working well together and the skills to construct maps of the content each member of the group wishes to tackle.

SODA attempts to address the psychological aspects of problem solving through focusing on the individual. The reality of a situation is considered as a construction of the individuals participating in the situation. The approach of mapping draws on the work of George Kelly in particular in relation to personal construct theory and repertory grid analysis (RGA) (Kelly, 1958). In RGA elements are paired with constructs to elicit meaning. In SODA, the map represents the meaning of a concept by relating it to other concepts. The link between cognitive mapping and Kelly's theory of personal constructs can be explained as follows.

Kelly designed the RGA technique. This technique can best be understood through his personal construct theory and the constructivist philosophy which he followed. In personal construct theory, a person's thought processes are psychologically channelled by the ways in which events are anticipated (reflections of the means–ends arrows in cognitive mapping). Constructs are the patterns which people invent in order to make sense of their world (reflections of the 'concepts' within maps in cognitive mapping). Kelly suggests that individuals strive to improve their constructs in order to increase their understanding of the world (reflections of the merged maps being studied by the group).

The constructive interaction ethos within this constructivist philosophy is what Kelly concentrated on. This ethos is used to describe situations where groups produce a collective performance which is superior to that of any of the individuals involved (reflections of the group work in SODA). Mutual evaluations and criticism provide a new, shared perspective and increase knowledge and understanding. Constructive interaction may be thought of as a methodological attitude – an attitude which clearly runs through SODA.

The relation, therefore, between SODA and Kelly is mostly philosophical and methodological. Whether this is enough to state that SODA is based on Kelly's theory is a matter for debate. Although RGA and SODA originate from the same psychological theory, the data they produce and the interface from which these data are analysed are very different.

In SODA it is assumed that each member of a client group has his or her own personal subjective view of the real problem. The individuals in a situation are taken to be involved in the psychological construction of the world rather than the perception of an objective world. That is, 'human beings are continually striving to "make sense" of their world in order to "manage and control" that world' (Eden, 1989:25).

The aim of SODA is to achieve understanding/agreement within the group. A view of organisations which focuses on the individual will inevitably also focus on the organisation as a changing set of coalitions in which politics and power are significant explanations of decision making. That is to say that organisations are a negotiated enterprise whose participants are continuously negotiating and renegotiating their roles within it.

The SODA method has four phases. The first produces individual cognitive maps. Each member of the client group is interviewed individually. The individual is asked to explore the issues in a general way to start with. The facilitator constructs a cognitive map of the discussion, identifying relevant concepts and the linkages between them. Concepts are recorded as a short phrase capturing the idea. After the interview has been conducted the facilitator takes the maps produced and reorganises them by identifying clusters of concepts or themes. This forms the basis of the second phase. The process of interview and clustering might be conducted several times until it is felt that the clustered maps truly represent each individual's views of the world. Once this is achieved the next phase is to construct a composite map that represents the combined views of all the group members. Here, it is important to ensure that as similar concepts are merged a balance of concepts from all members is retained. Once the maps are merged then they are again clustered into themes, as were the individual maps. These composite maps are then used as a basis for the third phase, i.e. the workshop.

The workshop uses the combined map as a focus for deciding collective and individual action. The workshop emphasises identifying emerging themes and core concepts. Conflict is managed and key options, assumptions and goals are identified.

Although the final cognitive map is the obvious tangible product of the technique it must be emphasised that its proponents consider this no more than a device to aid the individuals to focus on the problem. Since the developers of SODA have based their intervention approach on ideas of constructivist psychology that address the problem of how people perceive the world, the product of the technique is as much achieving the right sort of psychological state to enable individuals to make collective decisions and take responsibility for individual actions.

The last phase is to have a series of workshops focusing on encouraging the participants to raise and elaborate upon the strategic issues identified. Their involvement would not only increase the robustness of the outcomes through the capture of ideas and issues originating from different levels of the organisation, but would also increase the ownership of the strategy and their understanding of it (Ackermann et al., 1992). Each workshop could focus on a specific strategy making each group's task unique.

Later developments of SODA have resulted in 'Journeymaker', in which Eden and Ackermann (1998) provide an introduction to the process of strategy making. 'JOURNEY', or jointly understanding, reflecting and negotiating strategy, is presented in terms of the theory and concepts of strategic management, illustrations of case studies, and guidelines on methods, tools and techniques. Computer software to support the process also exists. We do not deal with Journeymaker in detail here for a number of reasons. Firstly, its focus on 'strategy making' is distinctly different from that of this book on decision-making, although naturally there are close connections. Secondly, Eden and Ackermann's emphasis is on the single organisation, only a part of our concern here. The book itself is an excellent source of case 'vignettes' which describe process (and incidentally say more about the task of facilitation, etc. than previous works by the authors), and thus provides a valuable resource for would-be facilitators.

STRATEGIC CHOICE APPROACH

This strategic choice approach was developed to help planners tackle complex decisions in a strategic way. In particular for use in the situation when planners face high levels of uncertainty, shortage of time, have limited resources and there exists among the participants a wide range of interest and the potential for conflict. Indeed the approach was developed to help participants 'plan under pressure'.

The approach developed from years of casework at the Institution of Operational Research at the Tavistock Institute of Human Relations, and through observation of these cases and reflection. The distillation of the work led to the approach being formalised in two books: Local Government and Strategic Choice (Friend and Jessop, 1969) and Planning under Pressure (Friend and Hickling, 1987, 1997).

The foundations of the approach have been claimed to be planning theory, decision theory and action research. The approach is directed to the problem of choosing strategically in the (complex) situation characterised by the involvement of more than one decision maker. Here negotiation with others who view the same problem differently or see different problems in the same situation makes choosing demanding and challenging. In such situations the authors say that the planners face pressure due to three types of uncertainties. These are:

- uncertainties about the working environment (UE)
- uncertainties about guiding values (UV)
- uncertainties about related decisions (UR)

They say that these are typically expressed as demands for more information, clearer objectives and for more co-ordination respectively. These uncertainties should be viewed in relative rather than in absolute terms, in that they are normally relevant to, or pertain to, a particular situation. The response to dealing with these uncertainties would normally be for UE to do more research, for UV to get clarification of aims through involving others and for UR to forge collaboration with other groups or processes (see Figure 3.2).

In order to achieve the exploration of these uncertainties in a group situation the authors suggest that we break with the orthodox approach to dealing with problems, i.e. its linearity, objectivity, certainty and comprehensiveness. Instead, a form of working that is cyclical, subjective, embraces uncertainty and works with selectivity would be more appropriate. The approach has a framework which they claim is highly flexible, cyclic and deals with subjective knowledge. The phases of the process are: *shaping*, *designing*, *comparing* and *choosing*. The processes can switch between these modes in any combination.

The *shaping* phase involves identifying decision areas which are no more than short descriptions of courses of action the participants might see as conceivable to adopt. These are presented to the group. The group can then link these areas where they think two are linked. Some links may be obvious and others not so obvious;

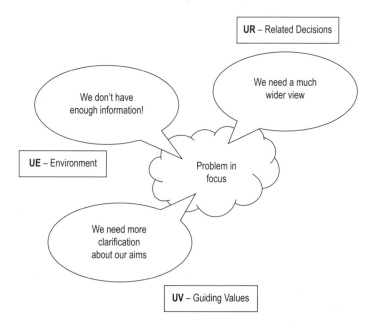

Figure 3.2 Types of Uncertainty

these are distinguished by full and broken lines. Also some areas might seem at that point in time for the participants as urgent, important or even both. These can be visually distinguished. It is clear that once the diagram is drawn a focus for the group to concentrate on might be readily given.

The *designing* phase is where the participants can explore the range of possible courses of action open to them. The problem focus identified can be explored using the *analysis of interconnected decision areas (AIDA)*. This is a process that looks for mutually exclusive options so as to reduce the set of possible courses of action. First the options in the different decision areas are elicited. Following this, all impossible links are identified. Those option links that the participants think are dubious are also noted. The pathways are then rearranged in graphs showing the feasible decision schemes.

The *comparing* phase is where a set of comparison areas are identified. These are concepts that can be used to evaluate each decision scheme with respect to each other. They are not restricted to areas which can be quantified. Each scheme can be assessed using the comparison areas. It is also in this phase that uncertainties can be aired and acknowledged. The process often used is for each scheme to be compared to each of the others in turn. Thus for each pair of possible schemes the comparison areas are compared and contrasted with each other. The participants at this stage begin to air their uncertainties and doubts or conflict might arise. Alternatively pairs of decision schemes can be compared through comparative advantage. This graphical form of sensitivity analysis allows participants to search for the advantage of one scheme over another in terms of the impact on the comparative areas.

The *choosing* phase is where the participants find ways to manage the uncertainties arising. The aim of this phase is to develop a list or set of uncertainty areas. The next step is to try and classify them as UE, UV or UR. Some uncertainties may be more important to deal with than others. To consider how they might be managed they can be explored using an uncertainty graph, where each uncertainty area can be explored and action to alleviate them discussed. Here the participants are thinking about the incremental steps forward in dealing with the uncertainties and the problem as a whole. The courses of action can be seen as things that are important now or can be deferred to a later date. A *commitment package* is produced which allows the decisions to be presented as actions that can be taken now or explored or deferred to a future date. Various forms of commitment package are described in Chapter 6.

According to Friend and Hickling, each phase can be visited at any time and in any combination. They claim that between six and eight people provide the ideal size for a workshop, although there have been examples where larger groups have used the process.

TEAM SYNTEGRITY

Team syntegrity is a process developed by Stafford Beer as a response to the inadequacies of bureaucracy and hierarchy in organisations (Beer, 1995). It is claimed that the process has its roots in management cybernetics (Beer, 1979, 1981, 1985) and in particular the ideas on geodesics developed by Buckminster Fuller (1979). Beer approaches the problems of hierarchy and organisational democracy through the invention of a process which he believes has solved the conundrum of finding a design for organisations which is both non-hierarchical and participative. The process he developed offers a possible image of a novel organisational form. This is called a syntegrity: drawn from synergy plus integrity.

A syntegration engages 30 participants for three to five days in a process to discuss and develop action around a particular issue. The process has been used with members from the same organisation and also in situations where individuals come together to form a multiagency group (White, 1997). The 30 people are called the 'infoset' (information set) 'who share information and interest in some area of mutual enthusiasm, and wish to investigate it further' (Beer, 1995; 20). The aim of the process is to organise the 'infoset' round a geometric structure. The structure is the icosahedron which, Beer believes, can balance the synergy and integrity for the infoset (see Figure 3.3). The process that is developed aims to fit 12 topics and 30 people round the structure (for more details of this and the development of the protocol see Beer, 1995). A brief description is given below.

The process has three main phases: the problem jostle, the topic auction and the outcome resolve. There is also a fourth phase, which is called face meetings or planning meetings. First, the 'problem jostle' is introduced as an alternative to a meeting. Here the infoset works, via a form of brainstorming, on a wide variety of topics of interest to the members. The process starts with free-form thinking where participants are invited to write down statements on post-it notes that seem to be important in relation to the issue they are there to resolve. These are called 'statements of importance'. The participants are then invited to take any of these to one of 12 flip charts and begin a discussion on that theme. The themes that resonate with the participants are carried through to the next stage and are called 'aggregated statements of importance'. Participants work through these in order to reach an agreement on 12 'consolidated statements of importance' (CSIs) – each CSI is a succinct problem statement, which reflects the major concerns of the 'infoset'.

The next major phase is the 'topic auction' where the infoset and 12 CSIs are organised around the icosahedron (the members are the struts and the topics are the nodes), essentially making up 12 teams tackling the 12 CSIs. Since each strut is connected to two nodes, each person is a member of two teams. Each node conjoins five struts, hence there are five members of a team. Each node can also be connected to five other nodes through the internal space of the structure (excluding the one directly opposite to it). The five struts that can be connected internally from a node represent the critics to that node. Hence for each team (node) there are five members and five critics.

The third stage is called the 'outcome resolve' where each CSI is explored in three rounds of discussion to enable the infoset to reach a conclusion which is meant 'to be a convergence on 12 [Final statements of importance] with the whole infoset in agreement' (Beer, 1995:33). For the outcome resolve two groups of five topic

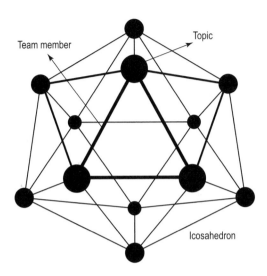

Figure 3.3 Team Syntegrity

members and their critics meet simultaneously. Each team is responsible for discussing their topic and producing a statement at the end of their meeting summarising their thinking. The critics play the role of 'devil's advocate' guiding the group
to reach their final statements. Each group is facilitated but the activity is limited to
timekeeping and scribing.

After the third session in the outcome resolve, the participants discuss their
statements in a plenary.

SSM (SOFT SYSTEMS METHODOLOGY)

SSM is a methodology used to support and to structure thinking about, and
intervention in, complex organisational problems. Checkland (1981) describes the
first decade of development in SSM; a later publication (Checkland and Scholes,
1990) describes the second decade seeking to show the 'flexible-but-rigorous use of
the methodology in the hands of experienced users' (Checkland and Holwell,
1998:12). How SSM has been presented by its originators and proponents has
changed over the years. The description of SSM given here draws on that given
in Checkland and Scholes (1990), Checkland and Holwell (1998) and that available
on the world wide web (at time of writing the web address on which this is available
was http://www.lums.lancs.ac.uk/mansci/HandlingStrategicProblems/index.htm).
Checkland and Holwell (1998) distinguish between what they label the 'formalized
process' or 'novice' SSM, in which the methodology is taken to be a prescriptive set
of stages to be followed in sequence, from what they label the 'internalized process'
or 'experienced' SSM, a more 'sophisticated way of using SSM in which the basic
model of the methodology is used as a sense-making device'.

The basic process of SSM can be described as five stages containing a total of eight steps, shown in Table 3.1. This particular form of presentation is a combination of that given in Checkland and Scholes (1990), Checkland and Holwell (1998) and the world wide web, it does not correspond exactly to any of them taken individually; if you like it represents the output of this author's sense-making endeavours. The eight steps do not represent a single process which can be followed from start to finish, after which a 'right' answer emerges. They are steps in a process: the process may have to be repeated many times before a reasonable accommodation or agreement may be reached. The whole process of SSM is a process of mutual learning, involving a facilitator (usually external to the parties involved) and members of the organisation(s) concerned. The most important site for this learning is in the comparison between conceptually derived models and the real world. When such a comparison is made, the learning gained usually means the model needs to be revised. At the same time, exposure to the model often changes the problem situation, or at least perceptions of what the problem consists of. Through this conversational process of thinking, discussing, accommodating and rethinking, practical ways forward may eventually be found.

Table 3.1 SSM as Five Stages and Eight Steps

Stage	Description	Comment
1	**'Exploring – 1'** is in two steps:	
	Step 1: Appreciation of the problem situation – involves gaining an initial understanding of the problem situation and the wider situation in the organisation(s). This under-standing informs the analyses performed later in the SSM process	No particular set of techniques recommended for this stage Rather, it is up to the facilitator to ask the questions that s/he feels need to be asked, and find the information which is relevant to the problem
	Step 2: Expression of the problem situation – organise description of the ideas and understanding of the situation, to enable and facilitate the analyses that will follow	Three separate analyses are suggested: 1. Identify 'client', 'would-be problem solvers' and 'problem owners' 2. Identify roles and behaviour expectations from those involved 3. Analyse different commodities of power (knowledge/experience, role/position, personal charisma, privileged access, control of resources). These are combined in a 'rich picture' Other possible tools (from outside SSM) are suggested for use here

(Table continued)

2   '**Conceptual modelling**' is in two steps:

Step 3: Formulate root definitions (including CATWOE) – systems to be modelled are described in the form of relevant root definitions. For each root definition, a further role analysis, called CATWOE, is also carried out

For explanation of 'root definition' and 'CATWOE' see Tables 6.11 and 6.12 respectively

Step 4: Build conceptual models – logically extrapolate a conceptual model from each root definition, to show each operational activity which would be necessary to carry out the process described in the root definition

A diagram is constructed to depict the system, this distinguishes:
- the system boundary
- dependencies between activities
- each model should contain 5–9 activities
- all activities should be at same level of definition (an activity which is a constituent part of another activity belongs in a model at another level)

3   '**Exploring – 2**' contains two steps:

Step 5: Compare models with real-world actions – the ideas generated in the previous step are compared to the real world. The thinking that has been done up to now (particularly the conceptual models of the systems in question) is contrasted to the relevant systems in the world

A comparison table is used to present this systematically, this shows:
- important differences between the real-world system and the model
- possible questions to ask of people involved
- possible courses of action which might be taken to change the situation
- necessary changes which should be made to the model

Step 6: Explore problem situation using models – generating understanding of interactions, options for change and their effects

4   '**Option appraisal**'

Step 7: Define feasible and desirable changes – the results from the previous stages are considered and weighed, and those which seem likely, if implemented, to have a positive outcome in the situation are recommended to those with the power to make the changes

5   '**Action needed to improve the situation**'

Step 8: Recommend actions to improve the situation – recommend changes and tactics for implementation of those changes

Explanations of component parts of SSM are given later in the book; in Chapter 6, Table 6.11 gives an explanation of 'root definition' and Table 6.12 explains CATWOE analysis of roles, while rich pictures are explained in Chapter 7. Those interested in a review of aspects of later use of SSM, not covered in detail here, can consult Taket (1999).

TSI (TOTAL SYSTEMS INTERVENTION)

Flood and Jackson's book (Flood and Jackson, 1991) describes lucidly their own particular approach to problem solving using different systems methodologies. They argue that the diversity of systems based approaches in existence represents a strength (rather than a fragmentation and a weakness), when linked with a framework for choosing between them in particular problem situations (including combining or alternating methods where appropriate). They call their framework 'total systems intervention' or TSI; it is built around two major components. The first of these is the use of five different systemic metaphors: machine/'closed system'; organic/'open system'; neurocybernetic/'viable system'; cultural; political (further subdivided into 'team', 'coalition' and 'prison' metaphors at a higher level of resolution). It is argued that these metaphors can be used to look at problem situations with a view to helping identify the nature of the problem context.

The second major component of the TSI framework is the system of systems methodologies (Jackson and Keys, 1984; Jackson, 1990); this is a classification of problem contexts in terms of the system(s) making up the problem situation (classification into simple or complex), and the relationship between participants (classification into unitary, pluralist or coercive). Thirteen different 'systems approaches' are placed within a classification (somewhat controversially, see later), giving us a matching of 'appropriate' methodologies for different types of problem context. The different problem contexts are also related to the systemic metaphors.

The TSI process of creative problem solving involves a three-phase systemic cycle of inquiry, with iteration back and forth between the three phases (see Figure 3.4). The first phase, labelled 'creativity', has as its essential task the use of systems metaphors as organising structures to help managers think creatively about their enterprises, and to identify (as the outcome of this phase) a 'dominant' metaphor which highlights the main interests and concerns, as well as any other 'dependent' metaphors. The 'choice' phase then involves choosing an appropriate systems-based intervention methodology (or set of methodologies) to suit the particular characteristics of the organisation's situation as revealed by the first phase. The 'most probable outcome' of this phase is the selection of a 'dominant' methodology, 'to be tempered in use by the imperatives highlighted by "dependent" methodologies'. The 'intervention' phase then has as its task the application of the methodology (or methodologies) in order to produce specific proposals for co-ordinated change. A later version of total systems intervention has been presented, local systemic intervention (or LSI), described in Flood (1996), where he links it to the

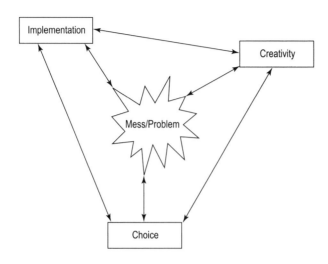

Figure 3.4 TSI

presentations for neophytes in Flood (1995) and for sophisticates in Flood and Romm (1996).

PARTICIPATORY APPRAISAL – METHODS FROM DEVELOPMENT PRACTICE

Participatory appraisal (PA, also known as participatory rural appraisal (PRA)) was developed from a variety of experiences and disciplines. It was developed to meet the criticisms addressed towards the limitations of rapid rural appraisal (RRA, known as rapid appraisal (RA) in the UK, however, the practice of RA is often very different from RRA). RRA as a tool emerged out of work in developing countries and it is based on ideas such as: the importance of a rapid process; allows working in the field; allows learning from local people; that it is semi-structured; and permits timely insights and best bets (Chambers, 1981).

RA is based on three principles: use of a systems perspective; triangulation of data; and an iterative approach to data collection and analysis. It has been used with communities that are relatively deprived. It uses selected people with knowledge of the area to identify key issues and to contribute to identifying solutions. The team undertaking the investigation is usually derived from different organisations. The key aims of the approach are: to gain insights into a community's own perspective on its major needs; to translate these into action; and to establish an ongoing relationship between service providers and local communities.

Proponents of the method have identified the following as key barriers to look out for:

- How do we gain access to communities and define the people who are knowledgeable about community problems? We would need to identify a sample of relevant 'key informants' in order to build up a complex and multilayered understanding. Key informants could be people who are in the best position to understand the issues being addressed, i.e. people who work in the community, community leaders, or important people within informal networks. They could be identified through snowball sampling.
- What other methods can be used and how do you check for rigour and validity? The methods that can be used are secondary data collection, observation and mapping. Validity of the approach depends on triangulation, with data collection from one source being validated or rejected by checking it with data from at least two other sources or methods of collection.
- What team composition to undertake the work is best? Here, it is important to consider how needs are going to be turned into action, and how to gain acceptance of the results.
- Can information be aggregated up from the community level first to understand the community and then to other levels dealing with policy and so on? How does the information relate to traditional needs assessment data?

The major problem with RA perceived by many researchers is that the method is too extractive and not empowering; we have reviewed the criticisms elsewhere (White and Taket, 1997b).

The difference between RRA and PA is that PA emphasises processes which empower local people, whereas RRA is mainly seen as a means for outsiders to gather information. The key elements of PA are the methods used, and − most importantly − the behaviour and attitudes of those who facilitate it. PA sees the facilitator as someone who works in partnership with the people so that the resulting knowledge is owned and shared by local people (Chambers, 1994a,b,c).

PA has much to offer the decision-making process. It provides a way to give people a voice, enabling them to express and analyse their problems and priorities. It can generate important and often surprising insights which can contribute to policies that serve the needs of the community. More fundamentally, it can challenge the perceptions of those in authority and begin to change attitudes and agendas.

It has been described as a family of approaches, methods and behaviours that enable people to express and analyse the realities of their lives and conditions, to plan themselves what action to take, and to monitor and evaluate the results. PA employs a wide range of methods to enable people to express and share information, and to stimulate discussion and analysis.

White and Taket (1997b) outlined the principles of PA as the following:

- *Learning rapidly and progressively*: with conscious exploration, flexible use of methods, improvisation, iteration and cross-checking, not following a blueprint programme but being adaptable in a learning process.

- *Offsetting biases*: especially those of the experts, by being relaxed and not rushing, listening and not lecturing, probing instead of passing on to the next topic, being unimposing instead of important, and seeking out the marginalised and disempowered groups, and learning their concerns and priorities.
- *Optimising trade-offs*: that is, relating the costs of learning to the perceived value of information, with trade-offs between quantity, quality, relevance, accuracy and timeliness. This includes the principles of optimal ignorance, knowing what is not worth knowing, and of appropriate imprecision – and not measuring more than needed, i.e. 'better to be approximately right than precisely wrong'.
- *Triangulation*: meaning using a range of methods of analysis, informants, types of information, investigators and/or disciplines to cross-check.
- *Seeking diversity*: that is, maximising the diversity and richness of information. Chambers describes this as deliberately looking for, noticing and investigating contradictions, anomalies and 'differentness' (Chambers, 1994b).
- *Facilitating – they do it*: facilitating investigation, analysis, presentation and learning by people themselves, so that they present and own the outcomes, and also learn. This often entails the outsiders starting the process and then sitting back and not interrupting.
- *Critical self-awareness*: meaning that facilitators are continuously examining their behaviour, and trying to do it better.

PA has mainly been criticised for not being able to move beyond appraisal (White, 1994; White and Taket, 1997b). That is, even though it is a less extractive process, it is unable to ensure shared analysis, planning, prioritisation of possible solutions, and lead to a commitment to act. It may be a good set of tools for understanding a situation but it does not explore the issues nor assess different options and choices for action. It simplifies and overlooks the inherent problems in developing a plan of action. What would you do if there were a conflict of opinions, different parties pursuing their own interests? It is apparent that there is a need for a further step that takes on these tensions by incorporating tools from elsewhere.

PA needs to build in an action component. It is not that it does not lead to action; in most cases it can help people develop action that they can take themselves. It gives a start to things they can handle. There is a need to engage with wider stakeholders to aggregate local knowledge and to involve policy makers. In other words to create partnerships between the different stakeholders.

Understanding that multiple 'socially constructed' realities may vary in any given situation has been the key reason for the development of our participatory approach. Methods need to be developed to enable a genuine synthesis of different intent and perspectives to be created. The framework should aim to link the multitude of voices. This can be addressed in particular through techniques using visualisation (see Chapter 7).

COMMENTARY AND CRITIQUE – PARTS OF THE ANSWER

As useful as these approaches have been, there are many potential criticisms that can be raised, pointing to problems with their use and gaps within the methodologies they provide. These indicate that there is considerable scope for further development of these approaches. The first of the criticisms that are relevant here is that the established methods draw primarily on theories of rational action (in this case applied to decision-making). Connected to this, through its privileging of a particular form of rationality, operational research/management science has been dismissive of intuition, emotion and feelings, manifested in a variety of ways: (a) a tendency to ignore them (bracket them out of consideration) – leading to criticism of operational research/management science being naive in its modelling of social interaction processes and individual action; (b) a tendency to regard it as interference, something undesirable to be minimised; (c) a view of it as a tool to be manipulated in the service of 'rational' ends. Thus so far, many of the existing decision support methods on their own offer little scope for recognising and/or incorporating and/or 'resolving' the feelings or emotions that may be involved in any decision process. This is not to say that individual facilitators have not recognised the important role that emotion and feelings play in group processes and adopted a variety of tactics to respond to these (see for example: Phillips and Phillips, 1993; White and Taket, 1994; Eden and Ackermann, 1998), rather that most of the established methodologies do not explicitly recognise this. More recently, some of the literature has begun to recognise this issue and debate ways of addressing these issues, see for example De Reuck et al. (1999), who provide a critique of traditional decision conferencing, noting that: 'It has been our experience over seven years of conducting Decision Conference workshops that only a small number of client groups return to use this decision-making technology on other occasions when important decisions for their organizations need to be taken' (de Reuck et al., 1999:200). They intuit (their term) that the reasons for this include: that the technology (particularly the quantification of judgements) is intimidating to the individual; effects of intense and highly structured processes on participation; possibility of unrecognised social compliance masking divergence in view; difficulties in gauging achievement of uncoerced group ownership. De Reuck et al. (1999) also discuss ways in which these points of critique may be addressed, including calling for the process to be made more transparent to the participants; we return to discuss this in more detail in Chapter 8.

It can also be argued that the methods do not stimulate or harness the creativity of the group. Indeed it can be argued that the concentration on structuring and rationality positively inhibits creativity and spontaneity, with most tools to encourage creative thinking (such as brainstorming) still relying on verbal communication.

The concentration on rationality and abstraction leads to another major concern about existing methods: the issue of access to participation in the processes involved. The methods are strongly verbally based, with the consequence that this can pose differential barriers to access to participation in the process. They thus make it difficult to enable equal (access to) participation; the argument here is similar to that advanced by some researchers that interviewing disadvantages particular groups in society who are less familiar with circumstances where they are asked to give their views about abstract concepts, see for example Calnan's discussions in relation to social class differences (Calnan, 1987). The methods can be technically complex (e.g. computer-based MCDA or other computer-based systems) and thus alienating to some.

A final relevant criticism is that the understanding of the potential roles of the facilitator(s) within the method is often not explicitly developed. For example, differences between active/intervening and less directive approaches may be seen in terms of difference in the individual style of facilitators rather than different types of facilitating role that may be appropriate in different parts of the decision process.

To illustrate these criticisms, let us scrutinise one particular approach we have described above, namely TSI; in doing so we draw on Taket (1992). TSI is particularly ripe for criticism, owing to its grand claims for itself. The first issue with the use of TSI is connected to the use of language, and concerns what seems to be a constant tension or contradiction in the book between open and closed views/ statements. This is perhaps best illustrated by a couple of examples. First contrast: 'And there are, of course, other systems methodologies which could be included in the TSI schema' (Flood and Jackson, 1991:241) with 'Hence we have employed the "system of systems methodologies" to help us make what is the broadest possible coverage of systems methodologies according to their underlying assumptions, without missing out any of the most powerful approaches that the reader should know about' (Flood and Jackson, 1991:59) or with 'Chapter 2 groups the most important of the available systems methodologies' (Flood and Jackson, 1991:xiii). As a second example, contrast 'We would argue that we are helping everyone to think within the very wide boundaries of knowledge in the managerial sciences and hence helping to avoid biases arising from limitations in knowledge. We are encouraging all users of TSI to expand their knowledge and broaden their horizons' (Flood and Jackson, 1991:243) with 'Our choice of methodologies has been guided by two assumptions. First, that systems approaches offer the surest source of theoretical guidance for implementing an intervention and change strategy. Therefore we have chosen only systems-based methodologies' (Flood and Jackson, 1991:59). Which are we to believe? At best, we would argue that the two closed assertions taken from p. 59 remain to be proven, and that, incidentally, we should not forget the interesting boundary debate (which we will not digress into) about what is, and what is not, a 'systems approach'.

Another issue that we want to highlight, without however giving it the full scrutiny it deserves, is the question of the assignment of particular systems meth-odologies to problem contexts. This is particularly important since, as Flood and Jackson recognise in their autocritique (Flood and Jackson, 1991:242), this is one of the legs TSI stands on. The particular assignments that gives us most concern are those of SAST and SSM to pluralist contexts (simple in the case of SAST and complex in the case of SSM), while CSH is assigned to simple coercive contexts. Our argument here would be that this assignment is crucially dependent on the particular readings of the methodologies used, and that the readings of these methodologies offered to us by Flood and Jackson may not necessarily be the same as those offered by their proponents or by other practitioners. Some brief illustrations of what we mean: Flood and Jackson argue (Flood and Jackson, 1991:244) that SSM tends to be ideologically conservative, and that it pays little attention to power relations (Flood and Jackson, 1991:187). A different reading of SSM would see plenty of scope for the analyst/participants to uncover power relations and their effects through developing, in suitable depth, the analyses making up Checkland's 'finding out' phase, and in particular the third so-called political analysis, see Checkland's description (in Chapter 4 of Rosenhead 1989), (this political analysis is characterised by Flood and Jackson (Flood and Jackson, 1991:187) as 'impoverished'), and by exploring a suitable range of different conceptual models. Similarly, we would argue that SAST, through its stakeholder analysis, can offer the opportunity to identify power relations and the existence of dominance, and warn us of any dangers of proceeding to a false synthesis based on the exercise of coercion rather than consensus. Ulrich's CSH offers its users extremely incisive interrogatory tools, very useful at identifying the existence of relations of power and dominance, and it certainly puts these issues clearly to the fore, more so than either SAST or SSM. It can produce a knowledge of what is or what ought to be, the latter according to its own critical standards, again, which we would wholeheartedly embrace, although we doubt whether everyone would. However, it does not guarantee us the production of an implementable prescription for intervention and change. This is a feature explicitly recognised by Flood and Jackson in their critique of CSH (Flood and Jackson, 1991:218). So we do not see that CSH necessarily gets us any further than SAST or SSM, and interestingly enough, in the example used to illustrate the chapter on CSH in Flood and Jackson (1991), the ideal of participation by all those affected was not achieved. There is much more that could be said, but we will refrain here from moving into a debate on the philosophical underpinnings of the various different methodologies.

In terms of the three phases of TSI, most detail is provided on the 'intervention' phase, whereas we suspect most difficulty in practice might be found in the completion of the other two phases – and this is where issues connected with the world-views of the participants in the TSI process and intersubjective issues come into play, we would have welcomed more attention to aspects of process here – such as the analyst's role in the facilitation of these two phases. It is here that we consider the 'self-contained' (isolationist?) nature of TSI is perhaps least helpful, and would want to suggest that there are a whole host of approaches within soft operational research (OR) (never mind elsewhere) that would merit admittance as potential tools that could add to the creativity and choice phases, for example: drama methods, cognitive mapping (this is actually mentioned in passing in Chapter 10, but not as a potential tool in the two earlier phases), hypergame analysis, etc. Even if it is regarded as desirable for didactic purposes to keep the basic structure of TSI simple, surely, in the open spirit of the quote given earlier from page 243, there are books that could usefully be recommended as supplementary reading, for example (Rosenhead, 1989; Bryant, 1989). It also remains a question for further research as to how sensitive the outcomes of these phases are to key players, including the analyst(s).

One key question for future examination is whether the practice of TSI lives up to the claims laid out in the philosophy of TSI. It is one thing to argue, *pace* Habermas, that 'Human beings have, therefore, an "emancipatory interest" in freeing themselves from constraints imposed by power relations and in learning, through a process of genuine participatory democracy, involving discursive will formation, to control their own destiny' (Flood and Jackson, 1991:49) and quite another to convince those in positions of power of the validity of this viewpoint, and of the actuality of the power relations they are implicated in. Flood and Jackson recognise this in their discussion of CSH, and in their lack of identification of a systems methodology for use in coercive contexts, but the implications of this for the totalising claims of TSI as set out in this book are not fully worked through. One further related point: 'Critical systems thinking is a politically conscious and self-reflective approach, distinguished by an openly declared emancipatory interest in an equal distribution of power and chances to satisfy personal needs, and in liberating people from dominance by other people and forces they do not currently control' (Flood and Jackson, 1991:244). Living up to that aim (one that we would wholeheartedly embrace as desirable), requires critical systems practitioners to engage in a constant process of ethical self-reflection, particularly in the choice of clients to work for/with (an issue that is not addressed in any detail in the book).

So do the later versions of TSI live up to the aim? Flood's later development into LSI and its manifestations as 'solving problem solving' and 'diversity management' have already been mentioned. Unfortunately, in our view, they do not address satisfactorily the criticisms raised above. As Checkland (1998) reviewing Flood (1995) and Taket (1998a) reviewing Flood and Romm (1996) point out, the two books are both strong on assertion and claim, but weak on helpful presentation and case studies. So it is still the case that only time will enable a deeper assessment of whether practice lives up to this laudable aim.

Earlier in this chapter we described a number of methods and approaches that have been used in one way or another in the multiagency setting. We would like to finish this section with a discussion of frameworks developed for the use of multiple methods in the multiagency setting. In particular we will discuss how the approaches fail to enhance or even work with diversity in that they generally aim at trying to find an overarching theory or meta-theory to explain how different methods are related.

It has been suggested that the emergence of a diversity of methods has created a brand new issue to be managed – and that is how to choose between models, methodologies and theories (Mingers and Gill, 1997; Flood and Romm, 1996). There seems to be a general agreement that since the end of the 1970s the management sciences (including systems and OR) have become more pluralistic – some might say fragmented – in terms of the methodologies employed. The proliferation of approaches for solving management problems have excited some quarters but left others worried that the management sciences are in crisis. Certainly, the proliferation of different methods has coincided with deep-seated changes taking place in actual organisational forms as well as the wider context in which these forms are located. However, it is often difficult to see the wider context which bears down on management sciences, and this has led to the perpetuation of a management science concerned with finding order. We now find many discussions offering to guide us through the rainforest of theories and methods.

The discussions have opened up a space for the generation of ways to account for the variety of methods, i.e. ways to embrace the pluralism. But as we will see, most attempts to deal with pluralism aim to control or master pluralism rather than embrace it.

> We need to retain rigorous and formalised thinking, while admitting the need for a range of 'problem-solving' methodologies, and accepting the challenge which that brings. The future prospects of management science will be much enhanced if (a) the diversity of the 'messes' confronting managers is accepted, (b) work on developing a rich variety of methodologies is undertaken, and (c) we continually ask the question: 'what kind of problem situation can be managed with which sort of methodology?' (Flood and Jackson, 1991:xi).

In the above quote, we can see elements of the need to tame pluralism, in that a particular vantage point (rigorous and formalised thinking – a version of the scientific method) is sought in order to deal with diversity, bias, mess. There is, however, a tension between this and the admission of a plurality of methodologies, and an appeal to a multimethodology (matching contexts to methodologies) is required to resolve this tension. Without such a move, the requirements of 'rigorous formalised thinking' make the alternatives (methodological imperialism, relativism or nihilism) unacceptably unpalatable. Or as Jackson phrases it elsewhere:

> instead of seeing [different strands of management science] as competing for exactly the same area of concern, alternative approaches can be presented as being appropriate to the different types of situation in which management scientists are required to act. Each approach will be useful in certain defined areas and should be used in circumstances where it works best (Jackson, 1993:575).

More recently we come to the work of Flood and Romm (1996) which is particularly interesting to us because of their claims to deal with diversity and to '[find] a balance between modernism and postmodernism' (p. 473). We would wish to note, however, that although we can find many points of similarity between their approach and ours, there are also many differences, not least in their reliance on

Habermas' theories of communicative competence and the possibilities of dialogue guaranteeing the achievement of unforced consensus.

Their aim is to design a scheme of thought that embraces two points: (i) diversity in types of model, methodology and theory and (ii) emancipatory practice. The authors discuss four types of responses they have seen in the literature (i.e. pragmatism, isolationism, imperialism and complementarism) that have addressed the two points, and they go on to develop their own brand of complementarism.

A 'standard' is described as 'the chances people have to make widely informed and locally contingent choices in the process of managing issues and dilemmas that characterise organisational and societal affairs' (p. 9). To achieve this standard the following are offered: managing diversity; triple loop learning; managing dilemmas; and the process of critique and complementarism.

Diversity management works with the tension between different methods, models and theories, as modes of knowing and intervening (i.e. their brand of complementarism). The tensions have to be kept in consciousness and their differences acknowledged. Triple loop learning loops (*sic*) three questions: Are we doing things right? Are we doing the right things? Is rightness buttressed by mightness or vice versa?

The main meta-theory that helps to deal with complementarism is reflexivity, i.e. 'to question in deliberate fashion the relevance and consideredness of unchallenged yet favoured points of view' (p. 34). 'It must locate diversity of, and irreducible differences between, theoretical positions', and there is no Archimedean vantage point to provide an objective adjudication between these theories. Instead their standard is offered which refers to the local contingent nature of choice making between theories.

Flood and Romm stress the importance of giving informed choice to those faced with deciding between the range of methods, methodologies and theories (i.e. interventionists/researchers). However, those who face the choice seem silent and passive throughout their work (the clients of the interventionists are not even mentioned). They are the 'other' in the work, kept in the dark, never shown to make a choice. Yet, in the end they are the ones who will be dependent on their ideas. It appears that they have to be given structure and guidance to avoid the 'messy world' or 'entering the pit'. They can even be taught to make the right choice. The impression is that they (or we) are not very sophisticated and must be protected from themselves (ourselves).

Another conviction in the book is a rejection of pragmatism. Flood and Romm claim that pragmatism (in terms of choice of methods) is 'mixing without [a] concern for the way mixing is done, whether or how mixing could be justified, and why some parts of models are being chosen for the mixing pot'. Thus, pragmatism is likely to maintain or increase the power of a select group and does not reflect over theory (p. 35). At the same time they assert that for the choice of methods 'there is no absolute standardised way of comparing, we need to be sensitive to other options', and that 'each choice ... can only be made using locally generated criteria informed by wider consideration'. This is all well and good, but what happens if the local circumstances change or a particular process does not work? Would one not have to be prepared to ditch the method and try something else? And is this not being pragmatic?

A further assertion by Flood and Romm is that a postmodern point of view on methodology choice means that nothing can be compared, and that relativism must be avoided. Perhaps this is so, however they agree that the world does not provide us with any absolute criterion of choice between alternatives. Instead, all we can do is compare methods (or the theories) with one another, with something beyond method called meta-theory or even a standard. Their standard (p. 9) is this: 'the chances people have to make widely informed and locally contingent choices in the process of managing issues and dilemmas that characterise organisations and societal affairs'. However, the authors would have to be prepared to accept the contingent aspect of this view, and that it may not be relevant to all situations pertaining to methodology choice or even that interventionists may just not want it. What happens then?

We had trouble with the notion of 'diversity management'. We are troubled with the authors' need to 'preserve diversity'. What is even more alarming is their view that 'difference may become divisive' and that 'divisiveness may lead to people talking past each other'. They seem to imply that diversity is a problem to solve. Postmodernists assume that human experience is fragmented and discontinuous – thus they search out discontinuity and difference rather than order and similarity. To put it provocatively – there are no patterns – these are merely sentimental illusions. We think, following Derrida, that we should give voice to silences and absences, i.e. all those things that are suppressed in the orchestration of order, i.e. to break the habit of organised routine and see the world as though for the first time.

Recently, Mingers and Gill (1997) have produced an edited book exploring multimethodology. In their introductory chapter, Mingers and Gill claim that multimethodology 'is about developing ways of mixing together or integrating a range of methodologies or techniques from different paradigms in the course of a particular intervention' (Mingers and Gill, 1997:16). The book has a number of chapters by various authors offering their own brand of mixing methods, as well as a number of chapters exploring the theoretical aspect of multimethodology; there is a chapter on our PANDA brand of multimethodology included. Within the book, Mingers provides a commentary on the different approaches and theory and concludes the book with a call for critical pluralism (Mingers, 1997). In particular he is concerned with the notion that critique in the use of different methods does not go far enough. He agrees with our critique of Flood and Jackson in that there is very little in their work to assist those using their approach to make choices. He also writes that for the move to multimethodology there needs to be 'a movement away from abstract methodologies towards an emphasis on the importance of the real agent(s) who will use them; recognising that critically oriented methodologies cannot guarantee their critical employment – this rests with the commitments of the agent; and accepting that any emancipatory potential must be local and contextual rather than general and abstract' (Mingers, 1997:408). We agree.

Mingers focuses on the agent and says that there are two types of activities the agent will take in an action situation: action in a situation in which the agent may need to use different methodologies or techniques; and reflection about the intervention to determine the course of combinations employed. The first activity should consider the relationships between the agents, methodologies and problem situation. The second activity is informed by Habermas' theory of communicative action mapped on to Habermas' three worlds, to clarify the dimensions of our actions (referenced in Mingers, 1997). Here the main principle for critique and action is to specify procedures so that individuals can determine and apply standards in a rational way. It is on this point that we depart from Mingers' view. Although he acknowledges that this is an ideal, he claims that identifying the procedures is possible, and that change and emancipation can be achieved through critical reflection, although it will be local and limited. To us critical reflection alone cannot guarantee change, particularly reflection that focuses on being aware of the underpinning paradigms of different methodologies in order to appreciate how they might or might not be used in a particular situation. This view reveals a contradiction in Mingers' view, in that he claims critique in other theories is too abstract to apply, yet his own version of critique can be criticised for its excess in abstraction — its abstract reason, and ethics. However, that aside, we find much to commend in his treatment of multimethodology, particularly its acknowledgement of action being local and contingent.

SUMMING UP AND MOVING ON – OUR MULTIMETHODOLOGY: PANDA

The framework that this book introduces is our version of multimethodology, formed from our practice and also partially in response to the critical observations offered above on other frameworks and approaches. The (so far) uniqueness of what we offer is our unashamedly postmodern/poststructuralist position and our acknowledgement and joyful celebration of the paradoxes this implies. But what we offer is also shared with many others. The form of multimethodology we espouse is mirrored in many other fields and specific case studies of various different types of practice. These come from extremely diverse fields, and we refer to them in more detail elsewhere in this book, and most especially in Chapter 10; however it is useful just to give a flavour of the diversity out there that seems to be closely linked to our type of multimethodology. In terms of broad fields, action research, especially participatory action research (Whyte, 1991), action learning (Revans, 1982), co-operative inquiry (Heron, 1996), critical management theory, organisational development and organisational change, development theory and practice (Thomas et al., 1998) all present strands which utilise a similar multimethodological approach. Note this is very emphatically not to say that all of the authors involved would label themselves as unashamed postmodernists/poststructuralists, some indeed may be quite horrified by our linking their work and ours, we shall see! Examples of case studies that illustrate this diversity include:

- an article by Heracleous and Langham (1996) discussing strategic change and organisational culture at Hay Management Consultants, which reveals Hays to be practising multimethodologists, and discusses the use of a device called a 'cultural web' as a diagnostic tool. We do not cover the 'cultural web' in any detail in this book, since we have not used it (yet);
- an article by Pizey and Huxham (1991) describing the development of a process for group decision support in large-scale event planning which provides a complex multiagency case study with multiple organisations and other coalitions, using SODA (usually, sometimes using HIVIEW and Metaplanning), and two facilitators (one for content and software, one for group process);
- a case study of the UK Open University's 'New Directions' organisational learning programme reported by Russell and Peters (1998), which 'deliberately created a "chaotic" space for random communication across organizational boundaries — so that the organization can begin to learn as a whole and respond faster to change' (p. 236);
- a case study of a multinational company, reported by Vennix et al. (1996), which involved group model-building (systems dynamics plus other methods) used for organisational learning and achievement of consensus on need for change;
- a case study of strategies used to overcome resistance to co-management in the case of natural resource management in New Zealand, reported by Prystupa (1998). A variety of strategies were used by indigenous groups to overcome the resistance of conservation agencies to co-management. This provides an example of how entrenched power relations can be overcome;
- a report by Aronoff and Gunter (1994) on the facilitation of participatory processes in technological hazard disputes in the USA.

Introducing PANDA   II

Pragmatic pluralism   4

*to think differently — this thought must enter deeply into our intentions, actions and so on —
our whole being. Bohm (1985:25)*

INTRODUCTION

In this chapter we introduce what we have called 'pragmatic pluralism' — a set of
theoretical principles which underpin our work. This is our strategy for working in
the multiagency setting, which we see as polyvocal, contingent, dynamic and
diverse. In Part I we described a number of methods and approaches that have
been used in one way or another in the multiagency setting. In Chapter 3 we have
already discussed how the approaches fail to enhance or even work with diversity
and they generally aim at trying to find an overarching theory or meta-theory to
explain how different methods are related. To us the use of multiple methods
requires negotiation that raises many complex issues.

In using the term 'pluralism' we intend this to read in several different ways and
on several different levels. In this chapter we will talk about pluralism in each of the
following features:

- in the nature of the client
- in the use of specific methods
- in the modes of representation employed
- in the facilitation process

We will argue that we need pluralism in order to deal with the diversity and
heterogeneity that abound in any multiagency setting.

Finally in this chapter we introduce our version of the process through which
groups in the multiagency setting must go through in dealing with issues. We have
called this the three Ds, which are deliberation, debate and decision.

Our use of pluralism is seen, drawing on our reading of Nietzsche, as a joyful,
playful becoming: a Dionysian creativity which is exercised with no fixed or pre-
conceived notion of where it will lead us. Our emphasis is on creativity and
reflexivity working in tandem with each other. To us the issue is how to create

an opening within which the Nietzschean/Dionysian creativity described above can flourish, we call this 'pragmatic pluralism'. The opening allows us a moment for reflection before acting.

PRAGMATIC PLURALISM

Our aim here is to present a framework we use for intervening which we call 'pragmatic pluralism'. It is also important to state that this is *not* an attempt at prescription (although there are some things in the course of our description that are proscribed). Since we espouse a postmodern or poststructuralist position in all this, we do not provide a 'justification' of what is presented in the 'normal' terms. To do so would be somewhat self-contradictory since we believe in the meta-narrative that there is no Archimedean vantage point from which what we describe can be seen to be absolutely right (or absolutely wrong for that matter!). Putting it another way, in the words of Rorty (1989:48–9):

> To accept the claim that there is no standpoint outside the particular historically conditioned and temporary vocabulary we are presently using from which to judge this vocabulary is to give up on the idea that there can be reasons for using languages as well as reasons within languages for believing statements. This amounts to giving up the idea that intellectual or political progress is rational, in any sense of 'rational' which is neutral between vocabularies. But because it seems pointless to say that all the great moral and intellectual advances of European history – Christianity, Galilean science, the Enlightenment, Romanticism, and so on – were fortunate falls into temporary irrationality, the moral to be drawn is that the rational–irrational distinction is less useful than it once appeared. Once we realise that progress, for the community as for the individual, is a matter of using new words as well as of arguing from premises phrased in old words, we realise that a critical vocabulary which revolves around notions like 'rational', 'criteria', 'argument', 'foundation' and 'absolute' is badly suited to describe the relation between the old and the new.

Instead of seeking a prescription we will seek guidelines, examples, stories, metaphors for use in planning an interaction, in carrying out the interaction, and in reflecting on it during and afterwards. In moving away from prescription, we seek to maintain an open and flexible stance, capable of responding creatively to the characteristics of a particular moment, continually disrupting the comfort of identification with a fixed theory or view, and seeking instead to mix different perspectives. We are interested in the move to action, arguing that:

> we can move away from theory to theatre (acknowledging in passing that they have the same Greek root). The call for action is the call for theatre, not for theory. The world is not just a stage provided by an invisible stage-hand. It is an ever changing scene. We need to act to change our scenes which then, in turn, change the way we act. We cannot unravel ourselves from the scene: we must aim to de-centre ourselves. There is no one theory providing the ideal plot, but many to choose from, like different soundtracks for different occasions (Taket and White, 1993:879).

OUR PRAGMATISM

Our approach is an attempt at moving away from the sorts of approaches that work piece by piece, analysing concept after concept, or testing thesis after thesis, and to work instead holistically and *pragmatically*. This approach encourages us to say things like 'try thinking of it this way' – or more specifically 'try to ignore the apparently futile traditional questions by substituting the following new and possibly interesting questions'. We can ask questions such as:

- How does this feel?
- Is this fun?
- Does this do what we want?
- Is 'h' better than 'f'? (In dialogue: do we prefer 'f' to 'h'; in action: select one, do it, change it if we do not like what we see.)

The focus with which the book is concerned is the process or task of intervention, and more specifically the exploration of three (overlapping and interacting) questions pertinent to those who would intervene:

- What is to be done?
- How shall we decide what to do?
- What can guide our actions?

As pragmatists we rejected the search for totalities in favour of a more eclectic approach. We do not have an argument or another theory to set in its place; rather we would like to think of what we do as 'critically reflective'. Thus, we question the usefulness of a view such as the need for an overarching theory and present an alternative view stressing the 'doing what feels good'. There are parallels between this and the stance taken by researchers in action research and action learning

(Schön, 1987). Bryant (1989) also reflects this view in management science. Our argument for thinking that the search for a meta-theory should be abandoned (following Rorty) is that the intellectual tradition to which they belong has not paid off, it is more trouble than it is worth, it has become an incubus. As Rorty said in rejecting the idea of a correspondence theory of truth: 'modern science does not enable us to cope because it corresponds, it just plain enables us to cope. The argument for the view is that several hundred years of effort have failed to make interesting sense of the notion of "correspondence" ...' (Rorty, 1989:xvii).

It is obvious that if this statement includes itself, then it is itself not interesting. We are aware that we cannot offer non-circular arguments and that we face a dilemma. However, if this view cannot support itself, then neither can other theories. The search for a totalising theory is no better than the circularity of pragmatism. Each is a story or perspective; what makes one 'better' than another is the use to which it is put.

We view our situation as a diverse conversation, in which we do not have a privileged status. By putting everything up for grabs at once the different views 'will not struggle dialectically for victory; there will be no glorious victor, no vanquished loser, only the passing of one era into another' (Rorty, 1989).

OUR PLURALISM

Pluralism, to use an illustrative simile drawn from Wittgenstein, is like a spun thread or rope, which gains its strength, not from a continuous strand that runs its entire length, but from the overlapping and entwining of many separate fibres. We have already argued that there is the need for pluralism in order to deal with diversity and heterogeneity. This is our reinterpretation of Ashby's 'law of requisite variety', which states that one needs variety to deal with variety, and that it is quite easy to fail to find a solution to issues because the solutions on offer have too little variety. Next we summarise some of the features of the different aspects of pluralism identified above.

The charge of relativism has been repeatedly made to our position, but to us this weakness is a strength, in that it frees us from the 'intellectual myopia' that is common in research and critical reflection and argues against 'standard write-ups' and 'normal science' whose ultimate aim is a regulation of texts. Thus we embrace relativism, since as intervenors we recognise that no cultural structure can analytically encompass the language of another cultural structure, since to encompass the 'other', it would have the effect of silencing the 'other'. This means that we aim to resist the seductive lure of the enlightenment vision, of ethical absolutism, the desire for a firm transcendent footing for our practice and the difficulty of embracing the shifting sands of postmodernism, the uncomfortable knowledge that the only certainty is uncertainty, and that all knowledge is partial, provisional and contingent. But, as Jacques observes: 'A world of multiple knowledge frameworks is not valueless; it is a world of possibility and of responsibility. It is a world in which we refuse to use "objectivity" as reason for avoiding personal involvement in our knowledge productions' (Jacques, 1989:708). This pluralism is not without potential criticisms, one such objection is to perceive a problem with the possible use of methods based on incompatible ontological or epistemological assumptions. Our response to this is that it only represents a problem from a strongly positivist standpoint; from postmodern or poststructuralist standpoints, this is not of concern, not least because the question of how to accord precedence to any set of ontological/epistemological assumptions is regarded as unanswerable. To draw on Luhmann's discussion of the pervasiveness of intransparency (Luhmann, 1995), we find ourselves inside operationally closed autopoeitic systems, with respect to the lack of possibility of checking what is known with recourse to anything that stands outside the systems. There are no mechanisms for such outside checks. We note also that such pluralism has the added advantage of imposing no requirement on participants in any intervention to negotiate a singular common set of ontological and epistemological beliefs as the first stage in the process (see Table 4.1).

However, it is extremely important to stress that this recognition of relativism does not amount to a position of 'anything goes'; in Haraway's words: 'the alternative to relativism is partial, locatable, critical knowledges sustaining the

Table 4.1 The Characteristics of the Scientific Rationality

1. Existence of stable, coherent self, capable of a 'reason' which offers privileged insight into its own processes and 'laws of nature'
2. Reason and its 'science' – philosophy – can provide an objective, reliable and universal foundation for knowledge
3. Knowledge acquired from correct use of reason will be 'true' in the sense of describing something real and unchanging about our minds and the structure of the natural world
4. Reason has transcendental and universal qualities, it is independent of the self's contingent existence
5. All claims to truth and rightful authority are to be submitted to the tribunal of reason. Freedom consists of obedience to laws that conform to the necessary results of the correct/right use of reason
6. By grounding claims to authority in reason, conflicts between truth, knowledge and power can be overcome. Truth can serve power without distortion; in turn, by utilising knowledge in the service of power, both freedom and progress will be assured. Knowledge can be both neutral (e.g. grounded in universal reason, not particular interests) and also socially beneficial
7. Science, as the exemplar of the right use of reason, is also the paradigm for all true knowledge
8. Language is in some sense transparent and can provide the medium through which the real can be represented. Objects are not linguistically (or socially) constructed; they are merely made present to consciousness by naming and the right use of language

Source: drawing on Flax (1987).

possibility of webs of connections called solidarity. ... Relativism is a way of being nowhere while claiming to be everywhere equally. The "equality" of positioning is a denial of responsibility and critical inquiry' (Haraway, 1991:191). So our pluralism is not 'anything goes' (even Feyerbend argues for reflection), but 'doing what feels good'. However, how does this fit in with methodological choice? In practice, our resolution to this is as follows. The first component is recognising and valuing the differences in the methodologies on which we draw and attempting to match these with variety in the local context worked within, the participants in the interaction and the purpose of the interaction. This is not to imply the existence of any simple mappings between these factors and the methodologies. The second component is the proviso that in the interaction we work to support disempowered or margin- alised groups, which are identifiable in any specific local context. This is our ethics of practice – a personal set of principles, which is necessary in the sense that to some explicit or implicit recourse to values enhances the role of the facilitator or interventionist working in the multiagency setting (see Chapter 8).

To us the question whether one method provides better truths than others has no meaning. What actually matters about the choice of, say, a method is not so much whether or not it provides 'truth' because surely all methods provide truths in one way or another, but whether or not it is capable of giving to those entertaining it feelings of freedom and em(power)ment, but we are not the judge of this, only the interlocutors. The kind of principle we can adopt is: we must work at the limits of what the rules permit, in order to invent new moves or perhaps new rules.

The picture that encapsulates our notion of critical reflection (and to some degree our notion of pluralism) is the rhizome as described by Deleuze and Guattari (1980). They stated:

> We enumerate certain approximate characteristics of the rhizome. 1 and 2. Principles of connection and heterogeneity: any point of a rhizome can be connected to anything other, and must be. ... A rhizome ceaselessly establishes connections between semiotic chains, organizations of power, and circum- stances relevant to the arts, sciences, and social struggles. A semiotic chain is like a tuber agglomerating very diverse acts, not only linguistic, but also perceptive, mimetic, gestural, and cognitive: there is no language in itself, nor are there any linguistic universals, only a throng of dialect, patois, slangs, and specialized languages. There is no ideal speaker-listener, any more than there is a homogeneous linguistic community. ... There is no mother tongue, only a power takeover by a dominant language within a political multiplicity. ... It is always possible to break a language down into internal structural elements, an undertaking not fundamentally differ- ent from the search for roots. There is always something genealogical about a tree. It is not a method for the people.

A method of the rhizome type, on the contrary, can analyze
language only by decentering it onto other dimensions and
other registers. A language is never closed upon itself, except
as a function of impotence (Deleuze and Guattari, 1980:7–8).

They claimed that a key characteristic of the rhizome is its 'multiplicative connectivity'. In this sense it can be seen as 'antisystemic', in the way it explicitly
connects incommensurate registers and different levels of the hierarchies set up
within systems thinking (as in the system of systems methodologies (SOSM) – see
Chapter 3). To us practice is a set of relays from one theoretical point to another,
and theory is a relay from one practice to another. Thus, theories (such as SOSM)
which put things into boxes in fact stop connecting things and they lose their
practical importance.

As Deleuze and Guattari stated (p. 12):

The rhizome is altogether different, a map and not a tracing.
Make a map, not a tracing. The orchid does not reproduce the
tracing of the wasp; it forms a map with the wasp, in a
rhizome. What distinguishes the map from the tracing is
that it is entirely oriented toward an experimentation in contact with the real. The map does not reproduce an unconscious
closed in upon itself; it constructs the unconscious. It fosters
connections between fields, the removal of blockages on
bodies without organs, the maximum opening of bodies without organs onto a plane of consistency. It is itself a part of the
rhizome. The map is open and connectable in all of its dimensions; it is detachable, reversible, susceptible to constant modification. It can be torn, reversed, adapted to any kind of
mounting, reworked by an individual, group, or social formation. It can be drawn on a wall, conceived of as a work of art,
constructed as a political action or as a meditation. Perhaps
one of the most important characteristics of the rhizome is that
it always has multiple entryways; in this sense the burrow is an
animal rhizome, and sometimes maintains a clear distinction
between the line of flight as passageway and storage or living
strata. ... A map has multiple entryways, as opposed to the
tracing, which always comes back to the same. The map has to
do with performance, whereas the tracing always involves an
alleged competence.

The centre of the rhizome is a plateau, in fact there can be many plateaus
'designating something special, a continuous self-vibrating region of intensity
whose development avoids any orientation towards a culmination point or external

end' (p. 21). A plateau is any multiplicity connected to other multiplicities whose effect is often difficult to describe.

The implication of this postmodern critique is the view that it is dangerous to see any form of methodology as *inherently* liberatory or emancipatory; there are no guarantees to be had. Whether we succeed in achieving some outcomes that can be seen as liberatory or emancipatory is only ever locally decidable. We can still, however, talk about guidelines that are useful to help us choose, but these must be used without allowing us to duck the responsibility of choice. From our reading of the postmodern literature we see guidelines for critical action including the following (explored in more detail later).

The first is a need to resist the seductive lure of grand narrative, replacing this by an attitude of positive scepticism. The second is the use of a form of deconstructive practice to replace the prescriptive application of a set methodology. The third is the need to move away from the binary thinking that dominates Western thought, and in particular from the negative–positive and normal–pathological couplets (see the discussions in Taket and White, 1993). The fourth is to call for resistance to the interpretation of postmodern stances as despairing, nihilistic and miserabilist, arguing that despite the actuality of oppression in many different violent forms, or as Shange (1992:19) puts it: 'Yes we still have to have romance in the face of adversity, this is a fact.' In discussing representation (through systems models for example), this should not be enacted to reinscribe the disciplinary relations of power, but to identify and work with points of resistance to such relations. The aim of representation is not then to accurately reproduce what existed at a particular point in time, but as a device to enable change. The fifth is the need to recognise and embrace plurality, multiplicity and diversity rather than homogenising (and sterilising) the diversity into a set of unitary distinct categories and according an unacknowledged privileged position to only one of these: the average rational economically active heterosexual able-bodied middle-class white male. The chapters that follow illustrate how pluralism in a number of aspects of intervention contributes to the achievement of our practice. In terms of what we will describe as pragmatic pluralism (our response to the questions identified earlier), we intend this to be read in several different ways and on several different levels. We will talk about pluralism in each of the following features:

- in the 'nature' of the client
- in the use of specific methods/techniques
- in the modes of representation employed
- in the role(s) of the facilitators/interventionists

Below we give an introduction to later chapters.

Pluralism in the 'nature' of the client

From our experience as interventionists, we have found that organisations/groups are increasingly exposed internally to the challenges of heterogeneity and diversity, while at the same time experiencing external pressure to reconstruct their collective identities along pluralistic lines. Individuals within organisations/groups, as well as organisations/groups within the wider setting, are increasingly subject to identity crises. As interventionists, in adopting a pluralist strategy for intervention, we seek to respect and acknowledge the views of a wide range of stakeholders, i.e. the heterogeneity within the group/organisation. The danger with this perspective, however, is its tendency towards relativism, and our attitude to this with respect to methods has been discussed earlier.

In Chapter 5 we explore approaches that can help participants to acknowledge the differences of others, and to help articulate issues that have remained private and personal and perhaps even unsymbolised. In terms of an intervention in the multiagency setting the chapter will explore many examples where we have employed the useful tactic of 'strategic essentialism' (Hooks, 1990; Butler, 1990) to deal with the problems associated with relativism.

Pluralism in the methods employed

In Chapter 3 we have described a number of methods that have been used to help groups make decsions in the multiagency setting. Recently, it has been suggested that the emergence of a diversity of methods has created a brand new issue to be managed – and that is how to choose between models, methodologies and theories (Mingers and Gill, 1997; Flood and Romm, 1996). There seems to be a general agreement that since the end of the 1970s the management sciences (including systems and OR) have become more pluralistic – some might say fragmented – in terms of the methodologies employed. The proliferation of approaches for solving management problems has excited some quarters but left others worried that the disciplines are in crisis. Certainly, the proliferation of different methods has coincided with deep-seated changes taking place in actual organisational forms as well as the wider context in which these forms are located. However, it is often difficult to see the wider context which bears down on management sciences, and this has led to the perpetuation of a management science concerned with finding order. We now find many discussions offering to guide us through the rainforest of theories and methods.

Flood and Jackson (1991:xi) offered one such map:

> We need to retain rigorous and formalised thinking, while admitting the need for a range of 'problem-solving' methodologies, and accepting the challenge which that brings. The future prospects of management science will be much enhanced if (a) the diversity of the 'messes' confronting managers is accepted, (b) work on developing a rich variety of methodologies is undertaken, and (c) we continually ask the question: 'what kind of problem situation can be managed with which sort of methodology?'

In the above quote, we can see elements of the need to tame pluralism, in that a particular vantage point (rigorous and formalised thinking – a version of the scientific method) is sought in order to deal with diversity, bias, mess. There is, however, a tension between this and the admission of a plurality of methodologies, and an appeal to a multimethodology (matching contexts to methodologies) is required to resolve this tension. Without such a move, the requirements of 'rigorous formalised thinking' make the alternatives (methodological imperialism, relativism or nihilism) unacceptably unpalatable. Or as Jackson (1987:575) phrases it elsewhere:

> instead of seeing [different strands of management science] as competing for exactly the same area of concern, alternative approaches can be presented as being appropriate to the different types of situation in which management scientists are required to act. Each approach will be useful in certain defined areas and should be used in circumstances where it works best.

More recently we come to the work of Flood and Romm (1996) which is particularly interesting to us because of their claims to deal with diversity and to '[find] a balance between modernism and postmodernism' (p. 473). We would wish to note, however, that although we can find many points of similarity between their approach and ours, there are also many differences, not least in their reliance on Habermas' theories of communicative competence and the possibilities of dialogue guaranteeing the achievement of unforced consensus. Along the same lines Mingers (1997) introduces his version of a map which attempts to address concerns relating to power.

Most thinkers see the need to respond to pluralism, by taming and controlling it, seeking to master it through some version of 'rigorous' or 'formalised' or 'intellectually disciplined' rationality, which reduces to some version of the highly problematic scientific rationality. In Chapter 6 we explore some ideas on mixing and matching methods in the multiagency setting.

Pluralism in the modes of representation employed

When we use modes of representation, many diverse meanings are possible for symbol used. In fact all representations refer to other representations, and hence nothing is authentic. This notion leads to two issues for representation. Firstly, that representation cannot have a direct relationship to the real world. Symbols, objects cannot represent anything; they have no equivalent in reality. Secondly, representations refer to other representations. Representations, therefore, could only have the validity of a copy, or a copy of a copy (a simulacrum) (Baudrillard, 1990). This has a further or wider implication for the management sciences in that authentic theory is impossible with representations, precisely because theory attempts to sketch out or represent reality.

The archetype that the management disciplines aspire to has two aims: theory and method. As Hacking (1983) says, 'theories try to say how the world is. [Methods] change the world.' In other words 'we represent and we intervene'. When one is applying this principle, a representation of a phenomenon is produced in order that something can be analysed and/or synthesised. In other words, 'we represent in order to intervene, and we intervene in the light of representations'.

Another problem we wish to explore is can we develop an activity of representation that enables a community of decision-makers to be involved? To answer this we wish to draw on some of the literature that talks about a new phase of 'modelling for learning' as expounded by Morecroft (1988) and others (Morecroft and Sterman, 1994; Vennix, 1996). We will use this discussion to develop our ideas further.

We assume for this argument that organisations today face messy and confusing problems. There is a lack of clear boundaries and different perceptions exist which do not lend themselves to easy modelling or formulation. These ill-structured problem situations are complicated by the possibility of many perceptions of the same issues and the many variables that will be or could be a factor in the situation.

Alternative ways of perceiving and ultimately representing an ill-structured situation have emerged (Rosenhead, 1989). When a problem is ill-structured one needs to communicate with others to determine what information is relevant. The interactive process allows groups to produce an outcome superior to that produced by individuals. Representation aids are purported to facilitate groups in this activity. It is possible through the process of representation to have a 'model' of the situation and to assist individuals and groups in representing and communicating problem perspectives (Rosenhead, 1989; Pidd, 1984; Eden, 1986). It is claimed by the proponents that representation aids or problem-structuring methodologies can be used to facilitate expressing individual perspectives and develop group understanding. The problem with the ideas is the over-reliance of experts in structuring the issues or problems as discussed earlier. We need to introduce a means by which the owners of the issues can play with their representations and learn from playing with them.

We would like to explore the idea proposed by de Geus, and others, that playing with representations of the real world may change the understanding of that world. Through this the owners of the problems may move into the next phase of development, i.e. they learn. The proponents for modelling for learning claim that modelling for learning works better in teams than individuals, where groups could play with their own representations of their world (Morecroft and Sterman, 1994; Senge, 1990; Wack, 1985).

A novel view of modelling as representation, taken from de Geus (1988:70), seems to capture this. It is that:

> We are no longer talking about the model as the understand-
> ing of this world as it has been acquired by a modeller or a
> planner. We are no longer talking about a modelled under-
> standing of this world as it has been acquired by an academic
> or some outside institution like a plan bureau to be used to
> make predictions. We are talking about the understanding of [a
> client's] world as it has been acquired by them. ... [M]odelling
> the world we give them a toy ... with which they can play,
> with which they can experiment without having to fear the
> consequences.

Or alternatively the view from Morecroft (1994:7):

> Models should capture the knowledge and mental data of the
> [client]; models should blend qualitative mapping with friendly
> algebra and simulations; models can be small; their purpose is
> to support team reasoning and learning; they encourage
> systems thinking. Simulations provide stories about the future
> not predictions.

Thus, the problem-owners and not the technical experts own these representations.
They are created in a group process, where greater insights into issues can be found.
These insights can be shared and disseminated to all the participants. The model as
a form of representation produced can embed learning. Modelling for learning
draws on cognitive psychology where links between mental models and learning
have been found (Johnson-Laird, 1987), and in child educational psychology where
links between play models and learning have been investigated (Papert, 1980). We
think that in the multiagency setting learning about, and dealing with, complex
issues can be facilitated by providing a space or opportunity to 'play'.

What we are witnessing is a shift in the notion of representation: from capturing
the world 'out there' to capturing impressions of the world. Similar shifts can be
noted elsewhere in the social sciences, all of which question a correspondence
theory of truth. As linguistic manifestations of this we can note the growth in
the use of terms like mind map, cognitive map, narrative representation. Once this
shift has been made, then the model is no longer a tool for prediction, but rather for
exploration, or 'learning' in de Geus's terms.

This recent recasting of systems dynamics displays a similar shift. So that for
example, Morecroft (1994) discusses mind maps as a way of capturing individuals'
views, which form the raw materials for exploration and learning using the plumb-
ing of systems dynamics. This draws on Seymour Papert's (1980) work on how
children learn by playing with representations of the real world to change their
understanding of that world.

This is where the work of Baudrillard is relevant. Writing about postmodernity,
he uses the notion of the simulacrum to refer to a replication of a replication for

which there is no original (Baudrillard, 1983). The implication of this is that no distinction remains between the real and the referent. The wider implication of this is that representations like simulation are furnished by other representations ad infinitum and there are no real world objects for study, only representations. To us these representations are not representations of reality; rather they *produce* reality. What we draw from this is that playing with the virtual world or simulacrum may become as real as intervening in the real world; this provides a challenge to action unless some method of viewing this process critically can be used. To return to Baudrillard (1990:91):

> Today knowledge about an event is only the degraded form of this event. A lower form of the energy of the event. Likewise knowledge about opinion is only a degraded form of this opinion.
>   When knowledge, through its modes of representation, anticipates the event, in other words, when the event (or opinion) is preceded by its degraded form (or its simulated form) its energy is entirely absorbed into the void.

However, this might mislead one to think that a meta-theory would need to be constructed to break up the resulting cycle of self-referentiality. The issue this poses is an obvious one, as it too (i.e. the meta-theory) only refers to itself and is no comment on representation, only a comment on itself. What does this mean in practical terms?

The representations produced by the use of methods described in this book have no correspondence with the world 'out there'; the codes, rules and diagrams give the world to the participants and that world is in accordance with those codes, rules and diagrams. These representations provide seductive toys. One reason for this is that they are controllable. What follows is an inability to move on and back out to intervening in the real world. In other words, reality has become the toys for gaming and the toys give us reality.

The difficulty posed by the self-referential situation can be tackled by viewing it as textual and constructed. As we have argued elsewhere (Taket and White, 1993), a variety of deconstruction strategies can be adopted to disrupt the taken-for-grantedness or matter in the words of our earlier paper:

> Deconstruction is attentive to suppressed tensions or conflict in text. It is suspicious of all 'natural' categories. The object is to look for what has been suppressed within the text, because it follows that whenever a discourse appears unified or whole, something must have been suppressed for it to appear as a unity. The process is to recover the suppressed and make the tensions and conflict within the text reappear. This leads to the

> exposure of the ideology assumed in the text, and spaces can
> be opened where different or more varied ideas can be offered.

Thus where do we go from here? We are informed by the work of Paulo Freire, particularly his writings on education (Freire, 1972), where he claims that education needs to be based upon genuine dialogue and it requires the sensitive use of linguistic codes in problematising interactions between different participants. We are also informed by work which draws on Freire, particularly work coming from the developing countries exploring visual forms of representation (Bradbury, 1994). We need to develop modes of representations in OR and systems that are transparent, mutually produced with the participants, are owned by the participants and can be interrogated by the participants. The representations are produced from shared analysis and results in shared meaning between all parties.

Seeking transparency and shared meaning, however, cannot be accorded the status of an unproblematic, universally applicable goal. This calls for a process of critical reflection on the processes used in the intervention (i.e. linking with different modes of methods), and the facilitator(s) (i.e. different modes of facilitation) must necessarily assume the responsibility for deciding what is most appropriate and suitable to each particular moment in the intervention.

In Chapter 7 we describe a range of methods for representing complex problem situations. These methods range from the verbal (such as brainstorming) to the visual (such as mapping) through to the vital (such as sculpting and doubling used in action methods).

Pluralism in the facilitation process

In our interventions we are conscious of the role we play as facilitators in aiding groups to work on issues or problems. The role of facilitation and the use of representation are inextricably entwined. To draw on the metaphor of the constellation used by many to express this problem, we can ask whether the constellation has existed as long as the stars it comprises, or did it come into being only when chosen and designated. We would claim that the latter is what happens. We make constellations by selecting and demarcating particular stars rather than others, so we make the world up by drawing boundaries around some rather than others. Thus as 'facilitators' we are usually in a privileged position to help individuals or groups to ascribe meaning through selecting and putting together some aspects of what we see rather than others. However, we are generally uncritical of the process of making up the world we are observing. That is, the modes through which the world is made up is often unchallenged.

One of the desires for management is the search for an approach which is designed for facilitators to help their clients work through messy problems. Here, we usually separate 'process' from 'content' (Eden, 1989; Cropper and Huxham, 1994), and the well-intentioned move which has made content essential and process contributory or even accessory. To refer to Eden (1986:21):

> an approach which ... aims to help to bring together two sets
> of skills ... the facilitator of process involved in getting a team
> to work effectively and efficiently and the construction of
> appropriate models and analysis of content which each mem-
> ber of the team is interested to address. ... [P]rocess and
> content are independent ... each informs the way the other
> skill is best utilised.

It can be shown (although not here) that even though actual development in
management science and systems may be giving us the view that it is leading us
away from the idea that the work of OR is primarily on content, the idea still exerts
an extraordinary hegemony. We want to suggest that this is because the idea is
perpetuated in the guise of a certain way of seeing management science that is
thoroughly ingrained among most practitioners, and so the project of representing
problems thus sustains the primacy of content over process.

Quite possibly, this is saying nothing new and may have well been said before.
However let us take a more sophisticated comment. It has been said that 'those who
advocate problem structuring methods are aware of the inadequacies of expertise in
complexity (i.e. orthodox management science) where the non-expert ... [Client]
has their own form of knowledge about systems and issues which are not
capturable in a mathematical net' (Rosenhead, 1989:348). This leads to the promotion of experts in process 'to surface knowledge ... by skilfully promoting interaction ... this is the consultant as catalyst' (p. 348). The statement goes further,
'the orthodox (experts in content) may have an oppositional view' (p. 348), and
positively, it is claimed that the way forward is a 'creative tension' between the two
to shape methodologies. It is taken that this tension may lead to the marrying of
process and content, and the product of the creative tension may be a method (or
methodology).

We would like to pose that if we reject this and say that all these concerns to find
an appropriate method have only allowed a divorce, or separation of process from
content, then what space is opened up by this? Possibly, it is a space in which the
consultant, expert or analyst may have been reinvented or replaced (White and
Taket, 1994). It is now possible to talk of an expert not as passing over, or
transferring, some knowledge, but introducing a realm where both expert and client
can enter and to which both can also have access. The now familiar view of the
facilitator being able to help shape perception(s) of the situation(s) may not be a
novel notion to us now, but it has had its consequences. To adopt an often quoted
extract from Foucault, 'the [expert] no longer has to play the role of the advisor.
The projects, tactics, goals to be adopted are a matter for those who do the
fighting. What the [expert] can do is provide the instrument of analysis' [in
Gordon, 1980:62].

As already noted in the above discussion, careful attention must be paid to the
role of the interventionist(s). Pluralism is required in terms of the adoption of
different roles or guises (White and Taket, 1995a) at different times in the course

of an intervention, and of different roles in relation to different individuals/groups involved in the intervention (at the same time). Another way of putting this is to argue that in practice, we can mix and match different guises in the course of an intervention, assuming in this way the role of the 'shaman' or 'shapeshifter'. Our practice here is to be understood in distinction from any notion of a meta-method for selecting guises (for example relying on any type of contingency table approach which would attempt to match guise to characteristics of intervention context), and which we find too rigid, formulaic and unhelpful to deal with the complexities of any intervention. We would like to say a few words about how the guises we use are to be understood, and to point to some future directions for exploration. The guises are discussed in detail elsewhere (White and Taket, 1995a; Taket and White, 1996b). The guises are not sharply separable, and in fact they can be interwoven in the course of a single intervention. In Chapter 8 we will explore the issue that intervention in a complex setting such as multiagency working requires adopting different approaches at different times over the course of an intervention. A range of roles will be explored that a facilitator/interventionist can play.

THE THREE Ds

As explored in Chapters 1 and 2, in the multiagency setting we would often find that different people may hold different views about the issues they face. In such a setting there is a continuing dynamic, where individuals are trying to find an appropriate *balance* in a circumstance where there is a continual shift in perspectives and views. There is also the situation where the participants in discussion and dialogue *beat* out their positions and present arguments. There is also the situation where the group *cuts* through the uncertainties and conflict and choices between options become clearer. In the multiagency setting these processes are continuously at play and not necessarily sequential. We call these processes the three Ds (see Figure 4.1):

- The first situation we describe as deliberation. The word is made up of 'de' – 'of' and 'liberate' or 'libra' which is to balance.
- The second situation is debate, which includes the part 'bate' or 'bateur' which means 'to beat'. This is where we argue our positions.
- The third situation is decision which is made up of the phrase 'de' and 'cision' – meaning to cut.

These processes are continually being worked through in the multiagency setting in many combinations and invariably back to deliberate and/or debate.

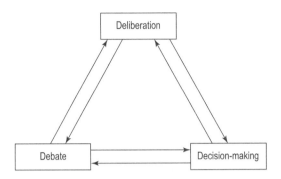

Figure 4.1 The three Ds

CONCLUSION

Our notion of pragmatic pluralism also involves a particular notion of the relationship between theory and practice – utilising the notion of praxis – where theory in itself is downplayed and instead the emphasis is on collective theorising for action and intervention, and theorising as a means of critical reflection on practice. So, in adopting a position of pragmatic pluralism, we argue for the need to move beyond conceptualising theory and practice as a dichotomy, following instead a strategy of mix and match, adopting a flexible and adaptive stance, and operationalising 'doing what feels good'. This means arguing for an end to theory as providing an abstract yet foundational basis for practice, but *not* an end to theorising as a part of a process of critically reflective practice. This position of pragmatic pluralism incorporates the following features:

- the use of triangulation (in terms of data sources, methods, analysis team)
- combining parts of different methods
- being flexible and adaptive
- critical reflection
- a reconceptualisation of the notion of praxis

Pluralism in the 'nature'   **5**
of the client

'The irrationality of a thing is no argument against its existence, rather a condition of it.'
Nietzsche (1986:515)

INTRODUCTION

From our experience as interventionists, we have found that organisations/groups are increasingly exposed internally to the challenges of heterogeneity and diversity, while at the same time experiencing external pressure to reconstruct their collective identities along pluralistic lines. Individuals within organisations/groups, as well as organisations/groups within the wider setting, are increasingly subject to identity crises. As interventionists, in adopting a pluralist strategy for intervention, we seek to respect and acknowledge the views of a wide range of stakeholders, i.e. the heterogeneity within the group/organisation. The danger with this perspective, however, is its tendency towards relativism, and our attitude to this with respect to methods has been discussed in Chapter 4. In this chapter we explore the issue of diversity in the client.

In this chapter we will present some strategies for dealing with the situation where there is a variety of views and values. In the multiagency setting this is often seen as a major source of conflict (Gray, 1996). Often the aim in such circumstances is for the group to find consensus. We will show that consensus as an ideal is not always possible. A better strategy may be to work towards a 'system of consent' (Taket and White, 1994). We will describe some examples of how this has been achieved in practice.

The mnemonic for this chapter is the three Cs:

- Critical – i.e. in the situation where there is a variety of views and values a 'critical perspective is important'.

- Consent – often consensus is impossible and the situation calls for a 'system of consent' to be found.
- Contingent – this principle acknowledges that reaching an agreement is always contingent on time and location. Once a decision is made uncertainty arises.

MULTIPLE RATIONALITIES AND PERSPECTIVES

There has been a significant change in the way in which the concept of the client or group is defined within OR and the management sciences. There was a strand of theoretical development in the late 1960s and early 1970s which converged with a systems-based approach that started to focus critically on the client as a single decision-maker and challenged the premise of homogeneous settings (see for example Ackoff, 1974b; Beer, 1981). However, by the end of the 1970s these systems-based conceptualisations and the scientific legitimation of the analysis they reinforced were being challenged (Vickers, 1965; Checkland, 1981) by a commitment to research based on social science (see also Lawrence, 1966). By the 1980s a rout ensued in that the whole programme of OR and management science was perceived to be in crisis (Ackoff, 1974a, 1979a, b; Rosenhead 1986; Dando and Bennett, 1981). For summary of the crisis see Rosenhead (1989) and Keys (1994).

The focus turned to soft approaches exploring working with clients in a social setting. Many issues came to the fore such as multiple clients, power and connections to wider societal arrangements. Around these conceptual and methodological issues a series of theoretical streams began to forge and widened the agenda for the management sciences. An array of alternative approaches that could not be accommodated within the once rigid intellectual orthodoxy began to emerge. The emphasis turned to looking at systems of organisation of the diversity of methods (Jackson and Keys, 1984; Rosenhead, 1989; Flood and Jackson, 1991; Flood and Romm, 1996; Mingers and Gill, 1997). The emphasis became making sense of the diversity of approaches that had emerged.

However, in among the concern for methods the issue of diversity began to flourish, particularly in relation to the client (Taket and White, 1994). Concerns were being raised about dealing with multiple perspectives, multiple realities and a diversity/plurality debate began to focus on the client or group. Viewing the client group as polyvocal was the problematic that was being engaged by these authors. In particular, questions around equal access and involvement in the process began to be raised, which led to a call for caution in the use of methodologies unreflectively (White and Taket, 1994; Taket and White, 1994).

RETREAT FROM RATIONALITY

In any given situation in the multiagency setting, different people may have a different view on the same issue. It is important to recognise the plurality of difference as a positive aspect of organisation and society today. Working with diversity has become the principal dynamic in working in the multiagency setting. Organisations are being characterised by their very heterogeneity and diversity (Clegg, 1990).

Decision-making in this environment is fraught with difficulties, in particular the issue concerning the concept of rationality for guiding and understanding choice among many options. A singular rationality is usually offered based on the notion of scientific reasoning. However, there is a growing suspicion that a singular rationality will not do. A number of writers have questioned the extent to which the behaviour of decision-makers can be regarded realistically as rational activity. Simon (1976) distinguished 'perfect' and 'limited' rationality. Knowledge of all possible outcomes is usually a prerequisite for rationality, but it is rarely the case that this is fulfilled; we usually have limited knowledge and limited capability. Another condition for rationality is that of the capacity for perfect judgement. In the multiagency setting, it is rare that objectives are single, isolated and well-defined. Simon claims that the reality is that a decision is made based on a 'satisficing' behaviour, rather than one which produces the maximum pay-off. Cooper (1992) has argued that Simon's concept of bounded rationality is an example of 'an isolated and singularised space' (p. 269). The rationality, he claims, is located 'within the limited cognitive capacities of individual decision makers'.

Lately Brunsson (1982, 1985) makes a distinction between 'decision rationality' and 'action rationality'. The first is the norms and/or rules which guide choice, and the second is based on informed conduct. Brunsson (1985) argues that all organisations deal with the tension between the two forms of rationality. The two forms are reconciled through 'organisational hypocrisy'. This he thinks is a fundamental type of behaviour in organisations where managing conflict is the major task. Although Brunsson's (1985) model goes some way to break with a singular dominant form of rationality to incorporate a political aspect, he is still operating within the school that believes in organised rationality which is singular and rational. Cooper and Burrell (1988) have called for a retreat from organised rationality. They say (Cooper and Burrell, 1988:108):

> Organisations do not first pre-exist and then create their relationships: they occur in existential gaps which lie beyond knowledgeable discourse.... Organised rationality, far from originating in beau-ideal and consummate logics of efficiency, is founded on sleight of hand, vicious agonisms and *pudenda origo* (shameful origins). This is the revisionary lesson that postmodernism brings to organisational analysis.

The study of decisions has been dominated for too long by the concept of a singular rationality. Rationalities such as exchange, trust, reciprocity and politics must be meshed together if they are to meet the challenge of organisations exhibiting pluralism and diversity.

To try and grasp the multiagency in its totality, in order to give coherence to our observations and interventions, has become discredited (see for example Lyotard, 1984). The postmodern position rejects all totalising theory and theory which aims at treating the whole as total. The simple reason for this is that the world is too complex. One cannot grasp society or organisations as a whole. It cannot be subsumed under a single totalising theory.

Those hostile to totalisation tend to celebrate plurality or fragmentation. The assertion of difference helps to undermine the group from being dominated by one viewpoint. Some have argued that diversity is there to be managed (Flood and Romm, 1996). This is not the principle we work to. Our principle is to let diversity flourish, that is, we believe that diversity should be enhanced and allowed to flourish, and not be managed. Working with diversity and multiple rationalities is the challenge we have set ourselves.

The groups we work with are not fixed homegeneous entities; they have identities that are floating, dynamic and contingent with individuals who have views that are not fixed or universally true at all times for all people. Multiple identities within groups are not naturally given, but socially constructed (Young, 1989). The groups are heterogeneous and diverse and cannot be grasped as a whole and this is to be celebrated.

As poststructuralists we deny the concept of an 'essential' identity and eschew instead the phenomenon of multiple social identities. In our work we understand that multiple 'socially constructed' realities may vary in any given situation and this has been the key reason for the development of our participatory approach. We believe that methods must be developed to enable a synthesis of different intent and perspectives to be generated based on a recognition of diversity.

In the multiagency setting there are competing claims for affiliation that cannot be reduced to one category. As well as organisational affiliations, there are gender, age, race, religion, ethnicity, music style and dress code, to name but a few, all are axes of organisational identity. There are also different rationalities and perspectives. In Box 5.1 we give an example of where we have worked with difference and diversity.

Poststructuralists like Lévi-Strauss would propose here 'anything goes' in which there is no commensurability between different worlds of meaning. If this were true, how would we be able to distinguish between different intent, meanings or theories. Each would be as valid on its own context as any other. Many argue that not all theories are equally valid and that we are required to choose between them, to decide which is true and which is not. They call for a need to find a totalising theory that gives us the capacity to make choices. For example Flood and Romm (1996) in their book *Diversity Management* argue that it is possible to make choices that avoid relativism and absolutism, that is, it is possible to decide what is true and what is not. They and others seem to suggest that we can stand outside the arguments and decide what is true, or that there are those with the ability to recognise what is true and what is right. In other words we should leave it to the 'experts' to help us make choices.

BOX 5.1   CASE STUDY ON BILINGUAL WORKSHOPS

The case study discussed here concerns a bilingual workshop held to produce a Bengali version of a health profile. The health profile was required to provide a measure of self-perceived health to be used in the assessment of needs for services and in the evaluation of the effectiveness of aspects of service delivery. The participants were bilingual community development workers (Bengali–English, Somali–English) and English speakers, including the facilitator. The workshop was facilitated in English with most of the substantive work done in Bengali. The control therefore rested with the participants who spoke Bengali, who were encouraged to use the English speakers as a resource, asking them to aid their understanding of the theoretical basis of the profile, plus the meaning of some of the terms before refining among themselves the Bengali version of the profile. The smooth progress of the work was aided by the monolingual English speakers giving up any goal of understanding the detail of the work in Bengali. The Somali speaker used the experience and knowledge gained to carry out the same sort of process in the community at a later stage to produce a Somali version of the profile. The workshop confirmed the possibility of facilitating in this situation, and of the necessary skill transfer.

Source: Taket and White (1994).

The problem with the above is that rather than liberate it in fact unwittingly reproduces the power relations it professes to overcome, i.e. the reliance upon experts. Some authors (e.g. Rorty 1989) believe that we must work in a locally contingent way and adopt a framework in which the local circumstances are prime, only then can the groups we work with be helped to decide at that point in time what is true. That choice is not absolute or eternal. It is specific to that particular time and place – it is contingent to the locality (following Rorty 1989).

By way of a further example, however, when views are reinforced by boundaries socially and linguistically constituted which act to oppress particular groups, for example those of race or ethnicity, then the interventionists, operating with an emancipatory code of ethics, need to separate these out in the course of the intervention and explicitly challenge any introduction of them into the process in a way which aids reinforcement of the oppression. Our practice is to provide a space where participants can acknowledge the differences of others, and which may also allow participants to articulate what before remained private and personal and perhaps even unsymbolised. During an intervention, we also act to contest as 'facts', any mythic stories which function oppressively to maintain or reinforce inequality or discrimination. Again the 'problem' of relativism rears its head here, we have found, like many others, that in the local situation, one useful tactic can be the deployment of 'strategic essentialism' (Hooks, 1990; Butler, 1990). This is acting in a way that acknowledges difference but being prepared to challenge views which are oppressing others. The challenge relates to the circumstances and not beyond. In Chapter 8 we describe tactics and principles which can help an interventionist in this situation.

Given the recognition of 'difference' and 'otherness', how can we act in working with diversity? We have written elsewhere about the practice of 'doing what feels good' (Taket and White, 1994; White and Taket, 1994), illustrating how practice does not fit in with a reasoned, rational process of selecting and applying techniques; and we have suggested that, instead, the approach used could be read as postmodern, where we recognise that the groups we work with will always be fractured, polyvocal, contingent and dynamic. Using other rationalities applies to both the process in terms of methods used with groups and in terms of the task of facilitation itself. We are used to singular rationality, and the view that all that is irrational is bad and in need of rationalising. Within this rationality there is no room for acting according to emotions, feelings, etc. unless they can be subjected to this rationality. We do not find such a view helpful, and instead conceive of rationalities in the plural: one might be labelled 'intuition', another (certainly overlapping to some extent) 'doing what feels good'. Some might insist on telling a story about these so that they can be seen to be 'rational after all'. We are not concerned with pursuing that myth. Instead, we prefer to tell a story of these as useful guides to action, both for the working methods of the group (drama methods, projective techniques – see Chapter 7) and for the working process of the facilitator (see Chapter 8).

To give a more specific example from our practice, when working as facilitators, deciding what to do next is not a rational reasoned process of identifying options, assessing likely costs and benefits of each, and choosing according to some strategy the preferred one for implementation. Instead it is better described as responding to hunch, intuition, feeling and selecting something (not consciously expressed as a choice), implementing and monitoring effects, responding, taking action and reaction. Within this process value judgements also come into play. Others may wish to debate whether the rational process goes on subconsciously … in our view it matters not. We do not find such post hoc rationalisation a helpful or necessary legitimation; it has the relevance of such debates as occupied medieval theologians on the number of angels that might stand on the head of a pin. The emotional life of the group is important and the combination of feelings between the group and facilitator(s) must be taken as an important gauge that helps in the choice of method of working.

IS IT POSSIBLE TO ACHIEVE CONSENSUS?

The idea of building consensus as an outcome of an intervention with a group that exhibits high variety will be addressed. Consensus usually means that there is a position where members of a group have reached an agreement on such and such an issue. This has in many circles been taken on in a Habermasian formulation, particularly where disputes or issues are not settled unless each member or party is prepared to listen to another's viewpoint on the basis that each would expect the other to listen to its own. It is argued that this ideal situation must exist if consensus or even communication is to be possible at all (Flood and Jackson, 1991; Habermas, 1985). The view taken here is that consensus, as an ideal, is problematic, because, in particular, it invariably leads to some people being forced to silence. Checkland (1981) talks about achieving accommodation between different interests and not consensus. In relation to SSM he says that consensus-seeking is 'an occasional special case within the general case of seeking accommodation in which the conflicts endemic in human affairs ... are subsumed in an accommodation which different parties are prepared to go along with' (Checkland and Scholes, 1990:29). Finding accommodation between different interests is the goal and can be seen as an outcome constituting an improvement of a problem situation. However, he is vague on how that accommodation can be found. Accommodation is described as being reached through acknowledging power relations. In Box 5.2 we describe a case study where consensus was not possible.

We have found the notion of a system of consent useful and have adopted it in our work with groups. We have found it a more workable notion than 'accommodation', in that accommodation feels like an ideal that is unachievable in a group setting.

EQUALITY OF ACCESS

The development of our position on access is drawn from and informed by a range of postmodern understandings. There are two related issues here. The first is making what we do as interventionists accessible to the groups we work with. The second is that it is important to us that all the members of the group are included in thinking about issues and thinking about the choices of methods. In other words, it is not on the outcome that we should concentrate our efforts to enable fairness but on the process.

In each situation we can adopt a principled position, that is, in order to address the issue of equal access we need to understand how inequalities are generated and sustained. Many of the processes we have discussed in this book, if used by themselves, will not give the participants a route to critique them. It is only by enabling the participants to have a choice that can critique take place and access increase.

We are interested in the participants' access to and control over the process involved, including the (implicit or explicit) theorising about themselves and their activities. The case study with Nucleus is an example of where the participants took control to theorise about themselves. We have found that it is possible to access the knowledges of the groups concerned, in that these are actively used as a part of the process. We have identified elsewhere (White and Taket, 1994) some guidelines that we have found useful in such practice, namely:

BOX 5.2   NUCLEUS HOUSING

A team was set up to help overcome problems associated with the growth of the organisation. The different individuals of the group made any decision-making difficult. It made collective action difficult. Through involvement with the group, it was recognised by the team that consensus would be a very difficult thing to achieve. The team thought that if consensus required everyone to positively agree with and support every decision, impassivity, apathy or indifference would undermine it. The team stated that the reasons why it would be difficult to achieve are that the efforts to achieve it would be time consuming and it may be a mask for autocracy. They wanted differences of opinions to be discussed and a position on an option would end up being negotiated to a point where each individual consented to accepting that option. It also meant that different people could take the lead on different issues. The team termed this working towards a 'system of consent'.

Source: Taket and White (1994).

1. Recognition of the co-responsible nature of the encounter, with the co-participation of the different parties involved;
2. Aim to achieve 'skill' transfer (both ways), and empowerment of all involved;
3. Recognising difference and working with it (difference as generator of multiple possibilities, acting to increase choice rather than constraining it), but working non-hierarchically;
4. Aim to break down stereotypes of the 'expert', the 'professional' and reduce the perceived distance between practitioner and client;
5. Work for consent (dynamic and contingent, not fixed and absolute, see for example the first case study above), not consensus;
6. Aim for flexibility, be ready to adapt and work in different ways at different times, be willing to depart from plans and from detailed methodologies.

If the above are guidelines for working with difference, we see this working in combination with flexible facilitation, and a judicious mix of methods and processes.

In this chapter we have tried to outline what we think is important to appreciate in working with multicultural groups, namely working with difference or otherness. We have chosen to talk about examples from our work, not only because they are interesting in themselves, but also because they illustrate particularly well some issues that are also relevant to practice in general; this can easily be appreciated by observing that one of the typical features of the organisations involved identified by Ritchie (1994) is their involvement of 'different kinds of stakeholders ... each group often have multiple roles', i.e. their multifaceted, polyvocal nature.

We want to sum up by talking about some aspects of how we have found it useful to think about the process of doing this kind of work. We find it is not helpful to think in terms of 'going into another culture'. We wish to challenge the notion that what is happening is a meeting of one culture with another, so that what is required is challenging the self-evidentness of 'us' going in with our homogeneous self into a (different) unified culture. We challenge this in (at least) two ways. Firstly, we notice that we ourselves have no fixed singular identity or culture, but rather this is always constantly created and re-created, negotiated and always fluid, dynamic and contingent. Secondly, we notice that any group contains inevitably more than a single culture (it is a collection of individuals each complex and fractured, sharing some things but different in others); this is particularly true of the multiagency groups with whom we tend to work. So it is always more complex than an encounter of One with AnOther. The notion of any singular client base thus becomes increasingly untenable. We would like to suggest that the basic minimum condition for productive interaction is recognising and acknowledging the other(s) and respecting the differences. Perhaps we might add to this the responsibility of the facilitator for critical reflection on her or his own part in the dramas/encounters. This might take the form of opening up a space for critical reflection by the group as a whole. This is facilitated by the establishment of mutuality, trust and respect. We would like to develop this further by examining what contributes to, or lays the ground for, this trust and respect. Throughout the remaining chapters we will demonstrate the importance of recognising and acknowledging the differences that exist within groups in this connection. This explicit recognition and acknowledgement are also a necessary prerequisite for facilitating widespread participation.

In conclusion, in order to acknowledge and work with the variety of stakeholders in the multiagency setting the mnemonic that may be useful is the three Cs:

- Critical – i.e. in the situation where there is a variety of views and values a 'critical perspective' is important. In particular, a situation may arise where views are reinforced by boundaries socially and linguistically constituted which act to oppress particular groups. A critical perspective is important and being 'strategically essential' may help in dealing with such a situation.
- Consent – often consensus is impossible. It may also be impossible to 'accommodate' the variety of views expressed in the multiagency setting. The situation may call for a 'system of consent' to be found.
- Contingent – this principle acknowledges that reaching an agreement is always contingent on time and location. Once a decision is made uncertainty arises.

Pluralism in the use of specific methods/techniques

6

INTRODUCTION: THE FOUR Ms

A number of methods (some of which have already been described) have emerged, claiming their applicability to solving complex organisational problems. In this chapter we will present some of these methods including: strategic choice approach, soft systems methodology, strategic assumption surfacing and testing, critical systems heuristics, action methods and so on. Chapter 7, which follows, continues the discussion of methods presenting those where a key focus of interest is on the mode of representation they employ. We will show that it is difficult to make a choice of which method/technique is 'best' (our postmodern/poststructuralist perspective as we have discussed in Chapter 3 implies that this is an unanswerable question). Choice(s) will depend on particular features of the local situation, and methods (or parts of methods) can be chosen and mixed judiciously; the choices made are relevant for that intervention, and the process of choice needs to be made afresh for each intervention. We will also show how parts of different methods can be used in different parts of an intervention. In terms of a mnemonic for this chapter (see Figure 6.1), this chapter can be encapsulated as the chapter of the four Ms, four different activities to be borne in mind while choosing and using methods or techniques:

- mix – use wholes or parts of different methods with one another and at different times in the course of an engagement;
- modify – change and adapt methods for their use in particular circumstances;
- multiply – increase possibilities by experimenting with different methods for the same task;
- match – choose methods in use bearing in mind the preferences (explicit or implicit) of the participants, including yourself as facilitator and the characteristics of the situation at the time.

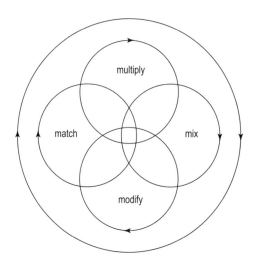

Figure 6.1   Choosing and Using Methods – the Four Ms

The reader is invited to note that, given our brand of multimethodology as set out in Chapter 4, and our use of methods within a framework of pragmatic pluralism, we deliberately do not spend time in this chapter exploring the philosophical underpinnings of the methods as set out by their originators or inferred by other commentators.

INGREDIENTS

There are a wide range of methods and techniques that we can draw on. Fairly obviously we cannot describe all of these in detail. Table 6.1 shows an overview of those we will discuss, distinguishing between those most usually associated with PRA, those most usually associated with OR, systems science and management science and those with other origins. This is by no means the only possible selection; this represents a selection from those that we have personal experience of using, and is not intended to represent all those that are available. Each individual facilitator, during the course of their work, will accumulate their own personal methods/techniques toolbox, from which they feel happy to draw in any particular intervention; these toolboxes will change over time. Table 6.1 also shows in brackets cross-references to where any examples of the use of the method can be found within the book.

Some of these methods have already been described in Chapter 3. The presentation of the others is divided between this chapter and the next. In Chapter 7 we have put the methods that have a particular focus on the use of different modes of representation. The others are dealt with in this chapter. Here we have divided the

Table 6.1 Illustrations of Methods/Techniques for Use

PRA[1]	Operational research/management science	Other
Transects (Table 7.14)	Strategic choice approach (SCA) and stages within it, such as AIDA (analysis of interconnected decision areas) and commitment packages (Box 6.1, Box 6.2, Box 6.4, Table 7.9, Chapter 10, Case D)	Brainstorming
Trend analysis	Strategic options development and analysis (SODA) (Chapter 10, Case C)	Nominal group technique (NGT) (Box 6.4, chapter 10, Case B, Case D)
Venn diagrams (Table 7.10)	Team syntegrity, and stages within it, problem jostle and hexadic reduction, outcome resolve (Box 6.2, Table 7.1)	Delphi technique
Wealth ranking (Table 7.14)	Strategic assumption surfacing and testing, and stages within it, such as stakeholder analysis (Box 6.1, Box 6.3)	SWOT (Table 7.11, Box 8.4)
Analysis of difference	Mapping and influence diagrams, including cognitive mapping (Table 7.2, Table 7.6, Table 7.7, Box 8.2, Box 8.3, Chapter 10, Case C, Case D)	Deconstruction[2] (Table 7.4)
Ranking/voting (Table 7.14, Box 6.2, Box 8.1)	Soft systems methodology (SSM), and stages within it, such as rich pictures, CATWOE and root definitions (Box 6.1, Table 6.11, Table 6.12, Table 7.5, Chapter 10, Case D)	Action methods (Table 7.11, Table 7.12, Chapter 10, Case B)
Stories/drama/ participatory theatre (Table 7.13)	Critical systems heuristics (CSH) (Box 6.1, Box 6.3)	Repertory grid analysis (RGA) (Table 7.3)
	TSI (total systems intervention) and its later development local systemic intervention (LSI) Systems dynamics models (Chapter 10, Case A) Open space technology (OST) (Box 6.4) Participative design (Chapter 10, Case E) IDONS (Table 7.8)	

[1] Good sources on methods and use of them are found in the RRA and PLA notes series published by the IIED (International Institute for Environment and Development).

[2] Deconstruction certainly did not originate in the operational research/management science field; however, it is recently beginning to find uses there.

methods up into two groups for convenience of presentation. The first are short and focused methods ideally suited to be used in their entirety, in some variant or other – methods to be modified and mixed with others. The second group consists of methods, or perhaps should more accurately be referred to as methodologies, that make much broader claims for themselves. These are methods that we rarely use in their entirety (although others may wish to do so), preferring instead to use parts of them.

Short and simple – methods for modifying and mixing

Brainstorming

Brainstorming is an aid to creative thinking which provides a means of getting a large number of ideas from a group of people in a short time. Guidelines include: suspend judgement and do not censor ideas; aim for quantity of ideas, do not consider quality; cross-fertilise between ideas. Table 6.2 presents one version and some variants. Wilcox (1994) suggests that a group of more than 5 and less than 20 is ideal. With larger groups care needs to be taken to enable everyone to have a chance to participate (see variants in Table 6.2). Nominal group technique, described next, is often used as an alternative.

Table 6.2   Brainstorming – One Version Plus Variants

Define problem, issue or question in advance of session.

In session:

- clarify problem, issue or question
- generate every idea possible
- do not discuss ideas
- do not reject any ideas
- record ideas on a list everyone can see
- stop when new ideas dry up

Note: facilitator has key role to play in stopping discussion, censorship and rejection

Variants:

1. Go round group and ask for new ideas from each in turn, individuals may pass if they have nothing immediately to mind (encourages everyone to contribute, prevents domination by few, gives some time for reflection on ideas already generated before next turn). *Must* be done fast.
2. Particularly for nervous or inexperienced groups, encourage loud applause for each idea
3. Once ideas have dried up, review one by one in group and cross off those that everyone agrees are ludicrous
4. For very large groups, consider splitting into subgroups and combining after agreed time

---

Nominal group technique

Nominal group technique (Delbecq et al., 1975) is a method that can be used to generate answers to specific questions and obtain reviews on relative priorities/importance. It exists in many different variants. The particular version (and variants) described in Table 6.3 is one that has been used in a variety of different settings by the authors. Its advantages are that it is relatively fast moving, assures input from everyone (which can be explicitly recorded by using individual worksheets at step 2), and builds in clarification and refinement of understanding. Problems occur when the initial questions are not well formulated.

Table 6.3 Nominal Group Technique – One Version Plus Variants

---

1. *Preparation*: beforehand, clarify the nature of the information required and formulate one or two specific questions
2. *Individually* (3 mins): generate an individual list of answers to the questions, noting views on relative importance of different answers
3. *In pairs* (10 mins):
   - expand and clarify answers on list (in turns)
   - identify top five answers to each question

4. *In fours* (10 mins):
   - share answers on lists (in turns), questions for clarification
   - identify top five answers to each question (by voting[1] if necessary/desired)
   - summarise on flip charts/post-its (for easy display)

Continue combining groups in this way until three, four or five groups remain

Whole group (20 minutes):
   - share answers on lists (in turns), questions for clarification
   - vote for top five answers to each question

Variants:
In voting allow individual to allocate more than one sticker to any answer
Vary number of stickers per person
Vary numbers of top answers sought (e.g. increase to more than five if dealing with extremely diverse situation)
Obviously group numbers will have to be changed to adjust to total size of group

---

[1] Voting: one easy way of doing this is by allocating each person five stickers for each question and ask them to place them against the five answers they consider most important.

Delphi technique

The Delphi technique consists of a multi-round assessment by relevant 'experts' of a particular question or set of questions (Delbecq et al., 1975). Between each round there is feedback of the results from the previous round. Usually the feedback does not identify the author of any particular view/statement and often the list of participants is not known to the participants; variants occur when this is known to varying degrees. The aim is usually to achieve a consensus, but variants aim at identifying several divergent positions or scenarios. The process can be carried out in several ways: by post; by e-mail/web; face to face (either in a single place or using video or internet conferencing).

The Delphi technique can provide a very useful structure to enable subjective assessments to be elicited and refined through a process of reflection. Selection of the 'experts' or participants is obviously important and needs to be done bearing in mind the purpose of the consultation. For example, is it to include a representative sample of those affected by the issue being considered, and/or those who have special technical expertise? Careful thought also needs to be given to the extent, if any, to which anonymity is dropped. Anonymity can serve to enable that individuals' contributions to be considered without imputing worth or value from their perceived authority or other characteristics (see also the discussion in Chapter 8 around group dynamics and conflict).

SWOT analysis

SWOT is a workshop technique useful for reviewing the current position. SWOT stands for strengths, weaknesses, opportunities and threats. In a SWOT analysis a group identifies relevant issues under each of the four headings. Guidelines and variants are shown in Table 6.4.

Table 6.4 Guidelines and Variants for SWOT (Strengths, Weaknesses, Opportunities and Threats) Analysis

---

Guidelines:

1. Brainstorm issues in group under each heading
2. Strengths and weaknesses refer to internal matters for the group
3. Opportunities and threats refer to matters external to the group
4. Check out cultural appropriateness of terms, it is important that terms are used that do not carry connotations of being unchangeable features, inherent flaws, etc. (see case study in Box 8.4)

Variants:

1. Get individuals to work on their own filling out an individual SWOT before sharing in the group
2. For each category go round the group in turn soliciting contributions, so that no one contributes twice until everyone has had a chance to add something (even if it is just 'pass' or 'nothing new')
3. After completing the SWOT, move into brainstorming about: how to build on strengths; make the most of opportunities; address weaknesses; and avoid or eliminate threats

---

Open space technology

A minimalist approach to structuring an opportunity for group work is offered by Owen's open space technology (Owen, 1992). However, as Owen explicitly argues, many of the multiagency settings that exist are not suitable for its use (see Table 6.5). Where the conditions are suitable however, Owen argues that open space technology can work in an empowering and fast fashion. The elements in the open space technology approach are summarised in Table 6.6. Of all the methods presented here, this is perhaps the one we have used least; one application is presented in White (1999) and described in Box 6.4 later in this chapter. We present it therefore, but not without some reservations.

It is fine to argue, as Owen does, that the law and principles provide a way of ensuring that proceedings run themselves, but particularly where individuals participating are drawn from the same or related organisation (or community) and have some sort of hierarchical relationship in existence between them, it seems quite possible that those lower in the hierarchy may find it particularly difficult to implement the law. Thus it is hard to see a guarantee that it will work (as with the other methods we discuss!), and certainly as facilitators we have found ourselves wanting to use/using many other devices (see Chater 8) to open up access to participation.

Participative design

Participative design (PD) is a method of involving work groups in redesigning their own work. It starts at the bottom of the organisation and works its way up. It was

Table 6.5 Conditions for Open Space Technology

In the author's own words:

'Open Space Technology is effective in situations where a diverse group of people must deal with complex, and potentially conflicting material, in innovative and productive ways. It is particularly powerful where nobody knows the answer, and the ongoing participation of a number of people is required to deal with the questions. Conversely, Open Space Technology will not work, and therefore should not be used, in any situation where the answer is already known, where somebody at a high level *thinks* he or she knows the answer, or where that somebody is the sort that *must* know the answer, and therefore must always be in charge, otherwise known as control, control, control.' (pp. 14–15)

'For Open Space Technology to work, it must focus on a real business issue which is of passionate concern to those who will be involved.' (p. 20)

'For OST to work the people must work because (and only because) they care. Put in slightly different terms, voluntary self-selection is the absolute *sine qua non* for participation in an Open Space event.' (p. 22)

Source: all quotes from Owen (1992).

Table 6.6   The Elements of Open Space Technology

Schema:

- set agenda (briefing)
- news sessions at beginning and end of each day
- rest is open space
- at end, celebration and closing

The space:

- one room large enough for all participants to sit in one (or 2/3) concentric circles, with one wall free for 'community bulletin board'
- break-out spaces – varied, etc. – for working sessions (not necessarily all rooms!)

In Open Space:

Each individual who wishes to identifies some issue or opportunity related to the theme for which they have genuine passion and for which they will take responsibility. The issue and individual's name is written down, announced to the meeting and stuck on the 'community bulletin board'.

Taking responsibility implies that the individual will designate a time and place and convene a session on the issue.

Once the market place is opened people sign up for sessions, persuading convenors to combine or reschedule if necessary.

The time involved:

- one day – for stimulating and intense conversation
- two days – recording becomes possible
- three days – reflection becomes possible

The event – stages of initiation:

- state the theme (and outline any specific expectations, e.g. written proceedings)
- described the process
- create the bulletin board
- open the market place

Four principles and one law to help it along

Principles:

1. Whoever comes are the right people.
2. Whatever happens is the only thing that could have
3. Whenever it starts is the right time
4. When it is over it is over

Law: If during the course of the gathering any person finds her/himself in a situation where they are neither learning nor contributing, they can leave and go to some more productive place

Facilitator's role:

To create space/time and hold space/time.
'Observably in performance, this means doing less rather than more. Under the best of circumstances, the facilitator will be totally present and absolutely invisible.' (p. 42)
'The job of the facilitator is not to keep things on time, but rather to enable the creation of safe time.' (p. 47)
'How does the facilitator manage all of that? It turns out to be less a question of *doing* than *being*.' (p. 48) The heart of which Owen argues is 'being present authentically', with four components:

- show up
- be present
- tell the truth or rather 'be the truth'
- let it all go – have no attachment to fixed outcomes

Source: all quotes from Owen (1992).

developed by Fred Emery as a response to the difficulties encountered in implementing organisational design following 'Socio-Technical Systems (STS)' (Emery,
1993). Problems with STS designs are that they deal only with small specialised
parts of the system rather than the system as a whole; they are never able to change
the underlying structure of the organisation and there is little or no ownership by
the majority of those involved in the design.

In PD the central assumption is that identified by the pioneering work of
Emery and Trist and that is in most systems the social system actually manages
the technical system, not the other way round. Another assumption is that those
who are responsible for the design are responsible for co-ordinating it and controlling and it is not controlled by the level above. Thus, the process of design is
non-hierarchical.

As with much of Emery's writing, participation and democracy feature
prominently. There are six democratic principles that guide PD, these are:

- people need to feel that they are in a non-hierarchical environment;
- people need to feel that they can learn and keep on learning;
- people need to vary their work and avoid fatigue and boredom;
- people need mutual support and respect;
- people need to feel a sense that their work meaningfully contributes to social
  welfare;
- people need to feel that there is a desirable future;

The key element in PD is to allow multiskilling. This, according to the Emerys,
increases interaction around tasks because people understand other tasks as well as
the challenges that surround them. The PD process can be described in terms of four
components: an educational workshop; the analysis phase; the redesign phase; and
finally the implementation phase. These are described in turn below.

The PD *educational workshop* begins with an organisational education process.
This helps the participants to understand the principles of PD and the differences
between a participative structure and a bureaucratic one. Workshops are held
throughout the organisation and forums may be established in order to give the
participants a chance to reflect on and absorb the participative paradigm. Following
these workshops the participants come up with the 'minimum critical specification
(MCM)' against which all designs can be measured. An example of this can be
'maintain same level of customer service'. The specification must be such as to be
general enough to provide participants with guidance and specific enough not to
lose sight of the detail.

The *analysis phase* starts with a brief review of the process and the MCMs. The
participants then analyse how their work is done and assess how much this falls
short of the six requirements. The participants then assess the skills required to do
the work for the redesign, and any shortfall in skills useful in assessing needs
required for redesign of the organisation in the implementation phase.

The *redesign phase* links in with the analysis phase in that the participants begin to redesign structure according to the six democratic principles and begin to draw up the new structures. The process of *mirroring* is used to redesign functions. This is where two groups work on redesigning one group then the other. The advantage of this is that it can provide an 'outsider's perspective'.

The *implementation phase* starts with the different groups of participants meeting with each other to share findings and to get feedback. This is where they learn from their efforts. The participants then develop goals and targets, identify and set up training requirements. The participants then finalise the design and run workshops to discuss and develop the design with the group.

PD was designed to provide the basis for systemic change and to bring this about by incorporating designs that are democratic and non-hierarchical. As such if the participants accept the participative paradigm, implementing new structures may be possible, although if only a partial acceptance is made then it is possible that the organisation may revert to the old organisational design. Thus, the process may only work in climates where there is a full commitment to changing the structure and where resistance is minimal. In terms of the multiagency setting the process holds out promise to organisations exploring strategic alliances, where processes such as *mirroring* may be able to enable creativity and effectiveness.

Deconstruction

Deconstruction can be viewed as the process of demystifying a text or narrative, taking it apart to reveal its arbitrary logic and its presuppositions. The text or narrative to be examined may be written (a plan or proposal for example), or may have been generated within the group. Deconstruction examines what is left out of a text, what is not mentioned, excluded and concealed. This can be viewed in another way: the process of deconstruction reverses the process of construction to show how artificial our ordinary taken-for-granted structure of the social world is. It aims at revealing the internal contradictions within discourses, and the identification of suppressed tensions or conflict in text. It is suspicious of all 'natural' categories. The object is to look for what has been suppressed within the text, because it follows that whenever a discourse appears unified or whole, something must have been suppressed for it to appear as a unity. The process is to recover the suppressed and make the tensions and conflicts within the text reappear. This leads to the exposure of the ideology assumed in the text, and spaces can be opened where different or more varied ideas can be offered. Another means of carrying out deconstruction can be through exploring the use of metaphor(s) to reveal hidden assumptions and challenge them, to arrest the 'taken-for-grantedness' of some aspect of a situation and thus see its limitations. For example, a metaphor often used within the business context is the desired goal of the 'lean and mean' organisation. If we examine this metaphor a little more closely, we might notice other less desirable characteristics, such as the unhealthy anorexic. This exploration thus aids our deconstruction. Table 6.7, which draws on Table 2 in Beath and

Table 6.7 Examples of Deconstructive Strategies

- focusing on marginalised elements
- exposing a false distinction
- looking at claims or assertions which depend on something other than what is clearly stated, especially those that make explicit or implicit recourse to claims of 'naturalness'
- examining what is not said or deliberately omitted
- paying attention to disruptions and contradictions
- examining use of metaphor
- examining use of double entendres

Orlikowski (1994) shows some specific examples of deconstructive strategies that can be used.

Action methods

Action methods enable a group to explore, in action, issues and difficulties that are important to them. An action method is a dynamic rather than a static approach, a process model rather than a mechanical one. It gives us ways of responding and managing in interactive dynamic systems. Sociodrama is a group action method in which participants spontaneously enact or depict hypothetical social situations and scenarios in order to examine shared concerns. A further description of the origins of action methods and the theoretical framework they adopt can be found elsewhere (Fox, 1987; Sternberg and Garcia, 1989). Sociodrama is systematic and practical and this highly structured, but flexible, approach facilitates the growth of spontaneity. This enables a group to explore its 'shared central issue' with attention to the feelings of the individuals and the complexity that this can generate. Differences are more tolerable if the facilitator (referred to as the director in the sociodrama literature) is seen to be able to deal with conflict in a clear and safe way. Once differences can be acknowledged and respected, the group can break through to shared concerns. This does not mean that all conflict is dissolved, but that it can be seen to be tolerable and the groups can learn effective ways of resolving difficulties in the future.

Moreno's theories of interpersonal relations (sociometry) play an important part in sociodrama. Sociometry has been extensively developed and expanded on by others into social network analysis. This can be used to assist in the study of social relationships regardless of whether the nodes represent people or other actors (such as corporations, governments, agencies or other institutions). It looks at patterns of relations between the actors, rather than the distribution of attributes possessed by the actors, and can be used to map social networks.

Sociodrama is a systematic method which contains a number of specific techniques for use in the process. Key concepts are: open tension systems, act hunger, shared central issue, role exploration, role rehearsal, role expansion, catharsis, action insight, resistance. Key techniques are: role reversal, doubling, empty chair, solilo-quy, aside, walk and talk, freeze frame, concretisation, sculpting, mirror, future projection. Sessions progress through a clear process from warm up through choosing the action to structured enactment and possible catharsis, then choosing action, sharing from role, sharing from self and processing.

Action methods have been widely used within a number of different fields:

- professional/staff education/training/development (i.e. work related)
- work with community groups
- other education/training (including for health education/health promotion)
- as a means of enquiry, i.e. as a research tool, including for the specific purpose of evaluation
- therapeutic

Action methods offer particular advantages. They:

- use of words allied to physical action, thus being more inclusive of people less verbally oriented
- require and facilitate collaboration
- are sensitive to context
- are concrete rather than abstract
- enable participation (for example in the research context see the use of drama methods by Ford-Smith, 1986; Griffiths, 1984; Sistren, 1986; in the education context see Berg, 1984)
- result in improvement in positive social interactions within groups (Miller et al., 1993)
- facilitate more spontaneous responses to change.

Despite recognition of their potential application in the workplace for exploring issues (Sternberg and Garcia, 1989), this field of application has not received systematic research exploration. Within the field of community OR (Ritchie et al., 1994), we have already begun to explore the use of action methods in conjunction with OR methods. In particular, Charles Ritchie has carried out a number of pieces of work with tenants' groups which were becoming involved in issues of housing management. Action methods have been used both to help groups create appropriate responses and policies on specific issues and to enable groups to test and evaluate the likely consequences of different policies. Further it has been possible to integrate action-based sessions within a structured approach to handling the overall problem situation. Ron Weiner and Liz Katis have used action methods with a variety of groups and organisations to explore teamworking and organisa-tional issues, including undertaking consultation with people with disabilities about provision of services in a particular area.

Some of the specific techniques associated with action methods are considered in detail in Chapter 7 on different modes of representation, where they are presented as examples of what are called vital modes of representation (as distinct from verbal or visual modes of representation).

More complex methodologies – for mixing, modifying and mutilating

The second part of this chapter's presentation of methods consists of methods, or perhaps they should more accurately be referred to as methodologies, that make much broader claims for themselves. These are methods that we rarely use in their entirety (although others may wish to do so), preferring instead to use parts of them. Our presentation here focuses on the parts that we have found most useful.

Critical systems heuristics

Ulrich's critical systems heuristics (Ulrich, 1983) makes use of 12 boundary questions which can be used to make transparent the presuppositions and normative value judgements underlying debate. Making these often previously implicit assumptions visible opens them up for debate. The boundary questions explore the relationships between seven different types of actor/stakeholder and a specific system under consideration (this can be one that already exists or one that is planned or being planned). The seven different types of stakeholder are introduced in Table 6.8.

The boundary questions are shown in Table 6.9. Two different versions are given. The first (on the left-hand side of the table) presents the form of the questions used to diagnose an already existing system or situation. The second version (on the right-hand side of the table) presents the form used when different possible options are being discussed or a specific plan is being produced.

Table 6.8 The Six Different Types of Stakeholder in Critical Systems Heuristics

Beneficiary	Those who stand to benefit from the system
Decision-taker	Those who have power to change the measure of success/improvement that is relevant for the system
Planner/designer	Those carrying out the planning or design of the system

(The above three types of stakeholder comprise the '*involved*'

Affected	Those whose lives (in whatever sphere, work, social, economic, political etc.) are affected by the system
Witnesses	Those representing the concerns of those who will be/are affected
Experts	Those contributing different types of expertise to the system
Guarantors	Source(s) of guarantee of system success, as seen by those involved

Comment: the possibility of overlap in these types (i.e. the same individual or group of individuals fulfilling more than one slot) ought not to be overlooked. Sometimes the guarantor is identified/expressed as though it stands distinct from any individual or group of individuals, for example as the validity of some data or some mathematical model; there will still be human agents involved in the production of these.

Table 6.9   Ulrich's Critically Heuristic Boundary Questions

Diagnosis	Planning
1. Who is the client (*beneficiary*)?	1. Who ought to be the client (*beneficiary*)?
2 What is the purpose?	2. What ought to be the purpose?
3. What is the measure of success/improvement?	3. What ought to be the measure of success/improvement?
4. Who is the *decision-taker* (i.e. has power to change the measure of success/improvement)?	4. Who ought to be the *decision-taker* (i.e. has power to change the measure of success/improvement)?
5. What components (resources and constraints) are controlled by the decision-taker?	5. What components (resources and constraints) ought to be controlled by the decision-taker?
6. What components (resources and constraints) are part of the environment (i.e. not controlled by the decision-taker)?	6. What components (resources and constraints) ought to be part of the environment (i.e. not controlled by the decision-taker)?
7. Who is/are involved as the *planner/designer*?	7. Who ought to be involved as the *planner/designer*?
8. What kind of expertise flows into the design (who is/are the *experts* and what are their roles)?	8. What kind of expertise ought to flow into the design (who should be the *experts* and what are their roles)?
9. Who is the *guarantor* (where does the planner/designer seek the guarantee that the design will be implemented and will prove successful, judged by the measure of success/improvement)? – is it the theoretical competence of the experts? – is it consensus among experts? – is it validity of empirical data? – is it political support of interest groups? – is it experience/intuition of the involved?	9. Who ought to be the *guarantor* (where ought the planner/designer seek the guarantee that the design will be implemented and will prove successful, judged by the measure of success/improvement)?
10. Who are the *witnesses* (representing the concerns of those who will be affected)?	10. Who ought to be the *witnesses* (representing the concerns of those who might be affected)?
11. To what degree and how are the *affected* given the chance for emancipation from the premises and promises of the involved?	11. To what degree and how ought the *affected* be given the chance for emancipation from the premises and promises of the involved?
12. Upon what world views is the design based? Is it the world view of (some of) the involved or of (some of) the affected?	12. Upon what world views of the involved/the affected ought the design to be based?

Source: drawn from Ulrich (1987).

Strategic assumption surfacing and testing (SAST)

SAST (Mason and Mitroff, 1981) is a method for encouraging and structuring debate around different options or perspectives on a particular topic. The application of SAST can be divided into four parts:

1. Group formation;
2. Assumption surfacing;
3. Dialectical debate;
4. Synthesis.

The content of each of these is described in Table 6.10.

Table 6.10   Stages in SAST

---

1. Group formation
Set of people available divided into small groups on the basis of:
- advocates a particular strategy/option
- vested interest
- personality, many from different areas, many from different organisations
Aim: Maximise similarity within group (in terms of view on strategy/option)
    Maximise different perspectives between groups

2. Assumption surfacing
Each group develops preferred strategy/option by going through the following three-stage process:
  (i) stakeholder analysis, performed using questions like:
- who is affected by the strategy/option?
- who has an interest in it?
- who can affect its adoption, execution or implementation?
- who cares about it?
  (ii) assumption specification – for each stakeholder, what assumptions are we making about them in believing that the preferred strategy/option is the best?
  (iii) assumption rating – for each assumption:
- how important is this assumption in terms of its influence on the success or failure of the strategy/option?
- how certain are we that the assumption is justified?

3. Dialectical debate
Presentations from each group, questions for information only (clarification of assumptions), then open debate:
- how are the assumptions of the groups different?
- which stakeholders feature most strongly in giving rise to the significant assumptions made by each group?
- are different assumptions rated differently by the groups?
- what assumptions of the other groups does each group find most troubling?
- assumption modification by groups takes place if appropriate

4. Synthesis
- draw up agreed list of assumptions
- identify research required to resolve disagreements

Comment: a useful presentation of SAST is given in Flood and Jackson (1991). This presentation also explores the underlying philosophy of SAST and gives some useful case study examples. A much simplified version of SAST is given by Wilcox (1994).

Source: derived from Mason and Mitroff (1981).

Other different useful variants can be obtained by mixing into SAST some of the critically heuristic questions formulated by Ulrich and discussed in the previous section. We might use Ulrich's classification of different types of actors to help in the stakeholder analysis stage. And/or, we might use the following as prompts during discussions in stage 2 or 3:

- What components (resources and constraints) of the strategy/option are controlled by different stakeholders?
- What components (resources and constraints) are part of the environment (i.e. not controlled by any of the stakeholders)?

We might also widen the discussion of strategies/options by asking:

- What elements, if any, of our analysis, could be changed to result in a preferred state of affairs?

This might be done during stage 2, 3 or 4.

Mason and Mitroff themselves recognise that, in common with many other methods, SAST depends on participants being able to identify and articulate their assumptions, i.e. it relies on a certain amount of awareness and honesty. The facilitator(s) obviously have a potential role here in questioning to elicit assumptions and clarifying them, this is also something, however, that the whole group can participate in, particularly if encouraged to do so. When working with groups who know one another, the possibilities of cross-questioning and challenge that exist can usefully be brought to bear here.

Strategic choice approach

The strategic choice approach as a whole has already been described in Chapter 3. Here we focus on one element or component which we have found particularly useful for mixing and matching, namely commitment packages. Another element, AIDA, is considered in the next chapter (Chapter 7) on modes of representation.

The definition of the commitment package offered by Friend and Hickling (1987:74) is that it is 'a combination of actions, explorations and arrangements for future choice designed as a means of making progress in a planning process'. In its basic blank form it is presented as shown in Figure 6.2. A row is completed for each decision area identified, where a decision area can be defined as 'an opportunity for choice in which two or more different courses of action can be considered' (Friend and Hickling, 1987:30). Where there are deferred choices the box includes when the choice is to be made as well as what it is. Contingency plans are entered in the form of 'IF ... THEN ...'

Variants immediately spring to mind. Incorporating the name of the individual(s) to carry forward explorations is one possibility, as is incorporating a date for completion. Individuals might also be assigned to make deferred choices and/or to carry through actions resulting from any contingency plans that become active.

DECISION	IMMEDIATE DECISIONS		FUTURE DECISIONS	
AREAS	ACTIONS	EXPLORATIONS	DEFERRED CHOICES	CONTINGENCY PLANNING

Source: Friend and Hickling (1987).

Figure 6.2 The Basic Form of a Commitment Package

There is a balance to be struck between wanting to insert more and more detail and ending up with something rapidly approaching illegibility. One variant, developed in 'Planning for Real' (discussed in Wilcox, 1994) is shown in Figure 6.3.

SSM (soft systems methodology)

Soft systems methodology as a whole has already been described in Chapter 3. Here we focus on some elements or components which we have found particularly useful for mixing and matching, namely root definitions (Table 6.11) and the CATWOE mnemonic (Table 6.12). Within SSM, the use of CATWOE is strongly linked into the production of a root definition. One variant is to use the CATWOE mnemonic to analyse involvement in, and the nature of, some activity, process or system, within such use the term 'transformations' may be in the plural rather than the singular. An example of such use is presented in the next section of this chapter, in Box 6.1. Other variants/extensions of the use of CATWOE have been suggested

Action	Now-important	Not so important

Source: Planning for real, discussed in Wilcox (1994).

Figure 6.3 An Alternative Form of a Commitment Package

Table 6.11   Explanation of 'root definition'

A root definition is a structured description of a system (which is relevant to the problem). It is a clear statement of activities which take place (or might take place) in the organisation(s) being studied.

A properly structured root definition has three parts, referred to as what, how and why:

- the 'what' is the immediate aim of the system
- the 'how' is the means of achieving that aim
- the 'why' is the longer-term aim of the purposeful activity

The following formulation is used:

A system to . . . . By . . . . In order to . . . .

For example, a root definition for 'constructing this table' might be given as follows: '*A system to* contribute to chapter section about soft systems methodology *by* writing and designing a table explaining root definitions, *in order to* contribute to explaining to the reader selected components of different methodological approaches for group work.'

Table 6.12   CATWOE – Analysis of roles

A CATWOE analysis identifies the various positions which individuals take up with respect to the specific system described in an associated root definition.
The categories are:

C (customer)	the victims/beneficiaries of the purposeful activity
A (actors)	the performers of the activity
T (transformation process)	description of the transformation effected by the system; what things change as a result of the activity and what do they change into?
W (*Weltanschauung*/world-view)	the view of the world that makes this definition meaningful, what views of the purpose of the activity are possible
O (owner)	those who could stop this activity
E (environmental constraints)	constraints in its environment that this system takes as given, what rules, roles, outside bodies, etc. exist which might restrict this activity

For the example root definition given in Table 6.11, this is a possible CATWOE:

C: the readers of Table 6.11
A: the author(s) of Table 6.11
T: requirement for an explanation of root definitions → that requirement met
W: that the book Table 6.11 is a part of will contribute to the literature on processes by which groups of people may manage the joint decision-making process in the multiagency setting
O: the authors; the publishers
E: the restrictions of linear printed text; the time available to author this table

Table 6.13   Variants/Extensions of the Use of CATWOE

---

1. Use CATWOE to analyse involvement in, and the nature of, some activity, process or system
2. Brainstorm lists under each of the CATWOE headings
3. Use the lists generated under Customers, Actors, Owners and elements of the Environment as a starting point for stakeholder analysis (described under SAST earlier in this chapter)
4. Use Transformations to prompt thinking about information and resource needs, monitoring and evaluation
5. Use World-view to identify groups of stakeholders
6. Use Owners and Environment as a starting point to think about barriers and action possibilities for their removal

---

Source: adapted from Wilcox (1994:32).

in the literature; Table 6.13 shows a list of suggestions based on those made by Wilcox (1994).

MIXING, MODIFYING, MULTIPLYING AND MATCHING IN PRACTICE

The first section of this chapter has introduced what we referred to as our in-gredients, a number of different methods/techniques available for use; in addition, Chapter 3 earlier introduced some broader approaches, methodologies, often viewed by their authors (and others) as being adequate to the task of aiding group decision-making used in isolation. In this section of the chapter, we present some examples to illustrate possibilities in mixing methods, splicing them with selections from methodologies. This will illustrate how often it is difficult to make a choice on which method/technique is 'best', and given this it can be unhelpful to think in terms of choosing the 'best' approach. Instead we might think of identifying a 'good enough' approach, and that choice(s) will depend on the locality of the situation. Experimentation can be used to aid the identification process. Within this experimentation, methods (or parts of methods and methodologies) can be chosen and mixed judiciously. This process of choice-making needs to be repeated anew for each intervention (and indeed for each part of each intervention). Later choices can be informed by the results of earlier choices in the same intervention, and indeed by earlier choices in other interventions, but remember that we have laid aside the possibility of hard and fast guidelines ever making this choice a deterministic one. We illustrate how parts of different methods can be used in different parts of an intervention. In terms of the mnemonic introduced earlier for this chapter (see Figure 6.1), we will illustrate how we can mix, modify, multiply and match our use of methods.

Box 6.1 presents our first example which illustrates mixing and matching at work. Here we were concerned with using wholes or parts of different methods or methodologies with one another and at different times in the course of an engagement.

BOX 6.1   MIXING AND MATCHING

A day workshop was undertaken, jointly facilitated by both authors, to help a civil rights group take stock of problems, possibilities and opportunities. The object of the encounter was to clear the ground for shared understanding of their situation, to encourage the whole group to be committed to taking action or to explore possible avenues, and to ensure everyone was sufficiently informed, so that there was as universal as possible support for any decisions made. The organisation wanted all the workers and staff to participate, hence the make-up of the group ranged from the General Secretary to the switchboard operator.

Once the agenda for work in the day had been created, the participants were asked to organise themselves into two groups for the subsequent session, working on building up a detailed picture of these two issues. Groups were chosen by the participants, in a way that mixed management and workers, campaign and administration in each group.

In this initial group session, one group concentrated on generating a rich/thick description of the problems/issues, exploring links between different factors identified (simple cognitive mapping if you like, although there was no explicit attempt to draw maps). Constraints and limitations affecting the different factors involved in the issues were identified. The emphasis was placed on generating diversity, and no attempt was made to reach consensus. At this stage, different (conflicting) views emerged and were acknowledged. The manner of work in this group could be viewed as the equivalent of the shaping phase in strategic choice, elements of stakeholder analysis were used, and some of the critical systems heuristics (CSH) boundary questions were also useful; see Figure 1 below. The feedback from this group to the group as a whole involved each individual contributing, there was no use of a rapporteur, this served to maintain the diversity expressed.

In the other group, guided by some simple prompts, they were asked to describe for themselves how they saw the problem. Following this and guided by the CATWOE mnemonic, they were asked to come up with, collectively, root definitions for their situation, see Figure 2 below. A debate ensued where different perceptions were aired, many bouts of conflictual comments were observed. The result was that it was possible to express the situation as a root definition. There was then an agreement that this provided a suitable basis to take forward and share with the other group. It is also worth noting that diagrams were used to map out various perceptions of the situation. This aided the debates because they were seen as quick summaries of the key points.

During the review session the findings of each group were aired and a discussion followed, then after lunch, during the afternoon session, the groups continued to work on the issues started in the morning session. For one group, the emphasis of this session was to get an impression of how or what improvements could result. Traditional OR encounters would be looking for some sort of model of the situation. What was done here was simply to guide them to describe what would be feasible for the future. The other group concentrated on the generation of realistic, feasible opportunities for change; discussion enabled negotiations and consensus on the feasibility of different options was reached. The opportunities for change identified were not expressed explicitly in commitment package form during the group session, owing to lack of time to fully air all the opportunities identified, this took place during the feedback to the group as a whole.

Figure 1: Elements from stakeholder analysis and critical systems heuristics used by the facilitator of the first group

In relation to the discussion of the current situation, including aspects that might be regarded as problems or issues needing attention, the following questions (adapted from stakeholder analysis and critical systems heuristics) were used to help people describe their views about the different problems or issues and to stimulate debate:

Who are the stakeholders?
• Who is affected by the problem/issue, who benefits, who does not?
• Who has an interest in it?
• Who can affect it, and in what way?
• Who cares about it?

For each stakeholder, what assumptions about them underlie the answers to the above questions.
For each assumption:
• How important is this assumption in terms of its influence?

Figure 2: the CATWOE mnemonic from soft systems methodology used by the second group

For the different activities involved in the problem who/what is/are its:

• *Customer(s)* – victims or beneficiaries
• *Actor(s)* – those who do the activities

• *Transformation process* – what input(s) are transformed into what output(s)

• *Weltanschauung* – the view of the world that makes the activity meaningful
• *Owner* – who can stop the activity

BOX 6.1 Continued

- How certain are we about the assumption?

What are the surrounding circumstances?

- What components (resources and constraints) are controlled by the different stakeholders in the organisation?
- What components (resources and constraints) are part of the environment (i.e. are controlled by the stakeholder outside the organisation)?

- Environmental constraints – the relevant constraints in the environment

Comment: One aspect of our approach in planning for the awayday was that we were not searching for a single method to apply throughout the day. Overall, we wanted to aim to work towards the outcome of some sort of commitment package at the end of the day. We discussed the potential usefulness of several different methods, and drew on some of these to draw up a series of worksheets to be used to allow individuals to explore their own views at various points during the day preparatory to group discussion. Apart from that, we made no fixed selection of methods. Not all of the worksheets were used on the day. Within the various sessions of the day, we aimed to be creative in responding to what we saw as the needs of the moment by selecting from, adapting and mixing various methods, which resulted in some of the plans being used, others not.

During the group work, the two groups took different paths, guided by the choices made by each facilitator for the group they were working with. Using different methods when working separately in the two groups did not preclude bringing the whole thing together when the groups recombined. During the day we deliberately worked to permit divergence of views, as well as divergence of methods used; the plural process allowed for sufficient negotiations by the end of the day to identify a commitment package. That it was a success we judge from feedback received afterwards. One interesting finding to emerge was the perceived value of the commitment package, particularly contrasted to the 'contract' which resulted as the output of the previous awayday. Comments made at the day included that it was a 'more matured process', 'more concrete', and the organisation told us afterwards that they found the written commitment package 'a valuable *aide-mémoire*'.

Source: Our original write-up of this case study appeared in White and Taket (1993). It has also been discussed in White and Taket (1994, 1997) and Taket and White (1996b).

Work carried out by White in Belize (described in White and Taket, 1997) presents an example of the mixing and modifying of different methods/methodologies. In this case elements from team syntegrity and parts of the strategic choice approach were used in the design of a workshop held to discuss and allocate priorities to the problems identified from an earlier participatory appraisal and to explore possible interventions. It was decided that the best way to ensure that the options and actions were shared and owned by the participants was to produce a form of commitment package. Elements from this work are shown in Box 6.2 to illustrate this. The case study also illustrates multiplying at work, through the use of multiple methods to help in identifying needs (group interviews, ranking exercises, map drawing exercises).

BOX 6.2   SOME WORK IN BELIZE

The case study described is concerned with how a development agency in Belize (called HELP) attempted to improve its relationship with the groups and the communities it works with. It was thought that a study with the groups would help to improve links with the rural communities.

The first part of the work was a PRA, to assess the needs of, and to evaluate HELP's work with, the groups and communities. The team devised a semi-structured interview schedule and in pairs, worked in different regions within Belize. In the respective regions each pair conducted group interviews, ranking exercises and map-drawing exercises. The pairs ensured that the information and maps were available to the participants for further interrogation and criticism.

A workshop was organised so that the representatives of the groups could bring with them all their concerns, problems and opportunities. For the workshop processes decided upon were elements from team syntegrity and parts of the strategic choice approach. The aims of the workshop were to discuss and allocate priorities to the problems identified from the PRA and to explore possible interventions. Another aim was to discuss how HELP could improve the existing services it provided and discuss new ways to meet gaps in its services. It was decided that the best way to ensure that the options and actions were shared and owned by the participants was to produce a form of commitment package.

Using the hexadic reduction phase of syntegrity and the shaping phase of the strategic choice approach clusters of major issues were brought out by the group. The issues were then examined in more depth by comparing different schemes using several criteria such as employment of women and youth, and sustainability, and then trying to bring out and resolve the uncertainties. This was done using the outcome resolve stage of syntegrity. A discussion of the uncertainties then followed. A form of commitment package took shape as the uncertainties were being discussed. The final commitment package was produced.

Comments: An approach was needed to aggregate local knowledge and to use this knowledge for further exploration with agencies and government. The needs generated from bottom-up local participatory planning through PRA were completely unconstrained. To select and implement ideas and solutions another round of debate to introduce constraints was needed, this is where the NGO as a stakeholder might come in. A problem for PRA is that it does not deal with multiagency planning, only with bottom-up needs assessment, so it does not help in taking this further step. This was done using other process. The choice of other methods must be appropriate to the circumstances and the participants, this may necessitate some experimentation until the most suitable mode is found, it may even be appropriate to use several different modes. It must also move the group to action, and it is in this that it is most different from PRA. The methods can be flexibly and creatively mixed and matched to enable local participants to obtain, share and analyse knowledge of their life and conditions and to plan and act according to that knowledge. Within this process we have mixed and matched methods, using only parts or stages of individual methods. One reason we do this, is in order to create for each situation a blend of methods that the participants feel comfortable with and engage with.

Box 6.3 provides an example of mixing and modifying of methods used in a case study of evaluation of innovatory health promotion projects, presented by Taket (1993). Here a hybrid of two methods (SAST and CSH) was produced to aid a process of formative evaluation. As a final example in this section, Box 6.4 describes work undertaken in the context of a patient participation forum, where the methods mixed were open space technology, the strategic choice approach and nominal group technique. The box explains some of the factors that went into the choice of these methods to match the features of the situation involved.

We now turn our attention to some other examples of where methods have been changed and adapted for their use in particular circumstances. A number of case studies reported in the literature on community operational research contain examples of where groups have gone on to modify and produce and use different variants of methods; see for example the case studies presented by Taket (1994b) and Pindar (1994). Pindar's case study reports on a multiagency intervention concerned with planning and implementing a network response to racial harassment that was occurring within a public housing estate. The initial workshop, which Pindar facilitated, used a combination of diagramming (see Chapter 7), SWOT analysis and the strategic choice approach. The approaches she introduced to the group were used in later sessions by them in different forms. Pindar also reports though that in this situation their use declined over time, something she links to change-over in the group's members and to lack of identification of the importance of paying explicit attention to process, with explicit facilitation of meetings. The case study presented by Taket (1994b) also describes a situation where modification occurred, firstly in Taket's use of different methods (the strategic choice approach

BOX 6.3 MIXING METHODS FOR GROUP EVALUATION SESSIONS

As a part of the formative evaluation in several health promotion projects, group discussions involving project workers and steering group members examined project progress and any problems that had arisen, using as a checklist a series of questions which had been produced by drawing on parts of SAST (strategic assumption surfacing and testing) and critical systems heuristics – see Table 1 below.

Table 1 Checklist for exploring particular issues/problems during formative evaluation

Initial session:

1. Identify the different actors (stakeholders) involved in the issue/problem:
   - who is affected by the issue/problem?
   - who has an interest in it?
   - who can affect it?
   - who cares about it?
2. What components (resources and constraints) of the issue/problem are con-trolled by the different actors?
3. What components (resources and constraints) are part of the environment (i.e. not controlled by any of the actors)?
4. Identify assumptions: for each stakeholder, what assumptions are we making about them in placing them in relation to the issue/problem?
5. Identify options for change: what elements, if any, of 2, 3, 4 could be changed to result in a preferred state of affairs?

In second and subsequent sessions, changes are identified (using a similar framework), together with the circumstances that allowed the changes to happen.

Comment: Note the differences in the above and Figure 1 shown in Box 6.1 above. The same methods are mixed in different ways for different circum-stances.

Source: drawn from Taket (1993).

and strategic assumption surfacing and testing), and later in the group's use of these methods in further modified versions. One feature she points out as being particularly important was the use of methods that employed visual forms of representation (described in Chapter 7). She observes that this type of method matched well with the situation, in creating easily understandable representations of the situation and decisions taken.

BOX 6.4   THE PATIENT PARTNERSHIP FORUM

The case is based on work with a health authority in London preparing to respond to the directive from the government to make public involvement a priority. The authority had to think about involving the public more in the development of its work and future strategies. In the past the authority adopted mechanisms such as representation on the board through the Community Health Council (CHC) and consultation with the public through surveys.

We decided to use 'open space technology' which is an innovative but well-respected technique and is particularly useful where a wide range of perspectives need to be applied to a complex issue. The approach is particularly powerful when people admit that they do not know the answer but want to work together to find creative and viable solutions (Owen, 1992)

The task of the event takes the form of a theme or question where the participants accept responsibility for answering in collaboration with each other. It was decided that the proposed theme for the event would be: *'How can we improve the health of the local population?'*

The day was planned to be intentionally unstructured to enable participants to set the agenda – indeed one of the key aims of the event was to allow those who attended the session to identify potential outcomes. Details of the event were advertised in a press release in the local newspaper, posters were displayed in local libraries and flyers were widely distributed to service providers, voluntary groups, church associations and the CHC.

The event took place in April 1998 and brought together a variety of people including people working in the voluntary sector, the wider public, service providers and key members of the authority including the Chief Executive. The day aimed at attracting anyone with an interest in health, including members of voluntary and community groups, staff from other statutory agencies such as social services, housing, education and local provider trusts, carers and service users. It was emphasised at the event that each person attended as an individual with an opportunity to have an equal say in what was taking place. Around 100 people participated in the day.

At the start of the session, the group facilitator asked participants to suggest topics for discussion around the broad subject of *'How can we improve the health of local population?'*, with the focus on asking people how the health authority can work with local people to improve the health of residents.

Twenty-one participants suggested a wide variety of subject headings for discussion, ranging from 'healthy diets' to 'primary care groups'. Each participant who had suggested a subject for discussion was asked to be the group convenor. The day was then divided into three concurrent sessions (with seven groups in each), each lasting approximately one hour.

Participants were then asked to sign their names against sessions, although they were also encouraged to move between different groups if there was more

than one subject which interested them running at one time. Thus, self-organis-
ing groups were set up to work on tasks and explore issues with a new and
different mix of people. There was a strong desire to see things happen differently. Some groups finished quickly, while others worked for much longer.
Groups were self-selecting and they set their own objectives. Each group convenor was asked to make notes on their session on a flip chart – listing key
issues and action points arising from the discussion and noting who participated
in their group. In some groups the convenor and facilitator used approaches to
stimulate deliberation and debate. Strategic choice and nominal group technique were used.

The work in small groups helped break down boundaries between individuals
and agencies. There was a mix of agencies and public in the small groups and
these worked well in tackling the tasks at hand. The day ended with the whole
group reflecting on the findings of the small groups and planning the follow-up
session.

The follow-up session was held on 29 April. Approximately half of those who
attended the first session participated in the follow-up discussions. All of the
points raised during this session were noted on flip charts by the facilitator.
Having run through the report in some detail, highlighting the main points, the
facilitator distributed eight red dots to each person and asked them to indicate
the eight action points on the flip charts which they felt were priorities.

In addition the participants were asked to sign their name against any action
point which they felt willing and able to help take forward at a later date. The
outcome of the session was a total of 60 action points to be taken forward which
were highlighted from the report of the open space event during the follow-up
session.

Source: White (1999).

An example of matching and multiplying can be found in another of Taket's case
studies, carried out in Pakistan. The most detailed description is contained in Taket
(forthcoming); the case study is also discussed in Taket and White (1996a,b, 1997)
and White and Taket (1995a), and elements from it presented elsewhere in this
book. In this case mixing different methods in the same session was vital in enabling
individuals with different (observed) preferences for different ways of working to
participate in the session; aspects of this case that illustrate this are shown in Boxes
8.3, 8.4 and 8.6. Finally, White and Taket (1994a), discussing cases of evaluation in
the non-governmental sector, illustrate graphically how it can be impossible to
comprehensively plan the methods to be used in an intervention beforehand and
how the process of choice-making through mixing, matching, multiplying and
modifying is necessarily a contingent and ongoing one.

SUMMING UP AND MOVING ON

In this chapter we have presented a number of methods and illustrated their use in interventions. We have discussed and illustrated the activities of mixing, modifying, multiplying and matching, which we engage in as we choose and use methods in an intervention. In Chapter 7, which follows, we continue the discussion of methods, presenting those methods where a key focus of interest is on the mode of representation they employ. The issue of representation has not been absent from this chapter; all methods/techniques rely on the use of some mode or modes of representation, but has not yet been explicitly discussed.

The examples from case studies we have presented, both in this chapter and in the rest of the book, demonstrate how choice of methods depends on particular features of the local situation, and that methods (or parts of methods) can be chosen and mixed judiciously. The choices made are relevant for the particular intervention, and the process of choice needs to be made afresh for each intervention.

Modes of representation 7

We should know we are making models and realise they are not models of ultimate reality, but proposals. They are part of the dance of the mind. They are not models of anything at all really. Rather we are proposing that if we carry out the dance in this way, that the general result will be more harmonious — not in the nature of something static — but rather in the nature of a creative movement. Bohm (1985:57)

INTRODUCTION

As we have explored in Chapter 4, deliberation, debate and decision-making (the three Ds) are an integral part of multiagency working. The use of representation is a crucial part of the process by which a group of participants can be facilitated to make sense of the situation and can be helped to understand the issues they face. Representation is no easy task given that issues faced by participants in the multi-agency setting are messy and often ill-structured.

There are many modes of representations, from verbal description, mathematical models, visual representations such as maps and diagrams, and physical mode of presentation such as role-playing. To us these are all modes of representations that can and should be used in the multiagency setting. We will introduce a mnemonic — the three Vs — as our categorisation of the different modes of representation. These are: verbal, visual and vital.

To us the issue of representation is important precisely because it re-presents. To explain this, when we re-present, i.e. as in a mathematical model, reality becomes an inscription or something that can be manipulated or played with. An individual or group could play with it, explore it, interrogate it and manipulate it; the possibilities opened up to us are endless. The representations are what representatives explore, say from different agencies, and it is through playing with them that agencies can find means to collaborate and conflict is managed. We, like Bohm (1985), would like to think of representations as nothing more than the 'dance of the mind'.

We often try to produce representations that try to achieve a 'likeness' of the real. In other words to produce representations that would correspond to the world. The world is then a jigsaw, which can be constructed from pieces of data strewn about, and the objective is to produce a big picture. Once we have a big picture we can control, change the world and be empowered (emancipated). However, we would argue that the representations can refer only to themselves, or refer to other modes of representations that attempt to imitate the world. Given this, representation becomes useful to us merely as a tool or toy.

Thus where do we go from here? The work by Freire on education is informative in this process. In his writings (Freire, 1972), he claims that education needs to be based upon genuine dialogue and it requires the sensitive use of linguistic codes in problematising interactions between different participants. Similarly, we would argue for the need to involve sensitive use of representations which are transparent and relevant to the participants (examples of these types of representations will be given shortly). We need to develop modes of representations that are transparent, mutually produced with the participants, are owned by the participants and can be interrogated by the participants. The representations are produced from shared analysis and result in shared meaning between all parties. Seeking transparency and shared meaning, however, cannot be accorded the status of an unproblematic, universally applicable goal. It calls for a process of critical reflection on the processes used in the intervention, and the facilitator(s) must necessarily assume the responsibility for deciding what is most appropriate and suitable to each particular moment in the intervention (see Chapter 10).

VISUAL LITERACY

Thus we see visual literacy as an emerging area that deals with what can be seen and how we interpret what is seen. It is approached from a range of disciplines which study the physical processes involved in visual perception, to the use of technology to represent visual imagery, and the intellectual strategies used to understand what is seen.

Berger said in *Ways of Seeing* (1972) that seeing comes before words, and that we look and recognise before we speak. This is taken up in with the emerging view that visual literacy is more universal than verbal literacy (Bradley, 1994). There is an ever-increasing body of research that shows that visual forms of representations are easily understood regardless of literacy.

Bradley (1994:7) stated that, 'Pictures give a "voice" to those who have little status in a community'. Thus, visual forms of representation can be a way of increasing participation between different individuals. Through our experience we are beginning to be aware that thinking calls for images and that visualisation is the ground on which thinking visually can take place. The source of inspiration is the work of Paulo Freire (1972) who used picture codes to promote education. The picture codes are used to help people reflect back the issues which they are concerned with and not to transmit the educators' messages. He claimed that pictures can promote participation. People can participate in the process of visualisation, it can help them to pool information about a group community and involvement will promote action.

As Bradley (1994:3) described, pictures can be 'employed by those who are primarily image users not language users, whose sense of identity and self are expressed better in pictures than in words'. Visual forms of representations can be produced by an individual, a group or a community to portray ideas which would be difficult to express in any other way. The images can act as a bridge between differences due, for example, to languages and cultures.

We are interested in exploring ways to enhance the skills of visualisation. We see the skills needed as:

- Viewing – an ability to look and see what is being represented
- Perception – an ability to interpret what is seen
- Discrimination – an ability to recognise and make links between various things represented
- Communication – an ability to communicate, preferably in a non-verbal way, any insights and/or views

Our use of visualisation enables a shared understanding between the facilitator and the group and between members within the group. The use of visual modes of representation (coupled with good facilitation and methods of working) is an empowering process. Our approach allows those who are disadvantaged to at least present an opinion. The researcher/facilitator should always try to enable everyone's voices to be heard.

There are many examples of the use of visual methods in the literature. Many are descriptions of experiences in the developing countries. We will not provide a comprehensive review here but provide some illustrative examples.

An approach that is widely used in the developing countries is participatory rural appraisal (PRA). It uses visual forms of representation to widen participation and encourage empowerment (see Chapter 3). Many of the tools that are used in PRA use pictures as discussion starters (Chambers, 1994a, b, c; e.g. Barnett, 1991; Linney, 1994).

Not all visualisation uses pictures. There is evidence that acting out of 'picture codes' is as important as just using picture codes (Fuglesang, 1982). It was revealed that intense and vivid 'memory pictures' were more concrete and meaningful than pictures drawn on paper.

Research has also shown that visualisations can give rise to emotional data being expressed allowing access to conscious and unconscious emotion (Vince and Broussine, 1996). In one piece of work the researchers used drawings with middle and senior managers in six public service organisations (local government and health care) as part of a process of working with management of change. They conducted several separate workshops by level and then joint meeting. They found a range of feelings which illustrate their theoretical hypothesis around articulating feelings. The managers reported finding the exercise useful – in terms of understanding, middle managers reassured by exposure of senior manager's feelings, senior managers realised they had underestimated needs of staff generally for communication and involvement in management of change. They conclude by setting out their process for working to comprehend and act on emotion in context of relations within organisations. In another piece of work Zuboff (1988) found that drawings helped clerical staff articulate feelings that had been implicit and hard to define. They drew pictures showing how they felt about their jobs before and after a new computer system was installed.

Meyer (1991) asserts that the pictures are capable of enabling participants to communicate information about multidimensional organisational attributes with clarity and precision. The respondents' pictures often possess more complex, subtle and useful cognitive maps of their organisations than they can verbalise. Meyer also found that the integration of visual with verbal data is a very useful form of triangulation.

It seems that visual data can enhance the capacity of respondents to make sense of things and to attribute meaning to events. 'Visual instruments seem uniquely suited to situations where a researcher aspires to some precision in measurement, but prefers not to force informants into his or her cognitive framework prematurely. Such occasions include investigations of amorphous concepts, efforts to build theory and research focusing on human awareness, interpretation and consciousness' (Meyer, 1991:232).

DIFFERENT MODES OF REPRESENTATION

In order to increase the capacity to participate in analysis of issues, we would need to address two problems – the limitation of our minds to hold a wide range of information and the limitation of working individually. Orthodox involvement usually happens in quite a linear way, which places on the memory the burden of recollecting complex information such as patterns of connection. It is inadequate if unsupported by, say, visual representation. We are generally constrained by the 'magic number seven plus or minus two' as our limit to short-term memory and attention (Miller, 1956). In orthodox approaches we record statements on flip charts or white-boards. This has become regular to help with our limitations of attention and memory. This leaves us with a checklist or a diagram of some kind, both of which are inflexible.

We need a form of visualisation that exploits the basic wisdom that a picture is worth a thousand words. We also need a form of visualisation that will enable participation of all where each will have the power to influence patterns of ideas.

Visualisation is important in order to make our work more participative. It makes the process of finding out and learning open to all. It can be used to help participants verify, amend, cross-check ideas and concepts, and for the findings to be owned by all. Everyone can see what is being said. Visualisations can be the focus of discussions that can help to resolve problems. This draws on ideas from Freire who used pictures as codes in that they are specific enough for exploring concepts, but general enough to be able to identify with them. These codes do not necessarily have to be diagrams, but non-verbal such as play and so on can help break down barriers to participation (Bradley, 1994).

Participation is achieved because visualisation is an equaliser in that all can understand what is being shown. People can participate in making visuals that pool information about, say, a community. It can shift autonomy away from experts to those who own the issues or problems. It treats local knowledge as valuable and promotes action. It allows sharing activities which can generate enthusiasm and solidarity. In fact visualisation can affect levels of participation and action.

This requires a supportive environment which can accommodate a series of work processes from issue conceptualisation to exploration. Facilitation skill (see Chapter 10) is the special expertise that supports people in representational thinking. It is the art of empowering the group to engage properly and productively with the transitional discipline.

We have found that in the multiagency setting — in particular in dealing with diversity — that a variety of modes of representation would be needed in order to help a group to visualise issues, share in their understanding and facilitate learning. Within our practice we are also experimenting with the use of other modes of representation. Firstly, there are the set of action methods, including sculpting (building a physical representation to explore an issue or situation using people and objects), and sociometric diagrams (using spatial distributions to depict aspects of relationships between actors or things). Secondly, there is the use of scripts, storytelling, narrative analysis and so on. From within operational research and systems, we also make use of such modes as cognitive mapping, influence diagrams, decision trees and rich pictures.

We have also found in our practice that the phases that participants go through are *deliberation, debate* and *decision-making* (see Figure 7.1). Different modes of representation can and should be used in each phase and preferably in combination.

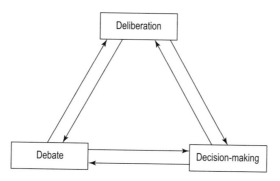

Figure 7.1 The Three Ds

Deliberation allows parameters to be explored in the context of issues to be shared and the scope of the work to be defined. Debate between participants is important particularly on the implications, feasibility and acceptability of what is being discussed. A new form of argumentation or dialogue is needed that enables participation. The use of appropriate modes of representation in combination with appropriate facilitation is a start to designing a novel form of argumentation or dialoguing. Here, participants can engage with each other and be able to adopt a critical distance to minimise conflict and to enable collaboration.

We will now go on to explore the different modes of representation in more detail. Huff (1990) and others have claimed that it is possible to group or classify modes of representation into five categories, from the verbal to more complex graphical maps that reveal influence, causality, structure and schemas that guide cognition. Bryant (1989) also offers a typology for capturing the complexity of shared views — these are: structuring debate, gathering evidence, and patterning meaning.

Here we introduce our three Vs framework. We classify the different modes of representation as verbal, visual and vital. The modes of representation can be used in any combination with the stages of development (i.e the three Ds) (see Figure 7.2).

Verbal deals with the use of language either as a list of key words or linking concept themes in order to represent causality or structure. Visual uses icons, diagrams or graphs. Vital refers to physical forms of representation such as role-play, drama and so on, that replays real-life situations. We will elaborate on these below.

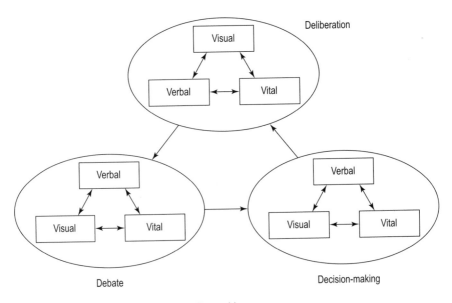

Figure 7.2   The Three Ds with the Three Vs

Verbal

The verbal mode of representation deals with the use of language. Normally what is being represented is represented using words. There are many types of verbal representation, from statements on the problem such as statements produced in team syntegrity (Table 7.1), to maps that show causality between one concept and another as in cognitive mapping (Table 7.2), which in effect can also be a cross between verbal and visual in that these types of maps are graphs. In many group settings or workshops there is usually a scribe taking down and summarising the

Table 7.1 Statements of Importance: Team Syntegity

The team syntegrity process has five main activities: generating 'statements of importance'; the problem jostle; the hexadic reduction; the topic auction; and the outcome resolve. The first three activities produce 12 topics for debate, the fourth allocates participants to topics or teams, and the final activity involves three rounds of debates on each topic.

Generating 'statements of importance' is where the initial 'playing field' is created around the overall reason for holding the syntegration. The participants are free to generate as many ideas as they can, record them in 10 words on cards or memo notes and place them on a bulletin board. This becomes the focus for the group to share ideas and to cluster statements on the issues to hand.

Example: A recent use of team syntegrity was to explore how the new authority for London should operate. The event involved 30 experts on issues relating to London. During the problem jostle phase over 120 ideas were elicited. These were scribed on a wall and the participants were asked to organise them into 12 themes. This proved very difficult to the group, in that the linear form of representing these statements did not allow the group to explore relationships between them. Also, with the range of interests and backgrounds present, it was difficult for anyone to agree on any set of statements to belong to any one category. Some individuals became concerned that their ideas were being lost once the categories were decided upon. The protocol (Beer, 1995) suggests that these hidden or lost views should and will resurface, although there is no guarantee that they will. The 12 topics eventually decided upon were:

- Strategic planning
- Transport
- Children of the city
- Sustainability
- Exclusion and inclusion
- Money/finance
- Serious media coverage
- Arts and education
- Demographic diversity
- Representation
- The complexity of London
- Community involvement in governing London

Source: White (1997).

Table 7.2   Concept Mapping

Concept mapping is where an issue is placed at the centre of a flip-chart paper or on the wall and the group is asked individually to spend a few minutes to make a list of what the issue means to them. They can write down as many views as they have for the concept. Then in a round-robin fashion each is asked to write around the concept on the flip-chart paper the one they think is most important to them and why. A form of a cognitive map is then drawn for each individual. As each member of the group explores his/her views links can be made between the different maps. A model of their impressions is built around the issue. This can be used to help the group explore the issues together (see Figure 7.3).

Example: The Migrant Resource Centre (MRC) is a voluntary agency set up to provide advice and information on immigration, housing, health and welfare rights for refu- gees and migrants in London. It also co-ordinates several other activities such as a luncheon club for the elderly and a health project. The MRC had many problems, ranging from attempting to stem the loss of volunteers to deciding what kind of services it should be providing. It found that many of the issues were linked but there was no way to untangle them sufficiently to deal with them. The team had felt paralysed by the overwhelming task of untangling the many issues and to decide on a course of action. The use of concept mapping was useful as a means of displaying the different issues and exploring the relations between them. For example, the group wanted to explore getting funding for a new worker, but was unsure what role this person should play. At the centre of the flip-chart paper, 'role of new worker' was placed and each member wrote, alongside the statement, his or her version of the role. The issues began to be addressed, such as should the person be an administrator or development worker.

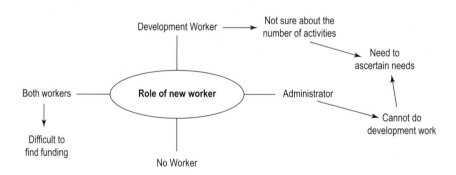

Figure 7.3   Concept Map

Source: White (1994b).

discussion. Often this is sufficient; however, when the variety is high in a group setting not everyone can engage with the descriptions or a mode of languaging may dominate. Concept mapping, mind mapping and cognitive mapping are useful means of breaking with the linearity of scribing what has been said or 'bullet-pointing' a discussion. Other examples of the verbal mode of representation are given in Tables 7.3 and 7.4.

Table 7.3 Repertory Grid Analysis

This process is relatively simple to undertake, but extremely effective in enhancing thinking in group situations. For a given situation a number of 'elements' need to be drawn up. This could be people or stakeholders involved in the situation or physical entities and so on. They are then individually represented on pieces of card. The process proceeds by the group choosing three cards at random and the group is asked to examine them and then to try and associate two and ask why they differ from the third. The response is called a 'construct'. For any given triad of cards there can be between zero and five constructs elicited. The process is then repeated with a different set of triads and this continues until the number of constructs have been exhausted.

The constructs and elements can then be arranged in a grid. The group would then look at the grid and tick for each element whether the first pole of the construct is associated positively with the element. If not it is left blank. The visual picture then becomes the focus for group discussion.

Example: Some work was carried out on a housing estate in London on the health needs of the residents. One of the groups that were involved was the elders on the estate. The workshop with this group used a combination of nominal group technique (NGT) and repertory grids. The emphasis of the workshop was to use visual forms of representation to facilitate debate on identifying their needs. NGT allowed the group to share concerns and prioritise which were important. However, the repertory grid analysis brought out more interesting issues.

The group was presented with a list of elements representing the estate, e.g. resource centre, shops and so on. Three were chosen at random and they were asked to associate two, then discuss why they did so. This process was repeated several times. At the end a list of key constructs was produced which began to shape into a story about their needs. The major one was that they were reminiscing about the 'old days' on the estate when there were a number of amenities, which brought the community together. They believed that a lot of the problems were based on a lack of facilities to bring people together and the general health of the community was deteriorating due to the isolation and fear that had come about due the break lack of community facilities. This issue was explored further in the validation workshop.

Source: White (1997).

Table 7.4 Deconstruction

Deconstruction uses a series of analytical strategies to examine texts closely and to look for contradictions and ambivalences. The strategies are used to take apart the texts to reveal implicit meaning and unacknowledged biases. These can include: looking for use of rhetorical devices, exposing a false distinction, paying attention to disruptions and contradictions, and looking at claims or assertions which depend on something other than clearly evident.

Example: The Forum Project was set up at a Community and Mental Health Trust in the south-east of England in the beginning of 1997. The project team comprised consultant physician, general practitioner, Parkinson's disease nurse, nursing team leader and independent project consultant. The team developed and piloted an integrated model of health and social care in the community. The intervention entailed bringing the inputs of the consultant and specialist nurse to a community setting, to combine with those of the general practitioners, community nurses and social services. Earlier on in the project the team members had to work out their relationship with each other. There was a tension between the nurses and the doctors. During one of the earlier sessions each member of the team was asked to describe how he/she saw the project developing. In the descriptions there was clearly a difference in the use of language. The rhetorical device used by one of the doctors was the need for a 'whole systems approach'. This image, however, had no meaning for the other members of the team. It was clear that the doctor had seen this notion as having scientific legitimacy. However, by being challenged by the rest of the group, the concept began to take on a new meaning based on interprofessional working. Whole systems became the catchword for joint thinking within the team.

Source: Taket and White (1999).

Visual

The visual mode of representation deals with the use of icons, diagrams or graphs. This mode can use simple procedures such as drawing 'rich pictures' to more sophisticated devices such as decision trees and networks. The visual facilitation methods described here require a supportive environment that can accommodate a series of work processes from deliberation, debate on complex issues, to decision-making. The use of simple technology such as on 'whiteboards' is excellent for gaining the 'hands on' involvement of a group. There are also a number of computer packages that have been used to great effect with groups.

This mode of representation can be used to sequence entities, or used to compare schemes, or simply relate or link concepts. There are modes that can help describe a situation, such as rich pictures (Table 7.5). Other examples of the visual mode of representation are given in Tables 7.6–7.8.

There are some techniques that can help a group compare the range of options in order to facilitate choice (see e.g. Table 7.9). There are also visual techniques that can help link concepts and help explore the relationships (see e.g. Table 7.10).

Table 7.5   Rich Pictures

This is a process where visual representation of a problem situation can be expressed graphically by adopting three devices. The devices are structure, process and climate. These are simplifications of system notions of elements, process and environment. A rich picture is a sketch that depicts certain aspects of a situation. The picture pulls together the three devices. Structure represents those factors that are slow to change such as organisational structure and physical aspects such as buildings, locations and so on. Process are things that are carried out within or around the system. Process represents the flows of resources, i.e. information, materials or money. Climate is the general feel, resulting from the interaction between structure and process, about how the factors gel together. Rich pictures can also represent issues expressed or felt by the participants such as complaints, criticisms or any feeling of discontent of the current situation being represented. Rich pictures aim to capture the richest point of view. It is a valuable aid to enabling shared understanding of the situation, to open up dialogue. Rich pictures can be drawn individually or in groups. The selection of relevant features is vitally important. It is important not to be overly elaborate; it is better to have an approximation than attempt to represent everything.

Example 1:   As part of a visioning exercise for the WHO, the participants were asked to describe their images of the past, present and future. These visions were represented as a form of rich picture (Figure 7.4).

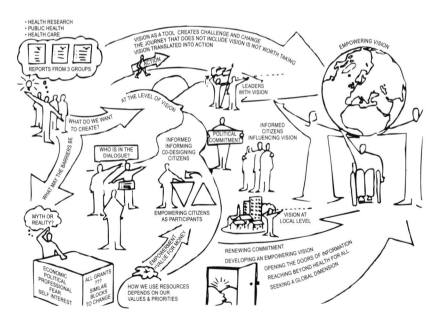

Figure 7.4   Rich Picture – WHO visioning exercise
Reproduced by permission of Don Braisby

(Table 7.5 continued)

Table 7.5   (Continued)

Example 2: The setting for this case study was work carried out in Lahore, Pakistan. The work was concerned with strengthening of the health services in the province. There were a number of organisations involved. The worked centred on the College of Community Medicine in Lahore. A rich picture was drawn up of the situation as seen during the first day of the work (Figure 7.5).

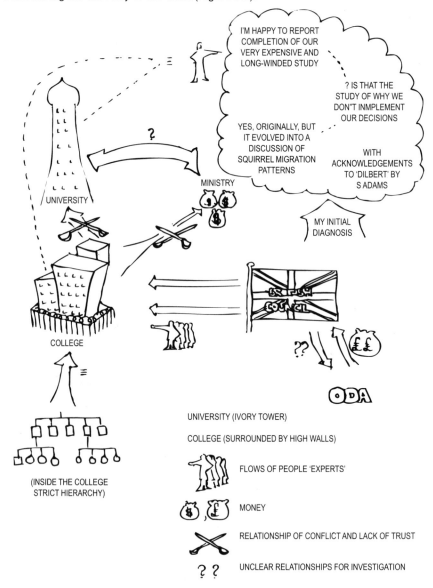

Figure 7.5   Rich Picture, Pakistan case study

Table 7.6 Cognitive Mapping

Cognitive mapping is an example of a mode of representation which is both verbal and visual. In SODA it is used as a modelling activity. It is premised on the view that language is 'the basic currency of organisational problem solving' (Eden, 1989). Language is assumed to be an adequate modelling medium. It is a mode of representation designed to display the way a person defines an issue. It is coded from what a person is saying.

In Figure 7.6 the arrow indicates the way in which one idea may lead to another. Note that '. . .' is read as 'rather than' and separates the first pole of the concept from the contrasting pole. Concepts, and their opposites, are written and linked with other concepts on the map.

Concept 3...Concept 4

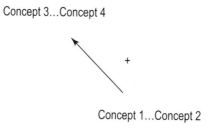

Concept 1...Concept 2

Figure 7.6 Cognitive Map

The links are in the form of arrows with positive (+) and negative (−) signs associated with each link − positive signs are sometimes omitted, being the default value. A positive sign at the arrowhead means that the first pole of one concept relates to the first pole of the other concept, and vice versa. A negative sign means that the first pole of one concept relates to the second pole of the other concept, and vice versa. The polarity of defining concepts along with their opposites assists in clarifying the meaning of the concepts.

The map is built as a series of means and ends, each concept at the arrowhead being an end and each concept at the arrow's base being a term of means. Higher-valued ends, in themselves concepts, are placed at the top of the map and defined as desirable goals to be reached.

Example: Often community health staff, working with families where there are children who face the threat of abuse, may have to deal with quite stressful and distressful situations. In many cases child protection work occupies a considerable proportion of the time. A project providing support to staff on child protection issues via a number of specialist child protection advisers (CPAs) was set up and evaluated.

As part of the study cognitive maps of the individuals involved in the project were produced (Figure 7.7). The combined maps became the focus of the workshop with the different stakeholders and brought about shared understanding of the issues. One of the main issues was the question of whether the CPA role should be full or part time.

Via the maps the participants were able to explore the benefits of both options and they enhance the discussion within the group.

(*Table 7.6 continued*)

Table 7.6   (Continued)

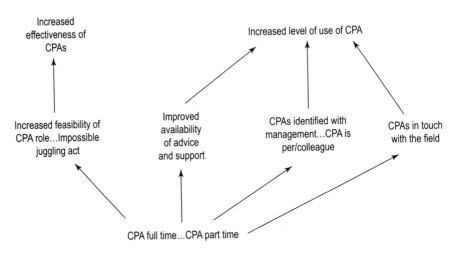

Figure 7.7   Example of a Cognitive Map

Source: Taket (1994b).

Table 7.7   Influence Diagrams

In many situations elements that make up the problem often interact with each other, often in a reinforcing or debilitating way, or in a way that attempts to maintain the effects within a certain range. We can represent this pattern as an influence diagram or causal-loop diagram. Figure 7.8 attempts to show which element causes other elements to change. We usually represent the links of causation as a loop. Complex systems behave with a combination of amplifying (i.e. small change amplifies a big change in the system), stabilising (maintaining a balance) behaviour and 'feedback'.

The entities are represented as blocks and causality as arrows. The convention is that the direction of the arrow indicates the direction of the cause. Often a sign is put on the arrow to indicate the effect of the causality. So if an increase in one entity leads to an increase in another, when all other elements remain constant then a positive sign is used. If an increase in one leads to a decrease in another then a minus sign is used.

(*Table 7.7 continued*)

Table 7.7   (Continued)

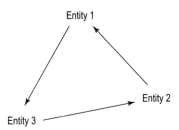

Figure 7.8   Influence Diagram

These diagrams can be developed into more formal models using levels and rates for system dynamic simulation.

Example: In the case study described above some of the cognitive maps were easily seen as influence diagrams (see e.g. Figure 7.9). In particular, when the group discussed the appraisal of their practice circular, dynamic arguments emerged and when it was represented visually everyone was able to comment on the dynamics. They were able to follow the cycles as virtuous or viscous and they were able to identify interventions that could either stem the flow or enhance it. This form of qualititative modelling helped the group explore tacit knowledge and assumptions.

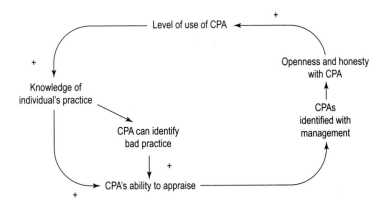

Figure 7.9   Example of an Influence Diagram

Table 7.8   IDONS

IDONS are used as a type of visual facilitation. It uses hexagons as a flexible mapping technique to bridge the gap between thoughts and models. By using movable hexagons for capturing data, a simple visual medium for handling flexibly the content of conversations is created. As the statements come out in conversation the facilitator captures each distinct idea as a summary headline on a magnetic backed hexagon which can be placed initially at random on a large steel whiteboard, clearly seen and accessible to the group. Each point is checked, as it is written up, for mutual comprehension but without at this stage debate about its validity. The initial phase can produce anything from 20 to 50 hexagons arrayed on the board. The next phase is to look for relationships. The simplest technique for doing this is to start grouping the hexagons, a process called clustering. This produces an 'issue map' which represents a new perception and grasp of the vague concern and provides a platform for formulating the next steps of thinking and decision-making needed by the group.

    The issue map will tend to point to the interconnectedness of things. The group will have explored some of the systemic implications of the issues.

    Mapping with IDONS is the process of rendering tacit models visible and shareable by the use of representational mapping. This mapping is done by means of a variety of techniques which are like 'moving diagrams'. The hexagon is only one example of a range of symbols that can be used in visualisation. A simple variant is the use of 'post-it' notes.

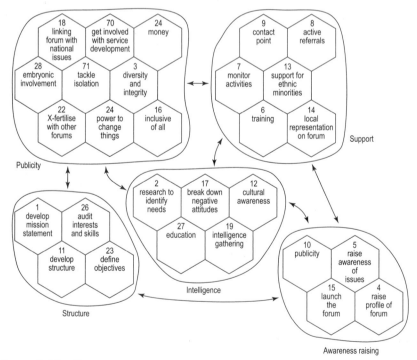

Figure 7.10   Hexagons

(*Table 7.8 continued*)

Table 7.8 (Continued)

Example: This example draws on work that was carried out to help establish an Ethnic Health Forum to help inform a health authority on services needed for the black and minority ethnic community in a borough in London. The forum was made up of representatives from voluntary agencies that work with the black and minority ethnic community in the area. IDONS were used to help the group explore the range of issues it would need to address if it were to be an effective forum. Each member of the group was given a number of IDONS to jot down the issue they thought was important or urgent. These were then put up on a whiteboard. The group was then asked to cluster the IDONS that were similar. Following this they were asked to see if there were any relationships between the clusters (see Figure 7.10). It was during the exercise of clustering and looking for relationships that the debate between the group was richest. Insights that came to the fore were noted down and became the basis for decision-making and prioritising.

Table 7.9 Analysis of Interconnected Decision Areas (AIDA)

This has been developed to explore a range of options that can be organised in a number of different arrangements. These options form a range of decision areas. In any given situation there may be several decision areas and thus there is a need to represent them in order to explore the range of choices on offer. The decision areas can be arranged and represented graphically as a decision graph. The decison area is represented by a circle and any decision area may include two or more options represented as dots within the decision area circle. A line can connect the circles if there is a relationship between them. The first step in the analysis of the graph is to eliminate incompatable combinations of options between the decison areas. This can also be repesented graphically by drawing option bars, i.e. lines depicting an incompatible combination. The feasible schemes of options can then be represented as a decision tree for subsequent analysis. For example, criteria can be drawn up and the range of possible effects on the criteria can be decided upon. Each scheme in the tree can then be assessed on how well it would perform on each criterion. This can be done graphically by exploring different modes of shading.

Example: The White Lime co-operative is a collection of smallholder farmers in Belize, Central America, who came together to produce high-quality lime, and to market their produce. The co-operative was facing a number of difficult dilemmas. The kilns they used to burn the lime require a great deal of fuel, mainly wood from cleared farms, however, the supply of wood could not meet the demand. Clearing wood from Crown forest reserves was illegal, and it is also the main cause of degradation and environmental hazards. The co-operative also had a problem transporting the lime to the markets among other things. Strategic choice approach was used with the co-operative (see Chapter 3). A decision graph was produced (Figure 7.11) which related decision areas the group found urgent and/or important. The decision areas included transport, marketing, input (fuel) and expansion. The focus mainly centred on transport and marketing (i.e. whether they should buy a truck, and whether they should be selling to other markets than just citrus. The options for each decision area were then identified (see Figure 7.11), and a set of feasible decision schemes was produced. A list of comparison areas was drawn up. Three comparison areas were finally chosen and these were rated on a visual scale depicting high, medium or low benefit to the community. Each scheme was compared in a pairwise manner, and this helped the debate on the merits and demerits of each of the schemes. The group decided to look at improving the kilns, and to set up a reserve for growing fuel wood.

Source: White (1994a)   (*Table 7.9 continued*)

Table 7.9 (Continued)

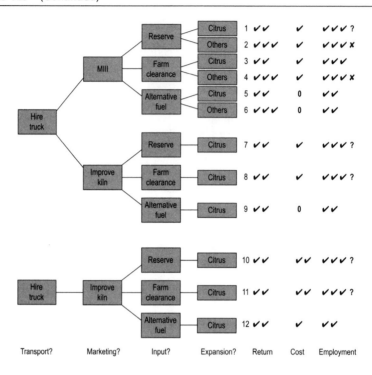

Figure 7.11 Decision Graph in AIDA

Table 7.10 Venn Diagrams

This idea for visual representation is taken from a branch of mathematics called set theory. Here circles representing a set are shown to overlap with each other if there are members of the set that belong to more than one circle. This can enable a group to explore the relationships between entities in terms of which one relates to which.

Example: For exploring issues with the village representatives one of the easiest ways of mapping the relationships between things was via a Venn diagram in Belize. Each circle represented a group in the community and where the members overlap. The circles were shown to overlap according to the number of members of each group that overlapped. This showed up who the key members of the community were in terms of a core that seemed to belong to a range of groups within the village.

Source: White (1994a).

Vital

This mode of representation uses real-life objects such as ourselves in exploring issues. It uses physical movement and creativity to explore different individuals' or the group's own experience and can lead to a general sharing of the issues and a common vision. Many of the techniques are simple and range from role-playing to scripted drama. Many of these techniques are used as warm-ups for the group and are useful aids in helping a group find out about itself. Exercises can be used to promote inclusion in a group, or to develop a sense of bonding. Techniques used in sociodrama are a source of inspiration. For example, sculpting and doubling (Table 7.11) are both techniques that can bring about involvement while at the same time

Table 7.11   Sculpting and Doubling

Sculpting and doubling are drawn from action methods or sociodrama. Sculpting uses people or objects to build up a picture depicting the underlying dynamic of a situation. There is no need for the participants to take on a speaking role. Thus, in a sculpt. People can be used to illustrate positive or negative dynamics in a situation. For example, in depicting how a group collaborates, the person who is sculpting this out may arrange the group in a circle where they are all facing away from each other depicting that there is no dialogue between them, or s/he may arrange them where groups of two or three are huddled together, showing that there are cliques within the group.

Objects can also be used in sculpting. The sculptor may be asked to find an object in the room that represents him or her in relation to the other members of the group. After this the others could walk around and explore common themes.

Doubling is a device to explore what is not being said or revealed. It can be used to add to a role-play situation where someone else in the group might see something that a person in the role could say. Doubling can also give support to a person in the role. The form is for the person who is doubling to come alongside the period in the role and hold the same posture. They can speak or just hold their position in empathy with the person in the role.

Example: Sculpting was used to help a feminist collective reshape its organisation. The collective was heterogeneous, in that their backgrounds were so varied. Yet, they had one thing in common which was that they described themselves as feminists. As a collective, the basis for decision-making is that it should be non-hierarchical, democratic and based on a consensus. Thus, any form of working must not violate these principles. This examples describes how sculpting and doubling were used to diffuse a situation that arose between the paid workers and the collective. The organisation was reshifting its focus and the differences in views needed to be accommodated. It followed a SWOT analysis and the group wanted to explore a threat – the paid worker perceived that the collective did not feel the same way about the threat. The sculpting took place with the paid worker using the other members of the group to shape her perception of the threat. Doubling took place as other members played the role of saying things that were 'unsaid'. Through doing this the collective demonstrated that they also understood the threat in the same way and the paid worker could see that the collective appreciated how real the threat was for her.

Source: Taket, reflective diary.

strengthening the bond between members of the group. These techniques are invaluable to people who are alienated by more formal or verbal participation methods. Role-playing can be a good device to share understanding of issues and to simulate situations familiar to the group. Indeed most of these vital modes of representation are simulations of part of the reality for the group. One of the more exciting techniques available is participatory theatre (Table 7.12), derived from the 'Theatre of the Oppressed' developed by Augusto Boal (1979). This has been used in Brazil and a number of developing countries to increase the involvement of disadvantaged people and to explore complex issues in a sensitive environment.

Many of the tools used in PRA are a combination of the visual and vital. Table 7.13 gives some examples.

Table 7.12   Participatory Theatre

A theme is decided upon and the players perform a short play showing the problem or dilemma the group faces. The performance is then repeated and the audience or 'spectators' are invited to say whether things could at any point be different or improved. They are also invited to come on stage and replace the actor to try out their ideas. It would be quickly evident whether or not the ideas or strategy would work. Thus all are invited to take part where they are constantly reflecting on the issues.

Example: One of the many ways Help for Progress (HELP) addressed issues with the communities they work with is through role-playing. During work on developing a strategy to bring HELP closer to the communities (White and Taket, 1997a) we decided to use participatory theatre. The scenario was how HELP worked with the groups in the villages. The workers from HELP were initially the players and they provided their version of how they worked with the groups. On the second run the HELP members were replaced by representatives from the groups and communities who showed that their perception was very different. It was clear that HELP did not engage enough with the groups or involved them in negotiating the problems. One scene by the community showed a HELP worker talking in Spanish to the community, then discussing decisions in English with the other HELP workers; the portrayal of the scene was very amusing, but it struck a chord on how the groups felt about HELP. This mode of working was also used to explore issues on taking things forward and developing a strategy.

Source: White and Taket (1997a).

Table 7.13   Tools from PRA

A good source of tools used in PRA can be found in RRA notes and PLA notes produced by the IIED, London. Below we list some of the tools we have used.

Pairwise ranking is used as a means of prioritising or ranking lists prepared by groups or communities. These can be lists of problems or projects for example. Ranking these lists can help groups decide which are the most important things to do or tackle. Often in a group when resources are involved the powerful ones are often heard and get their way. Also, each person within the group tend towards his/her own concerns and areas of interest. Ranking can help to give all those involved a chance to have their views heard.

Pairwise ranking is where each item on a list is compared in a systematic way with each other. Each item is given a letter. A matrix is drawn with the list for rows being the same for columns. The first item (usually given letter 'a') is compared to the second item in the column (usually letter 'b'); which ever is seen as the higher rank the letter is marked in the cell corresponding to the pair. This is done with all the other possible pairs. The total number of times each letter is seen as best can be found and can be ranked in descending order, thus giving the highest-ranked item at the top.

A variant of ranking is used for wealth ranking. A list of households is prepared on cards. The informant can be asked to put the cards into piles (or rows) each of which is a different level of well-being. They can make as many piles as possible and change the number of piles or location of a card during the exercise. For each pile the cards can be shuffled and the informant asked to rank the cards according to level of wealth or well-being.

Another popular technique used in PRA is transects. This involves walking along an area within a community with community members, drawing the area in detail, and asking questions about activities, resources, problems and opportunities. The final result can be used as a basis for discussion with the community or group.

Details of the use of these techniques are provided in a published case study (White, 1994a).

CONCLUSION

We have found in our practice that there is an enabling power in diagramming and visualisation. The modes of representation are open to all who are present to participate. Different people will augment the discussion, others will interrogate the detail, but more importantly everyone can see what is being 'said' because each view is represented.

We have also found that the different modes of representation can be combined and applied in many and different forms, and in our practice we continuously improvise and invent ways of combining the different modes of representation. Thus the activities of mapping and modelling, sequencing, comparing, linking and relating can be achieved individually or in combination.

Different modes of representation can help a range of people to participate in an inclusive way and at the same time create an environment where learning can take place not only about the problem situation and its outcomes but also of the perspectives of the people involved. The use of visualisations should create a shared picture of reality and result in shared understanding of issues and range of options to pursue in order to resolve them. The goal for using different modes of representation can follow the mnemonic PLAN. The aims in using visual, verbal and vital aids are:

- *Participation* of all in an equitable way
- *Learning* about enabling a shared understanding and vision of the issues
- Ensuring that everyone takes an *Active* involvement in the choice of representative devices and an active involvement in their execution
- Ensuring that the devices used help to connect different ideas from different places to build a *Network* of schemes and ideas.

Visual modes of representation are often created as a group activity. They can be used to aid learning processes of individuals and groups. Members of the group will use the different modes when it is clear to them that their ideas and knowledge are represented. Learning takes place when people discover for themselves the contradictions between observed behaviour and their perceptions of how the world should operate or even when the contradictions between different individual viewpoints are represented. As Freire puts it, 'there is no longer an "I think" but "we think". It is the "we think" which establishes the "I think", not the contrary. Thus, communication is the act of thinking together and implies that advantage is established as a shared act.'

Pluralism in the facilitation process

8

INTRODUCTION – THE FOUR Fs

The issue of facilitation is very important when working with groups. In this chapter we begin by visiting the literature on facilitation, drawing (briefly) on fields such as organisation development and organisational psychology. We will discuss the issue of facilitation and demonstrate that effective facilitation must pay attention to the process of: seeing the client(s) as 'experts', encouraging active participation, eliciting a wide range of views, working with the emotion(s) of the group, and working with conflict. We will also show, in this chapter, that an intervention in a complex situation requires the adoption of different roles at different times by the facilitators, in the course of the intervention. We will describe a range of roles that facilitators and group members can play.

In terms of a mnemonic for this chapter (see Figure 8.1), it can be encapsulated as the chapter of the four Fs, four different features to be borne in mind while planning or reflecting on facilitation:

- Flexibility – adapt facilitation to feedback, including feelings
- Forthrightness – be prepared to challenge and intervene, an alternative label for this would be forcefulness
- Focus – keeping a sense of purpose, progress and place
- Fairness – undertaking a process of critical reflection in order to enable fairness, in particular access to participation

Before the 1990s, literature within operational research, management science and system science paid only extremely limited attention to the task of facilitation within work with groups. The situation is now changing and we can find more papers and books explicitly tackling this issue, including: Huxham (1991), Phillips and Phillips (1993), Gregory and Romm (1994), Friend and Hickling (1997), Andersen and Richardson (1997) and Eden and Ackermann (1998). There is a much larger literature on facilitation and on group behaviour in terms of psychology,

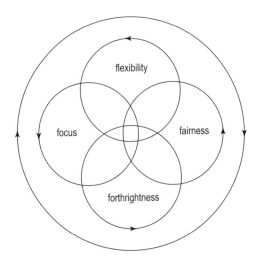

Figure 8.1   Facilitation – the Four Fs

organisational development and organisational behaviour. Much of the psychologically based literature, however, is not particularly helpful because of the strongly artificial and experimental nature of the settings in which empirical research has been carried out. Later sections in this chapter, in particular those on the characteristics of an effective facilitator, emotion and conflict, and the roles of participants draw selectively on this literature.

One relevant strand of the psychological literature examines participation in decision-making. Obviously a full review is out of the question given the volume of this literature, so we concentrate here on what is of particular pertinence, namely what can be said about the prerequisites for participation, in Wilpert's (1998) terminology (and on whose review we draw): 'the basic requirements for participation to occur at all, or . . . the conditions (contingencies) associated with participation to be successful' (Wilpert, 1998:43). Wilpert further distinguishes individual and social prerequisites. In line with our expectations we find that the review he offers does not present any determinative set of prerequisites that guarantee participation (let alone successful participation, however that might be conceived). In terms of individual prerequisites, he points out the existence of a version of the classic chicken and egg problem: that the literature shows that participation is contingent on requisite competences and skills, and also that participation is a major (individual) prerequisite for learning and competence development. In terms of social prerequisites, the review indicates the strongly contingent nature of the influence of most factors considered, which we might interpret optimistically to indicate the possibility of participation in most circumstances, as indeed Strauss (1998) concludes in a later chapter in the same book.

Before we move on to facilitation itself, we will first discuss briefly some of the notions of power and authority, which are closely connected with much of what we will cover later in the chapter.

A SHORT DIGRESSION ON POWER

As one starting point, we review briefly here some of the various different theories of power, in particular the contributions of Lukes, Clegg and Foucault, before considering some of the work of Bourdieu. This is not intended as a complete review of the literature on power (that would merit a whole book in itself), merely an introduction of some of the ideas and theorising that we have found helpful. We start by mentioning French and Raven's categorisation (French and Raven, 1968) of five different types of power in groups (reward, coercive, legitimate, referent and expert), noting that in this classification individuals are typically categorised on the basis of various socio-demographic, educational or personal characteristics in relation to the subject at issue, Although useful, this view conceptualises power as a somewhat static property of the individual. The alternative theories we move on to discuss present a rather more dynamic view.

Circuits of power

Clegg (1989) conceives power in a hierarchical model, termed circuits of power. At the top of the hierarchy are day-to-day episodes of power in which agencies with different resources and interests interact in a complex network of semi-causal effects, drawing on and reproducing social relations of signification and production fixed through the history of interaction. In addition, changes can occur at other levels, in particular the level of social integration, which fixes meaning and membership, where changes in the technology of production and discipline can alter the balance of power, facilitating the empowerment or disempowerment of particular groups. These changes feed up into the higher levels. Clegg's views draw on those of Latour in particular.

The three faces of power

Building on the earlier work of Bachrach and Baratz (1970), Lukes (1974) distinguishes three different faces/dimensions of power:

- A power relationship exists when there is a conflict over values or choices of action between two or more parties, where the wishes of one party are complied with by the other parties because they are fearful that otherwise they will be deprived of something which they regard more highly than what would be achieved by non-compliance.

- Power is exercised when one party devotes their energies to creating or rein-forcing social and political values and institutional practices that limit the scope of the political process to public consideration of only those issues which are comparatively innocuous to that party.
- Power is exercised where one party influences, shapes or determines other parties' values or preferred actions, particularly through the creation or reinfor-cing of the other parties' perceptions of the authority or legitimacy of the first party.

Another distinction made in discussing power, also attributed to Lukes, is that between 'power over' conceived of as control over other people or groups, exer-cised in different ways as outlined above, and 'power to' conceived of as the ability or capacity of individuals/groups to exert influence over and/or to change the conditions of their existence. Sometimes a further concept is also distinguished, that of 'power with', conceived of as the ability or capacity to exert influence over and/or change through joint action with others, see Johnson and Mayoux (1998) for a discussion of this and related issues. These notions of 'power to' and 'power with' interpreted as a potential or capacity have resonances with the work of Foucault, to which we turn next. In relation to 'power over', as we discuss in the next section, we often find it helpful to analyse this using the notion of 'authority'.

Foucault on power

In the *History of Sexuality* (1976:95) Foucault argued that 'where there is power there is resistance' and that power depends for its existence on the presence of a multiplicity of points of 'resistance'. He argued further that the plurality of resis-tance should not be reduced to a single locus of revolt or rebellion. This argument alongside the arguments of so many 'nouveau vague' philosophers is culminating to point out the problems associated with Marxism in particular and politics in general which reduce the 'struggle' to a single rebellion such as the struggle of the working class, and do not recognise the multiplicity of rebellion. In particular, Marxism is criticised by Foucault for passing over, in silence, what is understood by struggle when one talks of class struggle.

According to Foucault, power is conceived in terms of a multiplicity of forms, and by stating 'where there is power there is resistance', we take Foucault to mean that resistance is present everywhere that power is exercised. Foucault claims (1982:211) that the forms of resistance have the following characteristics:

- They are not limited to a particular nation, political or social formation.
- Their targets are the effects of power over peoples' bodies and lives.
- People direct their opposition to 'local' exercise of power – the concern is the local over the global where the global is seen as speculative, set in the distant future (i.e. liberation and revolution) and is assumed to be relatively insignificant.

- They are opposed to a government of individualisation.
- They contest the *régime du savoir*, i.e. the effects of power which are linked with knowledge of competence and qualification and they oppose 'the mystifying representation imposed on people' through constitution as the objects of knowledge in the population sciences.
- The concern is with 'who we are' rather than with abstraction and inquisitions which both ignore and determine who one is.

In other words, resistance stands opposed to particular techniques of power which pervade everyday life to categorise individuals, mark their individuality and constitute the individual as subject, i.e. 'subject to someone else's control and dependence and tied to an identity by a consciousness or self-knowledge' (Foucault, 1982:212).

Symbolic power and authorised language

We can take this further by drawing on Bourdieu's work on the production and reproduction of legitimate or authorised language (Bourdieu, 1991). First of all Bourdieu draws our attention to the inescapable relativism of linguistic practices and the existence of an (often overlooked) dominant linguistic practice.

> ... if one fails to perceive both the special value objectively accorded to the legitimate use of language and the social foundations of this privilege, one invariably falls into one or other of two opposing errors. Either one unconsciously absolutizes that which is objectively relative and in that sense arbitrary, namely the dominant usage, failing to look beyond the properties of language itself, such as the complexity of its syntactic structure, in order to identify the basis of the value that is accorded to it, particularly in the educational market; or one escapes this form of fetishism only to fall into the naïvety *par excellence* of the scholarly relativism which forgets that the naïve gaze is not relativist, and ignores the fact of legitimacy, through an arbitrary relativization of the dominant usage, which is socially recognized as legitimate, and not only by those who are dominant (Bourdieu, 1991:52–53).

One consequence of this is that linguistic practices tend to be measured against the dominant practice. This dominant practice is used to define the standard of what is legitimate, and its use confers symbolic power on the speaker. Bourdieu then goes on to argue that our understanding of what is 'common language' tends to erase its socially conditioned nature, furthermore: 'The competence adequate to produce sentences that are likely to be understood may be quite inadequate to produce sentences that are likely to be *listened to*, likely to be recognized as *acceptable* in all the situations in which there is occasion to speak.' (Bourdieu, 1991:54–55)

In terms of competence, Bourdieu does not find Habermas' ideal of universal communicative competence useful, drawing attention to the saturation of the communication situation by issues of power:

> It is only in exceptional cases (in the abstract and artificial situations created by experimentation) that symbolic exchanges are reduced to relations of pure communication, and that the informative content of the message exhausts the content of the communication. The power of words is nothing other than the *delegated power* of the spokesperson, and his speech – that is, the substance of his discourse and, inseparably, his way of speaking – is no more than a testimony, and one among others, of the *guarantee of delegation* which is vested in him. This is the essence of the error which is expressed in its most accomplished form by Austin (and after him, Habermas) when he thinks that he has found in discourse itself – in the specifically linguistic substance of speech, as it were – the key to the efficacy of speech. By trying to understand the power of linguistic manifestations linguistically, by looking in language for the principle underlying the logic and effectiveness of the language of institution, one forgets that authority comes to language from outside. ... Language at most *represents* this authority, manifests and symbolizes it (Bourdieu, 1991:112).

The arguments of both Foucault and Bourdieu can be useful to us in identifying and working with issues of power in the multiagency context, as the case study examples throughout the book illustrate. What we particularly draw from their work in this chapter is the insufficiency of asking the question 'who possesses or exercises power?' with its corresponding hierarchical view (we do regard this as a relevant question, but usually phrase it in terms of who possesses or exercises authority), and the usefulness as well of a view of power as non-hierarchical, exercised through a multiplicity of sites and simultaneously productive and repressive, or in other words that any point of exercise of power is also an opportunity for resistance and its subversion. As a consequence we must pay particular attention to the social networks involved in any situation, and ask questions about the relational aspects involved in these. In facilitation, one of the functions of critical reflection (discussed later) is to analyse power and authority at work and seek also the opportunities to offer resistance to this, and to subvert its operations where considered necessary. Sawicki (1991) provides an interesting case study that illustrates this at work in her chapter on the new reproductive technologies and their impact on women. In this she analyses the activities of FINRRAGE (Feminist International

Network on Resistance to Reproductive and Genetic Engineering) and shows how a Foucauldian understanding of power can provide a useful framework for criticism and for identifying possibilities for effective resistance.

FACILITATING ACCESS TO PARTICIPATION – THE CHARACTERISTICS OF AN EFFECTIVE FACILITATOR

The central task of the facilitator is that of enabling access to participation in the proceedings by all those who wish to participate. This will involve paying attention to group dynamics, encouraging contributions from everyone in the group, and sometimes actively intervening. The characteristics of effective facilitation that were introduced towards the beginning of this chapter will all come into play to achieve this, along with the creative use of different methods and diverse modes of representation, as illustrated in Chapters 6 and 7. In the sections that follow, we deal with different aspects that require attention during facilitation if this basic goal is to be achieved. The sections that follow cover: emotions and conflict, including interrupting the exercise of coercion; the importance of language; role(s) of the facilitator(s); roles of participants; how many facilitators?; practical details; devices for use; and finally, critical reflection.

We will mention just a few features from the literature at this point, which have a particular bearing on facilitation generally. The first is the phenomenon of 'group think', understood as a situation where leadership style, group cohesion and crisis combine to produce support for ill-considered options. The term has its origin in Janis (1972), and the classic oft quoted example is the 'Bay of Pigs' crisis, the phenomenon is also usefully reviewed in Baron et al. (1992). One of the challenges for facilitation therefore is to try and ensure that this is avoided at all times. Various of the methods described already, coupled with the principles of seeking out diverse perspectives, and the process of critical reflection, should provide some safeguards. The importance of active facilitation to involve all in deliberation, debate and decision is not just a principle or value to be adhered to, it is also important if certain arguments are not to remain unshared, since there is some evidence (Stasser et al., 1989) from analysis of tape-recorded discussions showing that unshared arguments are less likely to be expressed.

As part of facilitation we need to pay attention to what is happening within the group, this means paying attention to emotions and feelings and adjusting plans appropriately. While the explicit task of critical reflection (discussed later in this chapter) is relevant here, monitoring of group interaction and emotions needs to go on, on an almost continuous basis, with a continual adjustment of facilitation behaviour in response. Given that all this happens in real time, there is little space available for rationalistic analysis and formulation of responses. Instead, in facilitation we act on hunch, on gut feeling, on intuition. In earlier papers we have referred to this as 'doing what feels good', which has acted like a red rag to a bull for some of our readers. We still hold that this provides, for us, a good description of how we actually practise – any rationalistic analysis (and yes indeed there is a place for that) comes on a regular basis as a part of critical reflection, but we find it impossible to carry out on a continuous basis while 'on the job' so to speak. We are struck here by the resonances with the rapidly growing literature on 'emotional intelligence' (Salovey and Mayer, 1990; Goleman, 1995; Mayer and Salovey, 1997; Huy, 1999).

Table 8.1   Eight Characteristics of an Effective Facilitator

I.   **Respect:** a sincere belief that each member of the group possesses the skills and capacities to contribute and that the group can set its own direction and make sound decisions. Underlying this respect is the belief that knowledge gained from life and work experience is as valuable to the process as is organisational status and education.

II.   **Critical awareness:** ability to differentiate between thoughts and feelings, in self and others.

III.   **Self-disclosure:** willingness to articulate thoughts and feelings about oneself, others and what is happening, and awareness to share their feelings with one intention – to help the group progress.

IV.   **Self-confidence coupled with self-disclosure:** the quality of being in touch with who you are and feeling good about it, enabling the facilitator to take the risks necessary to model openness.

V.   **Questioning rather than telling:** makes no assumptions about why group members do or do not do things. Instead she/he questions. So instead of saying: 'you are avoiding conflict', he/she asks a question: 'this is the third time you switched the subject when the project funding was mentioned, what might be causing the topic jumps?'

VI.   **Observant:** able to:

     A.   watch and interpret non-verbal communication
     B.   note (in writing) what was said, by whom and when, especially when discussions are spirited and/or emotional
     C.   stay attuned to proxemics (where people sit in relationship to others and how they physically posture themselves)

VII.   **Direct:** stating what was seen or heard without dressing it up or watering it down. Example: 'Pat, you arrived 30 minutes after the meeting started', rather than 'some of us are arriving late'.

VIII.   **Confronting rather than confrontational:** issues raised immediately (rather than later), and in non-judgmental language (rather than evaluative language, for example 'you should have', 'why didn't you', 'I would have' etc.). The ability to bring people face to face with reality. This is needed when there is a discrepancy between:

     A.   what a group member is saying and what she/he is doing
     B.   what a member is saying and what he/she said earlier
     C.   what the group agrees to (for example ground rules) and their behaviour
     D.   the process the group has agreed to follow and what they are actually doing

Source: adapted from Gregory's version (Gregory, 1999) of Warihay's seven characteristics of an effective facilitator (Warihay, 1992).

Extensively popularised by Goleman (1995), the concept of emotional intelligence was first formally defined by psychologists Salovey and Mayer (1990). In their definition emotional intelligence includes four groups of competencies: the ability to perceive, appraise and express emotions accurately; to access and evoke emotions when they aid cognition; to comprehend emotional messages and the use of emotional information; and to regulate one's emotions to promote emotional and intellectual growth and well-being (Salovey and Mayer, 1990; Mayer and Salovey, 1997). As well as being taken up in the education sector (Salovey and Sluyter, 1997), emotional intelligence has also found currency in the literature on leadership, organisational change, organisational development and management (Huy, 1999; Cacioppe, 1997; Weisinger, 1998). The concept is still, however, under scrutiny within the psychology literature (Davies et al., 1998). Huy's paper (Huy, 1999), concerned with a multilevel theory of emotion and change, proposes a concept of 'emotional capability' analogous to emotional intelligence but operational at the organisational, rather than the individual, level. He understands emotional capability to refer to acquired and organised behavioural routines, which represent a necessary, though not sufficient, antecedent for organisational change.

We have mentioned in the above discussions a number of different characteristics which ideally should be present in those who assume the task of facilitation. Warihay (1992) has provided a very useful description of seven characteristics of an effective facilitator, which we consider summarises the position very well; we present an adapted version of this in Table 8.1 (with thanks to Wendy Gregory for drawing our attention to this). In the remainder of the chapter we deal with a variety of devices and aids to help develop and express these characteristics.

GROUND RULES/BRIEFING

At the beginning of multiagency work, ground rules and/or briefings are devices used explicitly to discuss and negotiate key aspects of the process that will be followed. Table 8.2 show a series of statements in the form of a 'Participant role reminder' produced by the Union of International Associations (1993) which might be used in briefing and/or explicitly incorporated into ground rules. The Union of International Associations' web site provides a much longer document which discusses roles and their interactions and ends with a commitment form to be signed by each participant (http://www.uia.org/uiadocs/contract.htm#reminder); this might be used. Table 8.3 shows an edited and adapted set of guidelines and ground rules used in a strategic planning workshop setting (drawn from Chisholm, 1996). These might be used in the context of group work not oriented towards problem solving, or decision-making, i.e. the deliberation stage in our three Ds framework. Another set of ground rules, taken from Warihay (1992), is shown in Table 8.4. These might be used in any of the three D stages.

Table 8.2   Participant Role Reminder

1. We are less rewarded for our involvement in a meeting when we assume that our role has been more central to its processes than when we are able to question its value to other participants.
2. We degrade and pollute the meeting environment more when we assume that any negative impacts of our initiatives on other participants are of little consequence than when we have doubts concerning the ability of the meeting to deal with them.
3. We exhibit a greater degree of ignorance in a meeting when we assume the adequacy of the knowledge we demonstrate than when we question its validity from the perspectives of other participants.
4. Our contributions are less nourishing and enlivening to other participants when we assume that they are naturally fruitful than when we question their fruitfulness to others.
5. We contribute more to the mismanagement of a meeting when we assume that our favoured procedures are the most useful to other participants than when we have doubts concerning their efficacy for others.
6. We are less productive in a meeting when we assume we are responding productively to other contributions than when we have doubts concerning the contribution of our efforts to the productivity of other initiatives.
7. We are more threatening to other participants when we assume that our role is not experienced as intimidating and discriminating by some than when we question how others may be threatened by our actions in the meeting.
8. We bring more malaise to a meeting when we assume that we are paragons of well-being than when we have doubts concerning our degree of health in the eyes of others.
9. We are more exploitative in a meeting when we assume that our initiatives do not impoverish the experience of other participants than when we question this possibility.
10. We make more inappropriate contributions to a meeting when we assume that they are naturally appropriate than when we have doubts concerning their degree of appropriateness to other participants.
11. The representation of reality that we endeavour to communicate to other participants is experienced as more incoherent when we assume that it offers unique integrative advantages than when we question whether this may be the case for others.
12. We are more effective in turning cultural and religious celebrations into meaningless rituals when we assume that they are not experienced as such by some than when we question why this may indeed be the case.

Source: Union of International Associations (1993)
http://www.uia.org/uiadocs/contract.htm#reminder

EMOTION AND CONFLICT

As was discussed in Chapter 3, many of the decision-making/problem-structuring approaches arising from the management sciences have been open to the criticism that they draw primarily on theories of rational action (in this case applied to decision-making) and tend to be dismissive of intuition, emotion and feelings. We have argued on the other hand that it is important to look for scope for recognising and/or incorporating and/or 'resolving' the feelings or emotions that may be involved in any decision process.

Table 8.3 Guidelines and Ground Rules

GUIDELINES
- activities are designed to create a shared understanding
- use open sharing of information and views to explore issues

GROUND RULES
- no problem solving – focus on awareness, understanding and learning
- all ideas are valid – there's no need to agree
- no lectures – emphasis on dialogue
- no pleading self-interests or personal agendas
- only one person talks at a time
- task oriented – stick to time frames, work efficiently, start and finish on time
- participants are responsible for participating

Source: adapted from Chisholm (1996).

Table 8.4 Ground Rules – Another Variant

- all people participate equally
- we reach agreement by consensus/majority vote/75% agreement
- each of us is responsible for gatekeeping – opening the gate for quiet members and closing it on those who tend to take too much air time
- no side discussions
- it is okay to disagree
- individual positions must be supported by at least two reasons why
- no decisions are made until each person states her/his point of view
- we respect each other – no low blows
- each participant is responsible for pointing out non-conformance to the code of ethics

Source: adapted from Warihay (1992).

So what is to be done? What devices etc. can we use to help in working with, dealing with and managing emotion and conflict. Simply first of all, we can note that it is very often valuable to acknowledge the existence of emotions/and or conflict. A wealth of literature from counselling and personal development literature informs us of the value obtained from affirming (acknowledging in a non-judgemental fashion) an individual or group's strong feelings or beliefs in any particular area; the literature on emotional intelligence discussed earlier in this chapter points in exactly the same direction. Once more we emphasise that this is not always a guarantee of 'success'; one of the authors (AT) is reminded of one occasion when such acknowledgement was followed by a rapid storming out of a meeting, followed some time later by an extremely acrimonious departure from the voluntary organisation concerned. However, maybe this was the best achievable outcome in the circumstances.... An example of a more apparently successful case is shown in Box 8.1. Such simple affirmation, which can be supplied by the facilitator

BOX 8.1   WORKING WITH EMOTION: AFFIRMATION AND ACTION

A day workshop was undertaken, jointly facilitated by both authors, to help a civil rights group take stock of problems, possibilities and opportunities. The object of the encounter was to clear the ground for shared understanding of their situation, to encourage the whole group to be committed to taking action or to explore possible avenues, and to ensure everyone was sufficiently informed, so that there was as universal as possible support for any decisions made. The organisation wanted all the workers and staff to participate, hence the make-up of the group ranged from the General Secretary to the switchboard operator.

Each participant was asked to think about what things they liked in the organisation, and what they disliked as a warm-up. After this round, the first session, conducted in the group as a whole, concentrated on identifying strengths and weaknesses (problems/issues) of the organisation. Each participant individually completed a worksheet, items were then shared and recorded on flip charts, with some discussion. Our aim was to use this to move on to identify, by means of 'voting', which issues were most important, which were most urgent and which were of most interest in terms of wanting to work on them during the remainder of the day. During the discussion, however, it became obvious that one of the participants held very strong feelings that a recent past event in which the organisation had been involved had left some 'unfinished business' affecting one particular individual. It was clear that this was not an issue shared by sufficient in the group to be carried forward for work in the context of the awayday. This was noticed and acknowledged by the facilitators, and the question posed as to what would be a satisfactory way to deal with this. Agreement was quickly reached that this be dealt with outside of the awayday, and a decision was reached on the first steps of what was to be done. The business of the awayday in terms of negotiating the shared agenda then continued.

Comment: The atmosphere created during the day was productive, sufficient 'safety' was created to allow the airing of difficult issues, and the acknowledgement of strong feelings that needed to be dealt with. As we discovered afterwards, the next steps formulated quickly in the meeting were carried out in the following week, resulting in action to the satisfaction of those involved.

Source: Our original write-up of this case study appeared in White and Taket (1993). It has also been discussed in White and Taket (1994, 1997a) and Taket and White (1996b).

and/or participants, can be coupled with many of the methods discussed earlier for exploring diversity of view and moving on through the three Ds.

There are other methods and processes that are to hand. Chapter 3, on methods, has already introduced action methods, which explicitly attempt to work with feelings and conflict. Non-verbal methods (both visual and vital in the terms used in Chapter 7 on representation) are also argued to access views/perceptions in terms of feelings and emotions, and use of different mode(s) of representation may allow these to come to the fore and be worked with. An excellent example of this is the work described by Rosenhead and White (1994), where use of cognitive mapping enabled conflict to be dealt with (see Box 8.2).

There are also many explicit processes that aim specifically at conflict resolution, through consensus building, mediation or negotiation. A full review of all of these would take us outside our word limits, however there are many further resources which may be useful. These include Coover et al. (1985), Fisher and Ury (1981) and

BOX 8.2   RESOLUTION OF CONFLICT – USE OF COGNITIVE MAPPING

The Nucleus group consisted of a number of projects – Nucleus Housing, the Youth Project, the Advice Centre and the Mother and Baby Unit. Money had been raised to set up a 'Core team' to provide central services for the 4 projects, 5 premises and 17 members of staff, so that the projects could concentrate on their own direct services to the community. The Core team consisted of a development worker, an administrative worker and a finance worker. The Core team, however, was failing to work together harmoniously, and was felt by the rest of Nucleus to be ineffective. The aim of the engagement was to work with the Core team, to draw out their problem situation and to guide them to a resolution.

Each team member was interviewed, and from his or her account of the Core, a 'map' was drawn showing the key concepts used to understand the situation, and the links between them. In this way it was hoped that some of the causes of conflict could be surfaced. The method also had the advantage, given the tense situation between Core members, that work could be started with each of them separately rather than in a group situation: indeed one interview was only agreed to on the condition that it was held outside the office.

These maps showed a number of reasons why members of the Core team felt they were, or were thought to be, ineffective. There was conflict within the team, partly due to a clash of personalities. There was lack of clarity about roles, with friction at overlap areas. There was uncertainty over future funding, and over whether the rest of Nucleus would endorse their proposals for the future of the Core. There was a feeling that no-one outside the Core had a clear view of what their role was or should be, and that the Nucleus Council of Management and its relevant subcommittee had not helped the situation.

The maps containing these, and other, concepts were merged, and the resulting combined map was presented at a workshop which was now organised with the whole team. The discussion took key concepts one at a time, and explored both what might be done to achieve or avoid the situation described in that statement, and what its higher-level consequences might be. The structure of the session succeeded in securing a suspension of hostilities, as team members focused on the tasks in hand.

> The options for action which emerged from this workshop included: the need for a management information system, a survey of the needs of the Earls Court area, an investigation of the structure of Nucleus, the specification of job descriptions, and the development of a fund-raising strategy. These options were judged and prioritised by the group, and a working list of actions was drawn up for the team. The three-hour session generated a commitment to planning and to working together to agreed priorities. Indeed the team became committed to changing the perspective of Nucleus – both on how the rest of the organisation viewed and used the Core, and on how Nucleus should be managed. They carried this through into a programme of action. Interestingly in subsequent team meetings they adopted their own variant of mapping to deal with issues which arose.
>
> *Source*: adapted from Rosenhead and White (1994); this work is also described in Taket and White (1994).

Floyer-Acland (1992). A list of elements which Coover et al. (1985) suggest are necessary for conflict resolution is given in Table 8.5, guidelines for negotiation based on Fisher and Ury (1981) are shown in Table 8.6. Guidelines or groundrules, discussed elsewhere in this chapter, when they are used, can also cue in participants to expectations in this area.

One particular case concerns the possible exercise of coercion in the decision-making process, here there are a number of particular devices that might be useful, discussed in the next section.

Interrupting the exercise of coercion

One of the criticisms that can be levelled against many group decision-making methodologies is that they often seem to assume that different individuals enter the process on a level playing field so to speak, and that an individual or group's view is

Table 8.5   Elements Necessary for Conflict Resolution

- enough time to deal with the conflict
- defining the problem in terms which are clear and acceptable to all
- dealing with negative feelings in a positive way
- helping people identify in specific terms what makes them unhappy with the situation – and distinguishing between feelings and reality in this
- each member of the conflict to identify their real needs
- an opportunity for individuals to unload feelings of hurt, fear, etc. in the presence of accepting, non-judgemental people
- to have at least one person, preferably uninvolved, to give special attention to seeing the process through

---

Source: adapted from Coover et al. (1985).

Table 8.6 Guidelines for Negotiation

1. Separate the people from the problem/issue. Put yourself in other people's shoes to see the problem/issue from their point of view. Do not attack the people, address the problem/issue.
2. Focus on interests, not positions. Try and find areas where the outcomes sought by the different parties overlap.
3. Invent options for mutual gain. Look for creative ideas which achieve overlapping interests.
4. Insist on specific criteria. Agree ways of measuring these. Agree ways of judging and reaching solutions/positions which are agreed to be fair.

Source: adapted from Fisher and Ury (1981)

treated 'on its own merits', divorced from who has espoused it. We have already discussed the use of different methods and modes of representation as a device for trying to achieve equality of access to participation, and an example drawn from our practice is given in Box 8.3. Crucial junctures come when we reach the parts of the debate or decision where diverging views or perceptions are being valued against one another. How can we attempt to treat these views or values 'fairly', rather than imputing value to them from the individual or group who espouse them? There are a number of possibilities.

SAST (described in Chapter 6) presents a framework, which, through its scrutiny and debate of the assumptions underlying the different positions being considered, encourages participants to move away from imputation of value. Critical systems heuristics (also described in Chapter 6), through its explicit identification of different

BOX 8.3 INTERRUPTING COERCION – USE OF DIFFERENT MODES OF REPRESENTATION

Work was carried out with the Faculty of an institute of higher education in Pakistan, two elements of which were:

- development of research policy and programmes, including the identification and development of specific action research projects in the health field that could contribute to improvements in the local health situation;
- work on the design of a database to support the work of the institute.

Some of the work on this first element arose in the context of discussions about the construction of an epidemiological database. In an effort to ensure that any such database contributed directly to the institute's mission in terms of the 'improvement of the health status of the population of Pakistan, and specifically of Punjab' work was undertaken by the group to explore the possibilities for use of different types of data. A particularly important part of this was the use of a form of influence diagram to depict the connection(s) between different elements of data and possible action(s) to identify and/or remedy significant health problems. The switch to this form of representation was found particularly helpful in allowing participants to debate the implications and feasibility of different options regarding database content and to reach agreement on their relationship to the achievement of the mission statement.

The visual form of representation was important in enabling all the members of the group to participate, in particular those at lower levels in the academic hierarchy, who in many of the more verbally based sessions tended to remain silent for long periods. On reflection, two reasons were identified for this. Firstly this form of representation overcame some of their hesitation about their abilities in the English language, by and large these individuals had much less prior experience of speaking English. Secondly, this form of representation allowed participants to give voice to alternative ideas to those expressed by their seniors in the Institute hierarchy, something they found difficult to do in direct response to a verbal statement from such members. The use of this form of representation 'out there' on a board allowed them to make contributions without being seen as being disrespectful to their superiors in the hierarchy, and provided a safe method to surface differences of view, to debate these and to reach a group consensus. It was also observed that the form of representation allowed individuals to change their views during the course of the sessions.

Comment: The sessions from which the above example is taken took place towards the middle of the three-week period of work involved. The facilitator had observed in early sessions the hesitancy of those lower in the institutional hierarchy about expressing their opinions and was deliberately experimenting with different approaches to try and counteract this. The use of visual rather than verbal representation turned out to have a number of locally desirable effects.

Source: taken from a reasonably full description of the piece of work given in Taket (forthcoming), the case study has also been described in Taket and White (1996a,b, 1997) and White and Taket (1995a).

types of stakeholders and the provision of questions which can be used to interrogate options under consideration, foregrounds the question of 'value to whom' and thus attempts to move away from imputed values.

De Reuck et al. (1999) suggest that setting up technology so that anonymous entry of an individual's input can be achieved provides a way to guard against positions acquiring authority from the person or rank from which they sprang. This is certainly possible, provided that we can assume that participants cannot accurately impute the speaker from the way the contribution is expressed (facilitator input could be used to minimise the risk of this). This is certainly possible to introduce at particular stages, e.g. generation of options and evaluation of options,

Table 8.7   Challenges to Validity Claims

- Do you understand what is being said?
- Is the speaker being sincere?
- Is the speaker's point acceptable to you?
- Do you agree with the speaker's use of information and/or experiences?

Source: Gregory and Romm (1994, forthcoming).

but it would be rare that the whole process could be managed without face-to-face contact. While this might be the case in some (rare) circumstances, it is unlikely to be perceived as desirable in much multiagency work, where participants typically may already be known to one another, and even if not, better knowledge of each other is assumed to be desirable and attains the status of a goal in itself.

Table 8.7 presents a set of questions provided to participants to aid them in debate; its originators, Gregory and Romm, draw on the work of Habermas to produce this list, a pragmatised version of Habermas' four validity checks, which he argues may be used to achieve communicative competence and thereby communication free of distortion caused, for example, by some individuals having more power to influence than others. As a part of the ground rules that they, as facilitators, set up for the multiagency work they were engaged in, these questions were to be accepted as available for all to use to interrogate different speakers' positions. In the case study described in their paper, they illustrate how these questions served to enable debate, how their use was modelled by facilitators, and also adopted by participants, resulting in what they judged to be positive outcomes from the process. They also illustrate how the facilitator can adopt a challenging role to some of the positions put forward in order to surface new possibilities for debate.

THE IMPORTANCE OF LANGUAGE

From the discussion we have had already in this chapter and elsewhere, the reader should have been alerted to the importance of careful use of language during facilitation. This is perhaps an issue particularly where some participants are working in languages that are not their mother tongue. At the most basic level, the facilitator(s) need to incorporate into the work sufficient space to check out the meaning of important concepts and terms as they arise and are used, spending time to check that a common understanding is present, and if it is not, encouraging discussion for clarification, and agreement where necessary on the meaning to be given to certain concepts/terms. Some of the methods we have already introduced in earlier chapters of this book can be helpful in this task, for example: generation of constructs (from repertory grid analysis); deconstruction; use of metaphors; action methods; root definitions.

Attention also needs to be given to the way certain terms used in methods are described. The terms need to be understandable and appropriate to the cultures present in the group. This may involve finding alternative terms to describe certain parts of methods in order for those methods to be successfully used. If this is not done, progress may grind to a halt, as the example in Box 8.4 shows.

BOX 8.4   THE IMPORTANCE OF LANGUAGE: USING SWOT IN PAKISTAN

While carrying out work, in English, with faculty members and students at a higher education institute in Pakistan, on a number of occasions, different forms of SWOT (strengths, weaknesses, opportunities, threats) analysis were used.

Initially, difficulties were found with the traditional presentation of this method which uses the term 'weaknesses'. In the context concerned, this term carried connotations of inherent inbuilt flaws, which were considered impossible to change. Discussions could not move further forward into generation of options, evaluation and selection of chosen actions.

Later sessions used an alternative formulation of SWOT, replacing the term 'weaknesses' by 'factors to be developed', and the work did then proceed.

Source: taken from a reasonably full description of the piece of work given in Taket (forthcoming), the case study has also been described in Taket and White (1996a,b, 1997) and White and Taket (1995a); other examples from this case study are presented elsewhere in the book.

Box 8.5 presents another example dealing with issues of language. This time problems were caused by a translation of a measurement instrument which, although literally correct, had not been translated with knowledge of the context in which it was to be used. Important concepts and issues were no longer covered. Prevention of this type of problem involves the use of translators who are adequately briefed as to the context in which the material is to be used.

BOX 8.5   THE IMPORTANCE OF LANGUAGE: PROBLEMS WITH TRANSLATION

The example here is a particular measurement instrument, a health profile, which was to be used in some multiagency work in a multicultural setting. The major (and seemingly obvious) point here is that straightforward translation of instruments produced and validated using English mother-tongue populations is not enough, a translated instrument *must* be revalidated. The potential difficulties can be illustrated by considering a Bengali version of a health profile obtained by translation (and used by other agencies in several community surveys prior to our use of it). The health profile concerned is a self-administered questionnaire measure of self-perceived health, yielding scores on six dimensions (sleep, pain, physical mobility, emotional reactions, social isolation, energy); it uses simple, but colloquial English expressions, which the respondent either affirms as true for them at that moment or not. On examination by project workers, the Bengali version was found to be very misleading, the relative seriousness of different items had not been maintained by the straightforward translation that had been used (we stress it was however a correct literal translation, but the translators had not been given information about the purpose and use of the instrument), meanings shifted radically, and in some cases colloquialisms had not been understood as such, some examples are presented in the table below. In each case statements which were supposed to be to do with emotion and feelings had been rendered into factual and physical issues. The use of English colloquialisms also makes the instrument inappropriate for use in a respondent's second language.

Dimension of health	Original profile statement	Back-translation/ misunderstood as
Emotional reactions	I'm feeling on edge	I'm walking along a cliff-top
Emotional reactions	I feel as if I'm losing control	I'm incapable of managing things – like keeping track of spending money, losing my keys
Social isolation	I feel there is nobody I am close to	All my immediate family are dead
Social isolation	I'm finding it hard to make contact with people I'm finding it hard to get on with people	Practical difficulties like: I don't have a phone or can't write, or live in a (physically) isolated place

Source: taken from Taket (1993)

It is also possible to work in more than one language, and sometimes this is vitally necessary. It is also possible to facilitate sessions when some of the work is carried out in a language that the facilitator does not speak; effectively this involves other participants in the task of facilitation as well. Box 8.6, as well as demonstrating some of the challenges in working cross-culturally, gives an example of both of these. Box 8.6 describes the work that was undertaken to avoid the problems illustrated in Box 8.5.

BOX 8.6   WORKING IN MORE THAN ONE LANGUAGE

This example involves cultural difference, but coupled with language differences as well. It presents a very clear example of the possibility of facilitation focused on process rather than content. The work here arose from a long-standing involvement between the facilitator and a group of voluntary sector health projects, run by a voluntary organisation. The facilitator is a member of the executive committee of the voluntary organisation and acts as 'research adviser' to many of the projects, as and when required.

The specific example to be discussed here concerns a bilingual workshop held to produce a Bengali version of a health profile. The health profile was required to provide a measure of self-perceived health to be used in the assessment of need for services and in the evaluation of the effectiveness of aspects of service delivery. The workers in the projects were particularly keen to use measures that relied on self-perception in addition to the more traditional measures of health and need for service, which are often based on unsatisfactory proxy measures (such as use of services). The participants in the workshop were bilingual community development workers (Bengali and English, Somali and English), and English speakers ('experts' in the English version of the health profile, plus community workers), including the facilitator, who had no knowledge of Bengali or Somali. The workshop was facilitated in English, with most of the substantive work done in Bengali.

The control therefore very much rested with those participants who spoke Bengali, who were empowered to use the English speakers as a resource, asking them questions to aid their understanding of the theoretical basis of the profile, plus the meaning of some of the terms (English colloquialisms), before refining among themselves the Bengali version of the profile. Important things to note are how this illustrates that the facilitator does not have to understand everything that is going on, her/his understanding of content is not the point, results are owned and authorised by participants. The smooth progress of the work was aided by the monolingual English speakers giving up any goal of understanding the detail of the work in Bengali. In this way there was, for example, no requirement on the Bengali speakers to account for, or explain, the detail of what they were doing except when they considered it necessary to provide the context for questions they wanted to ask of the monolingual English speakers.

The Somali speaker at the workshop used the experience and knowledge gained through his participation to carry out the same sort of process (although not in the course of a single workshop) in the community at a later stage to produce a Somali version of the profile. In doing this he drew on the English speakers as a resource when he needed them. His involvement in the workshop thus achieved the necessary skill transfer for him to take charge of modifying the process as appropriate.

> The facilitator was particularly interested in being involved and facilitating this workshop out of a curiosity to explore the dynamics and feasibility of such a multilingual enterprise, as well as a direct interest in furthering the work of the projects concerned. The workshop confirmed the possibility of facilitation in this situation, and of the necessary skill transfer.
>
> *Source*: adapted from Taket and White (1994).

ROLE(S) OF THE FACILITATOR(S)

A criticism we have raised of many of the decision-making/problem-structuring methodologies from the management sciences is that the understanding of the potential roles of the facilitator(s) within the method is often not explicitly developed. For example, differences between active/intervening and less directive approaches may be seen in terms of difference in the individual style of facilitators rather than different types of facilitating role that may be appropriate in different parts of the decision process.

As already noted in the discussions earlier in this book, careful attention is required to be paid to the role of the facilitator(s). Pluralism is required in terms of the adoption of different roles at different times in the course of an intervention, and of different roles in relation to different individuals/groups involved in the intervention (at the same time). The adoption of different roles can be necessary to maximise participation in the work, as well as to challenge explicitly particular points of views, perhaps most especially when the views of the most powerful groups in the situation seem to be dominating other perspectives.

Elsewhere (White and Taket, 1995a) we have explored a number of different metaphors which have been useful to us as guises to assume in facilitating group interventions; these are summarised and developed in Table 8.8 in terms of some key characteristics and devices. Those interested in our derivation of these guises and their sources are referred to the earlier paper (White and Taket, 1995a).

Illustrations of some of these in action are shown in the case studies later in the book. The reader will probably have noticed that the guises discussed are not sharply separable, and in fact they can be interwoven in the course of a single intervention. Another way of putting this is to argue that in practice, we can mix and match different guises in the course of an intervention, assuming in this way the role of the shaman or shapeshifter. Our practice here is to be understood in distinction from any notion of a meta-method for selecting guises (for example relying on any type of contingency table approach which would match guise to characteristics of intervention context), and which we find too rigid, formulaic and unhelpful to deal with the complexities of any intervention.

Table 8.8 Different Guises for Facilitation/intervention

Guise	Some characteristics and devices
The anarchist (subtype – the guerrilla)	Learning to live comfortably with disorder subversion – using opponents' arguments against them leaderlessness
The rebel (*l'homme révolté*)	integrity 'solidarity' moderation maintenance of 'relativity'

The trickster (sometimes referred to as the clown)	use of humour
	subvert notions of saviour, superhuman, etc.
	subvert constancy of identity
	constantly deconstructs him/herself and his/her actions
	facilitate challenging people's accepted norms
	reconstituting different views of themselves
	breaker of taboos
	ambivalence
	  – no culture of dependency is induced
	  – strategic/tactical device

The innocent or naive inquirer	asks simple, basic naive questions to uncover 'taken-for-granted' assumptions and reveal new/different perspectives. innocence may be real (for example, if an external facilitator is being used) or assumed/feigned

Many of the different guises which may be used by the facilitator(s), are based on forms of intransparency. These might be used to interrupt inappropriate actions, to interrupt authoritarian statements or to prevent interactions within groups reinforcing, and being reinforced by, oppressive relationships within society at large. This may necessitate, at times, calling on the perceived authority of the facilitating role and acting in what may well be perceived as a strongly authoritarian fashion; this is a judgement call on behalf of the facilitator. This calls for a process of critical reflection on the processes used in the intervention, and the facilitator(s) must necessarily assume the responsibility for deciding what is most appropriate and suitable to each particular moment in the intervention. Careful choice of methods and approaches which offer opportunities for improving access is important, as is facilitating the interruption of racism, sexism, classism, heterosexism, ableism and the oppression of other groups. An example of the use of different roles in facilitation, drawn from the same case study as used in some other boxes (Boxes 8.3 and 8.4), is given in Box 8.7 and demonstrates what is discussed here. A further example is contained in Box 8.8.

This discussion on the role of the facilitator should not be taken to imply that we believe facilitation requires the use of an 'expert' or 'experts'. Far from it, as we have

BOX 8.7   DIFFERENT ROLES IN FACILITATION – THE FACILITATOR AS SHAPESHIFTER

Work carried out with the Faculty and students of an institute of higher education in Pakistan. A very important feature was the plurality of roles adopted by the facilitator. Pluralism was required in terms of the adoption of different roles at different times in the course of a series of sessions, and of different roles in relation to different individuals/groups involved in a particular session (at the same time).

At some times the facilitator acted as a naive inquirer to open up previously unacknowledged assumptions for debate. At other times, participants were provoked into challenging the views of previous 'experts' and also into challenging their own initial view of the facilitator as the expert who should tell them what to do (the facilitator as devil's advocate). The use of different roles helped to achieve participation from all present and empowered them to the extent that they were able to critique some of those experts' recommendations, and to build alternative action plans. Different roles were used by the facilitator to encourage participants to subject any assumptions about sources of legitimation to critical evaluation, through considering aspects of the relevance, applicability, feasibility and acceptability of the *content* under discussion to the local situation, rather than imputing these from any perceptions about the standing of the *speaker*. The use of visual forms of representation discussed elsewhere helped in this process.

Another area where adopting different roles and styles in facilitation was important was in responding to the different make-up of some of the small working groups in terms of the balance between the sexes. To a considerable extent the options available for use with the men in the groups were considerably restricted from those that the female facilitator could use with the women participants. Completely different physical cues and behaviours were appropriate towards the two sexes within this particular cultural context (for example, eye contact, physical contact, tone of voice).

One component of the work involved a series of sessions held with the faculty to generate and explore plans for research development. In terms of the structures within which this work took place the facilitator was presented as an 'outside expert', contracted to work with Faculty. The facilitator's attitude in approaching this role was to present herself as a facilitator, with expertise in the subject domains to be covered, but without detailed local knowledge of the situation in Pakistan. Her aim was for the work to be carried out as a joint exercise, from which all parties could learn and to which all parties contribute substantive knowledge of different kinds. At the beginning of the first working session participants were asked to talk briefly about what they wanted/expected to gain from the sessions. Several of them were reluctant to do this and expressed instead the desire/expectation to be told what should be done, so that for example one participant said: 'Please tell us everything you know about the subject, how this applies to the situation in Pakistan and what we should be doing.' This view was very much in line with how the Institute presents itself as in need of outside aid and technical assistance. It was also manifest in the instructions given by senior management in the Institute to the video technician, who was instructed to film sessions, but only the parts when the facilitator was speaking (this was something that was stopped as soon as the facilitator had identified it – incidentally by utilising the authority vested in this false position of 'outside expert' to issue what were effectively commands during sessions). The view described above was not shared by all the faculty within the institute, others expressed the desire/expectation that we would work jointly on the issues involved, i.e. expressed a view in common with the facilitator.

In all the sessions, Faculty were invited to critically question the view that all the relevant knowledge was present in the facilitator and that their task was merely to hear it and follow instructions. One important requirement was to facilitate the recognition of the multiple perceptions involved. In this instance, this was achieved through organising the facilitation of sessions so as to actively question the presentation of various organisations, groups or individuals one to another (and to aid the identification of submerged or hidden points of view within each), thus actively breaking down the notion of each organisation, group or individual as a singular or static entity. As already mentioned, another requirement was to subject any assumptions about sources of legitimation to critical evaluation, through considering aspects of the relevance, applicability, feasibility and acceptability of the content under discussion to the local situation, rather than imputing these from any perceptions about the speaker. Both these requirements necessitate careful thought about the style and stance of the facilitation. One solution adopted in this instance was using the notion of the facilitator as shapeshifter, adopting one role or guise towards some participants, while acting in a different role towards others, particularly to interrupt inappropriate actions (like the video behaviour discussed above), authoritarian statements, or appeals to legitimation on the basis of who was speaking by some participants. This shifting of facilitation roles, together with the use of multiple methods, particularly different forms of representation discussed earlier, enabled the facilitator to interrupt unequal access and exercise of hierarchical power/status in order to maximise participation and provide a chance for everyone to have a voice in the discussions.

During the component of work on curriculum development, different teaching methods which might be utilised were discussed at length, and the facilitator introduced the various different ways that student-centred, self-directed learning might be incorporated. A considerable proportion of the Faculty expressed extremely negative attitudes to the students' capabilities and attitudes, for example, repeatedly asserting that students would not read things on their own, and that every definition and concept must be introduced in detail in a formal lecture. The facilitator's own experience when working with the students directly contradicted these statements, as the students proved capable of working in difficult areas to which they had no prior exposure with no lack of enthusiasm, willingness and effort. As a result of the facilitator's (and some of the other Faculty's) direct experience of the students managing to work and learn in different ways this perception was able to be changed.

Another component of the work dealt with the question of a database. The construction of such a database was championed by the session convenor (who was in a position of hierarchical authority within the institute); radically different views were held by the facilitator (and some of the participants). By taking the database 'seriously', and using the convenor's arguments against herself in discussing database construction, this subversion led to a change in the convenor's view. This is an example of the facilitator at work as a 'trickster', by (ostensibly) taking the database seriously, and encouraging people to work out how it would be possible (or rather impossible) to construct it, the participants identified its impracticality and undesirability in the originally proposed form.

Source: Taken from a reasonably full description of the piece of work given in Taket (forthcoming), the case study has also been described in Taket and White (1996a,b, 1997) and White and Taket (1995a).

BOX 8.8 DIFFERENT ROLES IN FACILITATION – THE FACILITATOR AS SHAPESHIFTER – MINISTERIAL ROUND TABLES AT THE WORLD HEALTH ASSEMBLY

One of the new features of the May 1999 World Health Assembly were sessions referred to as 'ministerial round tables', held on a variety of topics. During these sessions there was a moderated discussion on policy themes of particular importance: priority-setting in the health sector; dilemmas about investment in hospitals; financing health services; sustaining appropriate responses to the HIV/AIDS epidemic.

The participants in the round tables were the chief delegates from a selection of countries, usually a minister responsible for health, sometimes a civil servant. The facilitators were drawn from the media, with considerable experience in interviewing politicians. In some cases they had a lot of substantive knowledge about the topic under consideration.

The following examples were noted as particularly effective in getting ministers to address issues that are often evaded:
'I'm going to ask a politically incorrect question ...'
'It's my job to be politically incorrect ...'
'I'm going to put you on the spot here ...'

'I know this is an unfair question, but ...'

'Let me play devil's advocate ...'

'I'm going to interrupt this interesting story and remind you of the point I want addressed ...'

Comments: The questions draw on a number of different roles. What was particularly interesting was the openness with which the roles are alluded to in the question, without the effectiveness of the role being undermined. Not once did a minister make any response such as 'yes that is an unfair/politically incorrect/ naive question and I won't answer it'. The most effective sessions were those where the facilitator combined the form of questioning above with detailed knowledge of the subject under discussion. There are strong parallels here to the stance on facilitation discussed by Gregory and Romm (1994, forthcoming).

argued elsewhere (White and Taket, 1994), and have illustrated in Box 8.6, our principles when working as facilitators involve acting to break down the notion of the 'expert' wherever possible, encouraging others to join in the task of facilitation in a spirit of mutual learning, where a basic assumption is that all participants have something to learn and something to teach.

ROLES OF PARTICIPANTS

More widely, it can also be useful to think in terms of the roles adopted by different participants in different sessions, not just by the facilitator(s). Achieving some consciousness of these roles, and their interaction, and working explicitly with their complementarity can help the progress of group work. In this section, we introduce a range of different approaches that can help in this task. These can be used in a variety of different ways: by the facilitator(s) in planning or reflecting on progress; as a prompt for debate or discussion in the group itself; as a tool for formally assigning roles to group members (not all the approaches discussed are relevant here); provided for group members as a tool for personal reflection (and as a stimulus to changed behaviour).

Bales (1950) provides a framework for the behavioural analysis of group members which can be useful for analysis (see Table 8.9). One problem with this as a practical tool, however, is the plural nature of the behaviour used by group members in the course of any interaction, thus calling into question the practicality of using the framework in anything other than an impressionistic way in real-life, real-time settings. Another classic work in this field is that of Belbin (1981), who analysed different types of roles that can be utilised in effective teamwork, roles being defined in terms of knowledge, skill and aspects of interpersonal interaction.

Tuckman's stages of group development (Tuckman, 1965) can be useful in exploring the progress of a group over time. He presents a four-stage process,

Table 8.9   Categories of Group Behaviour

Supporting	Verbal or non-verbal expression of agreement with another's suggestion
Making proposals	Putting forward suggestion(s) for discussion
Expressing views	Expressing personal perception or opinion on topic to group
Giving information	Giving 'factual' information to group
Debating	Puts forward discussion points on topic under consideration
Leading	Exerts influence in chairing or shaping discussions
Attacking	Showing antagonism to others and their views
Expressing hostility	Displaying power, conflict and aggression, channelled towards the disruption of the group
Expressing apathy	Shows indifference to discussion
Hidden agenda	Seems to be working to an implicit personal agenda

Source: drawn from Bales (1950).

Table 8.10   Tuckman's Stages of Group Development

Forming	Initial stage when group is still a set of individuals
Storming	A 'conflict' stage while preliminary consensus or consent (see Chapter 5) on purposes, on leadership or norms of work is established, challenged and re-established
Norming	Establishment of norms and practices
Performing	Group at full maturity, having completed other stages, able to be fully productive

Source: drawn from Tuckman (1965).

summarised in Table 8.10, to which a fifth stage of adjournment or disbandment is sometimes added as a useful reminder that groups are not necessarily permanent (Tuckman and Jensen, 1972). A word of caution is necessary; as group members change through temporary absence or permanent departure, and new members join, stages may be cycled through in an iterative process, rather than passed through once and once only in a linear progression. The introduction of new techniques or methods of working by a facilitator can also be thought of as necessitating a revisiting of the storming and norming stages before performing can commence again.

Starhawk (1982) distinguishes between formal and informal roles in her description of groups (her work is oriented specifically at non-hierarchical groups); these are summarised in Table 8.11. Formal roles are those that are often formally assigned, while the informal roles are ones that all individuals may adopt from time to time.

Table 8.11   Formal and Informal Roles in Non-hierarchical Groups

Formal

'Facilitator'	Keeps meeting focused and moving on relevant theme
'Vibeswatcher'	Pays attention to feeling/emotion and may intervene to suggest feelings are acknowledged, personal attacks are stopped, etc.
'Priestess/priest'	Pays attention to the energy of the group, keeps it moving, channelled and grounded. Given that the paradigm Starhawk works within is one of spirituality and magic, it should not be a surprise to find this role identified, and that it is separate to the 'vibeswatcher'. Whether this role is considered meaningful obviously depends on the nature of the group.
'Peacekeepers'	Help to keep order and deal with crises
'Mediators'	Neutral objective person who helps resolve conflict
'Coordinator'	Centre for flow of information

Informal

The lone wolf	You don't commit, but love to criticise Ask yourself: Why do I want to hang around people I consider inferior? Am I afraid of my equals? How would my criticisms be different if I said 'we should' instead of 'you should'?
The orphan	Often from a background of loss and deprivation, wanting closeness from the group and terrified of vulnerability and rejection, feeling you have little to contribute Ask yourself: What work can I take on for the group, preferably in company with one or two others? What can I contribute?
Gimme shelter	Constantly demanding something from the group: advice; reassurance; help Ask yourself: What actual work can I do for the group? What tasks can I take on – and do in such a way that my work does not require anyone else to expend time or energy on the tasks? Ask yourself: How would I act differently if I felt I had power? – and act that way
Filler	Just take up space, and feel your opinions and ideas aren't very interesting or valuable Try: speaking out, taking on a task (perhaps with an orphan)
The princess	So sensitive that the group process is never smooth enough, feel compelled to comment anxiously on slight tensions and minor nuances of conflict Ask yourself: Who am I competing with, and why? Refrain from commenting on group process until you can do so affectionately
The clown	Makes fun of people and ceremonies, a role that is of value [see roles for facilitators] Ask yourself: Can I be serious when necessary? Can I move out of this role sometimes?
The cute kid	Charming, cute, wanting approval, wanting to be taken care of Ask yourself: Do I really mean that I can't, or that I don't want to? Am I scared of power or responsibility?

Table 8.11 *Continued*

The self-hater	Perfectionist, harder on yourself than others, however escalating your standards for the group and outraged when they are not lived up to Be nicer to yourself. Sandwich your criticism between expressions of appreciation
The rock of Gibraltar	Takes on thankless tasks and gets them done, remembers what everybody else forgets, everyone brings their problems to you Ask yourself: Am I afraid of showing my weaknesses? What tasks can I delegate?
The star	Talks a lot, interrupts, enjoys impressing people, feels nothing can begin until you are present Ask yourself: Do I want to impress people or help their empowerment? How do I feel about people who are constantly trying to prove to me that I can never equal them?

Source: adapted from Starhawk (1982).

The Union of International Associations (1993) sets out a detailed discussion of different roles which might/can be identified in use in meetings/group sessions; a very brief extract from this has already been given in the form of a participant role reminder in Table 8.2 earlier in this chapter. A more detailed description can be found on their web site; it covers a lot of the same ground as Table 8.11, individual preference will determine which you feel to be most useful. These role descriptors can be used by facilitators as a tool for planning and analysis, and an aid in critical reflection. They can also be used by the group (individually or as a whole).

HOW MANY FACILITATORS?

Facilitation requires a lot of work and attention to many different issues, as should be clearly apparent from the discussions so far. It often makes sense to share out the tasks and the responsibilities. It seems to us that one facilitator alone is never ideal, although in many circumstances, one is all that is available or possible. Where the possibility of more than one exists, sometimes different roles are distinguished, sometimes this does not occur (see the case study discussed in Boxes 6.1 and 8.1 for example).

In terms of different classifications of different roles, we adopt our usual device of presenting several different classifications, all of which we have drawn on at different times. Andersen and Richardson (1997), describing group (systems dynamic) model-building conferences (which have many surface similarities to decision conferencing), distinguish two to five 'support team roles': facilitator/elicitor; modeller/reflector; process coach; recorder; gatekeeper (the key contact person in the organisation being worked with). Vennix et al. (1996) use three of these: process coach (incorporates facilitator role); model coach; and recorder. Whiteley and Garcia (1996) coin a rather appealing name for the modeller/model coach, namely the 'chauffeur'. Pizey and Huxham (1991) working (mainly) with SODA use two: one for content (and COPE software), one for group process. Starhawk (1982), in her classification of formal group roles (discussed in the section above on roles of participants since her work is focused specifically around non-hierarchical groups), distinguishes six different roles, all of which can be regarded as facilitation roles, see Table 8.11.

PRACTICAL DETAILS

The task of facilitation often includes sorting out a whole host of practical details that go with running group sessions. There are good checklists in Friend and Hickling (1997) and Wilcox (1994). Our own particular version which draws on both of these is shown in Table 8.12, and is presented without discussion, except to say that: firstly, a different version would obviously be appropriate for group

Table 8.12 Sorting out Practical Details: Checklist and Guidelines

When facilitating a group session:

1. Plan space and equipment:
   - walls or stands for charts
   - space for group working
   - movable furniture
   - sufficient chairs and tables
   - coloured pens
   - post-it notes
   - chart paper
   - bluetack
   - coloured stickers/dots for voting
   - ?camera, film, tapes for visual and/or audio record
   - refreshments
2. Plan around your knowledge of the group's characteristics (literacy, colour blindness, physical ability, preferences, etc.)
3. Provide clear briefing on session purpose and structure
4. Obtain consent to guidelines if these are being used
5. Check out understanding of what is written up
6. Use small groups
7. Be happy to make mistakes and admit them
8. Be happy to deviate from plans
9. Stick to announced beginning, end and break times (but note that 'when it is over, it is over', and if the work is finished earlier than planned, end earlier than planned!)
10. Be clear about follow-up arrangements

sessions not based around physical and temporal co-presence, and secondly, every time we revisit this we tend to add another point.

DEVICES FOR USE

There are also a variety of devices that can be used to help work proceed at different points. This section contains those we have found particularly helpful.

One device that can help the facilitator in the task of enabling access to meetings is agreeing some specific mechanism for time sharing in meetings. One such system is shown in Table 8.13. Judge (1994) argues that this system allows participants to use time resources more flexibly and democratically, and with less abuse or with fewer oppressive control structures needed to deal with it. We might add it makes the facilitator's task easier, with less recourse to some of the more heavy-handed roles in the lists given above. One advantage of working with something like this is that it serves to make very visible people's entitlement to be heard, in a way that seems to aid group members to participate in enabling that time is to be shared, thus sharing out this particular part of the facilitation role.

Guidelines or reminders also are often helpful. Tables 8.14 and 8.15 present two sets that we have found particularly inspirational, which express (in different ways) the same elements sought in the PANDA framework; one focuses specifically on dialogue, the other, broader in scope, encompasses action as well. In terms of dialogue, the ideas presented in Table 8.14 have resonances with Bohm's work. Bohm (1985) developed a theory of dialogue which combined two principles: a holistic view of nature, and recognition of the interaction between thinking and action. Drawing on quantum physics Bohm (1984) suggested that the universe is an

Table 8.13 Time-sharing in Meetings

- The total time available is first estimated. Each participant is allocated an equal number of minutes (variants are possible with higher or lower allocations to specific individuals for particular reasons)
- Mechanism set up for time-accounting, could be physical (beads or counters) or through accounts held by banker
- Each participant pays for speaking (hands over the beads or has account debited)
- Participants may reallocate their time units to others, in this way participants acquire more right to speak according to how their contributions are valued
- Participants may renounce some of their time without gifting (the time value of units remaining may then be increased – or the session(s) could finish early)
- Devaluation of time units may be necessary if unforeseen delays or cancellations are imposed. Revaluation occurs if extra time is introduced
- Systems of fines might be agreed (e.g. for violation of ground rules)

Source: adapted from Judge (1994), which details other variants and also presents examples of use.

Table 8.14 Traps and Opportunities of Dialogue

1. Single framework of agreement: Believing that everyone can and should agree on a single set of principles and guidelines, whether in the form of a charter, declaration or pledge (and including this note).
2. Labelling inappropriateness: Believing that it is useful to label some perspectives as wrong or inappropriate, especially in the absence of any sense of a global functional context.
3. Assumption of simplicity: Believing that the way forward is simple and that any perceived complexity is the product of inappropriate understanding.
4. Avoidance of issues: Believing that unpleasant issues can be postponed or treated as irrelevant.
5. Tokenism: Believing that it is only a media exercise and that people are not increasingly impatient with expensive exercises in collective impotence.
6. Avoidance of interaction: Believing that symbolic processes are a substitute for effective interaction.
7. Incorporation of disagreement: Believing that the diversity of positions does not call for designing in healthy disagreement to maintain a pool of alternative perspectives.
8. Marginalisation: Believing that it is appropriate to marginalise bodies and cultures representing alternative perspectives (whether by use of geographical distance, procedural or linguistic devices).
9. Collective learning: Believing that collective learning, even at the highest policy levels, is not vital to the emergence of more appropriate structures and processes.
10. Wishful thinking: Believing that it is sufficient to wish to be 'on the other bank of a river' and that the technical challenge of 'bridge construction' can be ignored.
11. Single-factor responses: Believing in the adequacy of the 'one answer', whether problem-specific, technocratic, spiritual, ethical or based on common sense, or on particular values.
12. Despair: Believing that no major breakthrough is possible, despite the prevalence of short-termism, tokenism, opportunism, cynicism and outdated modes of thinking.

Source: adapted from Judge (1993),
http://www.uia.org/uiadocs/conftran/xsptrap3.htm

indivisible whole, thus at a quantum level the observed object and the means to observe it interact with each other in an irreducible way, therefore perception and action cannot be separated. Bohm discusses two types of discourse: dialogue and discussion. The latter he sees as confrontational, the purpose being to win through analysing and dissecting the points of view or positions people take as part of the discussion (discussion has the same root as percussion); whereas dialogue suggests a free movement or flow of words between people where the whole organises the parts. The aim is not to win in a dialogue, but to help individuals gain insights that simply could not be achieved individually. In his own words: 'the process of dialogue ... [is] a free flow of meaning among all the participants ... to maintain the feeling of friendship in the group [is] much more important than to hold any

Table 8.15   Guide for Everyday Politics

- free political action from all unitary and totalising paranoia;
- develop action, thought and desires by proliferation, juxtaposition and disjunction, and not by subdivision and pyramidical hierarchisation;
- withdraw allegiance from the old categories of the Negative (law, limit, castration, lack, lacuna), which Western thought has so long held sacred as a form of power and an access to reality. Prefer what is positive and multiple: difference over uniformity; flows over unities; mobile arrangements over static systems. Believe that what is productive is not sedentary but nomadic;
- do not think that one has to be sad in order to be militant, even though the thing one is fighting is abominable. It is the connection of desire to reality (and not its retreat into forms of representation) that possesses revolutionary force;
- do not use force to ground a political practice in Truth; nor political action to discredit, as mere speculation, a line of thought. Use political practice as an intensifier of thought, and analysis as a multiplier of the forms and domains for the intervention of political action;
- the group must not be the organic bond uniting hierarchised individuals, but a dynamic collection of multiplication, displacement and diverse combinations.

Source: Foucault's introduction to the work of Deleuze and Guattari (1984:xiii–xiv).

position. . . . A new kind of mind . . . begins to come into being which is based on the development of a common meaning that is constantly transforming in the process of the dialogue' (Bohm, 1994:175).

In dialogue the group explores issues from many positions. The members of the group are open about the assumptions they have and communicate these freely. Dialogue is where the incoherence of thoughts is revealed. Dialogue is a means of seeing the representative and participative nature of thought, it is also a space where it is safe to acknowledge the incoherence of thought. To Bohm, dialogue enables people to be observers of their own thoughts. Thinking then is a collective activity and in the right conditions people can participate in a pool of common meaning. Dialogue can help the members of a group to become aware of the incoherence in other people's thoughts and through the process of dialogue collective thought hangs together or becomes more coherent. As Bohm (1994: 175) puts it: 'the group . . . begins to engage in a new dynamic relationship in which no speaker is excluded . . . going . . . along these lines would open up the possibility of transforming not only the relationship between people, but even more, the very nature of consciousness in which these relationships arise'.

Last of all in this section, recognising the importance of the beginning and ending of a defined session of group work, thought can be given to appropriate warming-up and rounding-off exercises. Warming-up is useful for setting a good tone and atmosphere for the session. In addition, if the group has not worked together before, it can act as a good ice-breaker, and in this circumstance a rather longer time might be spent on warming-up. The type of warm-up chosen will obviously depend on the particular group concerned. Some examples are given in Table 8.16.

Table 8.16   Warm-up Exercises for Group Sessions

Very simple exercises that can be used with almost every group include:

- a quick round of something new and good
- a quick round of something enjoyable that happened to them in the last week (or whenever)
- a quick round of one thing the person likes about the particular multiagency setting (about their organisation or group, or about the partnership so far)

The idea here is to do this very quickly. Questions all focus on positive aspects. Individuals can be allowed to say 'pass' if nothing occurs to them, and if too many do this another round on something else might be a good idea.
Other possibilities include:

- a quick round of main hope from the specific session
- a quick round of main anxiety about specific session (usually used in combination with another round with a positive slant)
- any anxiety from the rest of your life that you want to acknowledge and leave to one side while group work continues (usually used in combination with another round with a positive slant, and in some cases what is revealed may necessitate some appropriate action being taken)
- physically based warm-up exercises, such as 'group laugh' where everyone lies down in a circle with their head on someone else's stomach, someone starts to laugh and this is transmitted around the circle (obviously only for use where appropriate: culturally; in terms of people's physical abilities; and in terms of its acceptability to the group. This one is usually greeted with horror and embarrassment when suggested as being far too 'touchy-feely', however, once started it is usually extremely effective.)

With all of these, the idea is to do them quickly. If this does not work the facilitator will have to diagnose why (on the spot) and take remedial action: reminding people to be quick; interrupting to thank someone (if they are going on too long) and ask the next person to start; changing the plan and substituting one exercise for another; responding appropriately if someone reveals something that is deeply distressing for them (recent bereavement, illness in family, etc.).
There are plenty of books which yield ideas for use here, including: Barker (1980), Ernst and Goodison (1981) and Lewis and Streitfield (1972).

Closing a session is also important. The checklist in Table 8.12 has already covered making sure that everyone is clear about the follow-up arrangements; this may involve devoting time during closing the session to summing up the position and the next steps and clarifying where necessary through questions (be wary of people attempting to reopen discussion though!). The closing part of a session also provides an opportunity for critical reflection in the group. This could involve a quick round of questions (see Table 8.17 for some favourites) or might involve a slightly longer period of time for discussion (maybe even using a specific method such as NGT for example). Another possibility is the use of written session evaluation sheets which everyone fills in. Yet another possibility is to carry out

Table 8.17 Closing Exercises for Group Sessions

Questions that aid critical reflection:

- one thing you enjoyed about the session
- one thing you learnt from the session
- something that you thought worked well during the session
- anything that could have been done differently in the session
- anything you'd like to remember for the next session

Questions to end on a positive note:

- one thing you enjoyed about the session
- one thing you learnt from the session
- something that you thought worked well during the session
- something you are looking forward to
- one thing you appreciate about the group

The aim is usually to do this in quick rounds, using one, or maybe two questions, only. The facilitator may need to encourage people to keep it short!

critical reflection after some time has elapsed (to allow for the session to be evaluated individually first of all after a little time has elapsed for reflection); in this case the closing session might not include any reflection at all. It is also useful to end the session on a positive note wherever possible. Table 8.17 contains some questions that can be used for this purpose.

CRITICAL REFLECTION

One aspect of facilitation which we want to highlight as being particularly important is the process of critical reflection that we engage in as facilitators, in order to help plan the work, execute it and modify plans where appropriate. To some extent this happens continuously, in real time, as sessions progress, and judgements are made on the spot, as to how things are going and whether anything needs to be changed. The basis of these judgements is the accumulated experience and knowledge of the facilitator(s), including the tool-box of methods, etc. with which they consider they are able to work. To search for a rationalistic account of the facilitation process that presents this aspect of real-time reflection as a conscious rational process of option appraisal and decision-making, with associated schema that can be used to guide choice, seems to us to do violence to the reality of practice. This is where the art or craft of facilitation is exercised and where gut feeling, hunch, intuition comes into play – a change is made because it feels good, it seems right, or seems to offer a chance of improvement. We observe the consequence in practice of this change and decide to proceed with it, to modify it, or to abandon it completely and try something else. The theoretical position we adopt offers us the comfort that there is no overarching framework to guide our decision here, no framework that will guarantee a desired outcome, instead, like all good action research or action learning, we must try it and see what happens, flexibly modifying what we do on the basis of actively learning what is working, and what is not, in the particular local situation we find ourselves in.

Table 8.18   Four Crucial Elements in Critical Ethical Reflection Applied to Facilitation

---

1. *Undertaking a process of critical/ethical self reflection*
   At any point where a dilemma arises there is no single 'right' ethical answer/ course of action. We are an intrinsic part of the 'system' or structures we study. I, myself, as an active (be it undercover or out in the open) facilitator must evaluate and weigh up alternative actions in each particular situational context. This necessitates forming a view on power relations in particular. No set of guidelines is ever going to be able to substitute for this self-conscious reflection on the part of the facilitator.

2. *Recognising subjectivity and responsibility*
   This process of reflection is necessarily personal and subjective, and one for which the facilitator must assume responsibility. The notion of a set of universal guidelines telling me 'what' is the ethical solution is self-contradictory, at best I can hope for guidelines as to 'how' I might decide. We must throw aside the notion that we can have an authoritative code of ethics, there is no external authority that can substitute for our own reflection, no set of absolute truths that can tell us precisely how to act, we must accept responsibility for our role as agents.

3. *Recognising non-neutrality*
   In most situations, it is impossible to remain neutral, as Becker puts it: 'We cannot avoid taking sides. . . . Almost all the topics [that sociologists study], at least those that have some relation to the real world around us, are seen by society as morality plays and we shall find ourselves, willy-nilly, taking part in those plays on one side or the other.' This involves recognising our own, and others', non-neutrality, and considering as part of the process of reflection the likely consequences of this in each situation.

4. *Recognising the pervasive nature of ethical issues*
   Questions of ethics arise at all times in the group decision-making process. This involves a recognition that that there is nothing separate from context. Our actions are part of a nexus of interwoven and interconnected relationships, constantly being shaped by the relationships they shape. So, for example, we must recognise that each of our choices brings about consequences, and that we cannot escape responsibility for these. Another corollary is that ethics must be a part of the entire process, it is not something that can be dealt with as a subsection entitled 'ethical considerations.' The process of ethical examination must be part of all stages: how I decide whether to get involved, how I present myself to other participants, how I get involved, how I behave during the engagement, how I write any report, what I include/exclude in any report, how I act following any report. . . .

Source: adapted from Taket (1994a).

As well as ongoing critical reflection, it is also useful to set aside specific times for reflection, apart from the multiagency work itself. This process of critical reflection can be done as an individual, and/or as a group activity together with some/all of the participants. We have already mentioned that elements of reflection can be incorporated into the closing part of a session; they can also be included in other parts as well! It should go without saying that the decision as to how reflection is to be used is necessarily a contingent one, and that furthermore, it is not one that can be made free of value judgements. An early version of personal guidelines for critical reflection was presented in Taket (1994a), the salient elements of which are reproduced in an adapted form in Table 8.18.

We would argue that it is important to widen participation in critical reflection as far as possible, although we clearly want to stop short of making it an imperative to involve everyone every time. We also argue that the process of critical reflection necessarily involves reflection on ethical issues. Following Kohlberg (1981), we would also argue that this requires the most advanced form of individual moral development, namely an ability to think critically and act responsibly. We will not enter into any more detailed discussion of ethics in relation to multiagency work, those who wish to read further on the topic are invited to consult Taket (1994a) and Maclagan (1998).

The importance of critical reflection is illustrated by a Nepalese case study reported by Taket and White (1998). Here training in PANDA was given to a variety of workers from local non-governmental organisations (LNGOs). The need for the work arose because the LNGOs felt they needed to understand more about how to work with communities. In the past they had used participatory methods with little success and this was put down to the fact that they were using them mechanically and found it difficult to transfer the ideas to their setting and adapt the processes to their needs. Little or no attention was paid to community involvement. In fact, it was believed that approaches were used without reflection. During the training phase it was emphasised that PANDA involves reflecting on the processes and interacting with the communities through methods such as games and group work. Following a period spent using PANDA in the field working with village residents, those who had been trained as facilitators met to reflect on their work. This included recognition that it was important that the groups had a good understanding of participatory approaches and appreciation of the importance of reflection so that the activities are not just carried out mechanically. In Nepal the use of participatory methods had become a fashion and as a result it was felt they had been used unreflectively. Through the use of PANDA, it was possible for the participants to reflect on themselves and their approaches to development, to go beyond a name to carry out work in the villages where their NGOs are working in partnership *with* local people rather than *for* local people.

SUMMING UP AND MOVING ON

We have now reached the end of Part II in which we have introduced the PANDA framework. Chapter 4 presented the theoretical principles on which PANDA is based, a position we have labelled pragmatic pluralism. Chapter 5 then discussed pluralism in terms of the nature of the 'client', understood to mean the parties engaged in multiagency work, noting the diversity that is to be found. Chapters 6, 7 and 8 then focused in turn on methods, modes of representation and facilitation. These are the three axes of design available to us in order to respond to the diversity that exists in the parties we would engage in multiagency work, and in the settings in which such work might be done. We are now ready to move forward to Part III, which is concerned with focusing on PANDA in action.

PANDA in Action

In this, the third and final part of this book, we focus on the use of the PANDA framework. Chapter 9 discusses its use for planning the process(es) to be used in multiagency work. It brings the content of Chapters 5, 6, 7 and 8 together in a discussion of preparing for facilitating a particular piece of multiagency work.

Chapter 10 then presents five case studies demonstrating PANDA in action. We have already presented many examples drawn from case studies in our practice to illustrate various points in the book. What we do in this chapter is rather different. Here for each of the five case studies in turn, we first describe the whole case, briefly, pointing out the main features of what happened. We then discuss how the case study fits within the PANDA framework. Each case study illustrates how the PANDA framework was applied in practice and the results this had.

The book is then concluded with a short final chapter, Chapter 11.

Using the PANDA framework for planning process

9

'I hear and I forget.
I see and I remember.
I do and I understand.'
Chinese proverb (Wilcox, 1994:31)

INTRODUCTION

We refer to the approaches we use in the multiagency setting as PANDA (participatory appraisal of needs and the development of action). In Part II, we introduced the different features of PANDA in chapters that discussed the client, methods, representation and facilitation. We have argued that PANDA is relevant and suitable because: it enables the affirmation of individuals and difference; a pluralist stance is used giving voice to individuals and groups; knowledge and technology are seen as contextual in time and space limiting their transferability; the future is recognised as uncertain and indeterminate.

In this chapter we discuss how we use the PANDA framework in practice, drawing together some of the material presented in earlier chapters. This serves as a short introduction to the case studies that follow in Chapter 10. We make this presentation conscious of an initial paradox (we consider some others below), illustrated by the quote that begins this chapter: although we can describe what we do, understanding is woefully hampered unless gained from direct experience. Our text and tales are but a pale imitation of the understanding that comes from experience. Our post-hoc rationalisations (as this text might be seen) are no substitute for action and critical reflection.

As we have already emphasised, we view the application of PANDA as an art or craft and not a science. We have already carefully distinguished PANDA from those approaches that drive selection of methods and techniques by attempting to classify characteristics of the situation in which work is to be carried out. The emphasis is on work that is informed by experience, by practice, by critical reflection, by theorising (about practice, ours and others), but is not determined by any of these. Appropriate metaphors for this might be found in music or in cookery. As we have noted elsewhere, we are not the only practitioners who work in this fashion. In the context of a model-building conference, Andersen and Richardson (1997:112–113) describe their preparation thus: 'Whereas the guiding image for the planning phase of group modelling may be preparing for a theatrical show, the appropriate image for the execution phase is a chess player, a jazz musician in concert, or a football coach executing a game plan. All three of these examples have in common the notion of flexible improvisation after compulsively detailed advance planning.' Arguing that PANDA is not to/cannot be applied deterministically is not to say that there is no need for planning. Far from it, it is just that the product of such planning is multiple, in the sense of identifying a number of different options for use at each point.

In the chapters of Part II we focused in turn on four different types of pluralism. Of necessity we divided this up and presented it in a linear sequence. This is, however, in some ways inadequate, since these chapters represent four different views into the same whole, four different aspects that need to be thought about and considered, but not considered in isolation, they interconnect. Instead of suggesting to the reader that we can reveal a privileged path or sequencing through this maze, we suggest that the reader needs to think their own way through, in the light of each situation in which they wish to use this book. Managing in the multiagency setting is a creative process, an art or craft rather than a positivistic science, it requires choice, even if that choice is to follow someone else's recipe. We have resisted the temptation to provide any detailed or complete recipe (or even a recipe for generating recipes), instead we discuss the ingredients we use, how we use them, and describe some of the meals we have consumed. The contents of this chapter need to be read in this light. They describe for the reader some of the steps we follow in planning and monitoring interventions.

The remainder of this chapter again necessitates the uncomfortable imposition of a linear sequence on the various items to be thought about in the planning process. We deal with the issues in the following sections. First, we acknowledge and discuss the paradoxes inherent in our approach, noting, as we have discussed earlier, that from our ontological and epistemologicial stance, these are to be expected, and the challenge is to live with them, working towards embracing them playfully. We note that our training in traditional operational research often makes us uncomfortable with such paradoxes, more so perhaps than those with other less 'scientistic' backgrounds, but we are learning to live with this. Here we use the term 'scientistic', following Hayek (1952), to describe the use of methods in a social context that inappropriately shape themselves on the physical sciences.

We then move on to delineate the different stages in the application of PANDA, noting as we do some of the different variants in categorisation that others have put forward. We refuse the lure of debating which is 'best' and instead move on to discuss the stages in a little more detail, dividing them according to the three Ds described in Chapter 4: deliberation; debate; and decision. There are two sections on deliberation, one at the beginning and one at the end; this is intended firstly to remind the reader that what we discuss is a cyclical process, and secondly to provide an opportunity to focus on the deliberation that goes on to explore a situation/issue (deliberation I) separately from the deliberation that goes on to monitor or evaluate the effects of action taken on the situation/issue (deliberation II). The chapter then concludes by looking forward to the case studies presented in Chapter 10.

THE PARADOXES OF PANDA

We have emphasised earlier that our position involves learning to live with uncertainty and change, recognising and affirming difference and diversity, being comfortable with the notion that contradiction is inherent in what we do. We might summarise this in the form of a number of different paradoxes (see Table 9.1), within which work proceeds.

These paradoxes arise 'naturally' from the postmodern/poststructuralist perspective we adopt. As we have emphasised elsewhere, in particular in Chapter 4, they are to be expected, and our challenge is to learn to live comfortably, even joyfully, with them. The first two of these paradoxes serves to remind us that the only thing we can say with certainty from our perspective is that there are no certainties, the possibility of knowing, in advance, that our plans will definitely 'work' (whatever that might mean), is precluded. Following on from this, we are prepared for the need to reflect critically on what is happening and to be prepared to modify our plans based on this reflection.

We have emphasised the importance of facilitation, whether this be enacted through the person of one or more individuals who explicitly take on (or are given) this role, or is viewed as a task to be shared in a more informal fashion between the different individuals involved in any multiagency situation. The third and fourth paradoxes are intimately connected with this task of facilitation, which we have discussed in detail in Chapter 8. The third reminds us that as individuals,

Table 9.1   The Paradoxes of PANDA

The only guarantee is that there are no guarantees
The only grand narrative is that there are no grand narratives
Use only what you feel comfortable with, ... but take risks and expand your boundaries of comfort
Wherever oppression/power is exercised there is the possibility of resistance, empowerment and change
Theory is dead – long live theorising
Have fun – but it will hurt too (or no pain no gain!)

with a unique personal history and experience, we will feel a different level of sympathy and comfort in the different methods/techniques that exist; our level of awareness of the existence of different methods and techniques will change over time, thus we might expect to expand our repertoire as time progresses. We cannot pretend that we can all use all methods/techniques without falling into a paralysis of inaction as we try to learn them all before selecting any for use. We can also remind ourselves that in line with the action learning approach that PANDA draws on, experience of using a method, for real, is an excellent form of learning. So, to stimulate learning and development of facilitation we need to experiment, to take risks and to learn from our experiments. This will mean making 'mistakes', trying something that grinds to a halt, but if we recognise this and change our plans, moving on to try something different, this need not be a 'problem' but experience gained (see Box 9.1).

BOX 9.1 CELEBRATING MISTAKES – AN EXAMPLE OF FACILITATION DEVELOPMENT

In the late 1970s, a highly informal voluntary sector coalition located in an inner-city area was engaged in actively seeking to promote dialogue around community change, in particular seeking action to make processes of decision-making and action-taking more inclusive of all sectors of the community. Each individual took on the responsibility of undertaking the facilitation role in the various settings in which they were engaged (in their paid employment, in unpaid volunteering roles, in social settings, etc.). We set up a regular series of informal meetings between us, the purpose of which was to reflect on our experience and learning. These were set up under the title of 'celebrating mistakes'. These meetings provided a supportive (and confidential) environment where in turn each individual described something they had tried that had not worked – to be applauded (yes, loudly and exuberantly with whoops, cheers and claps by the rest of the group), before reflecting on the learning to be gained, and answering the question what else did you/could you have done. By convention, everyone who attended a meeting would identify at least one 'mistake' for celebration, if time permitted we would go round again for a second or even third round.

Comments: This provided a highly effective mechanism in a number of ways. It enabled us to actively notice (and reflect on) what we were doing. Sharing our experiences enabled us to benefit from each other's experience in terms of sharing techniques, tips and tactics. It was an enjoyable experience, and helped us keep on acting in the facilitation role in other settings and not give up easily. In terms of wider effects, individually and collectively the group succeeded in widening participation in a number of different arenas, in particular in terms of membership of the management committees of two community centres and membership of consultative forums set up to contribute to decisions on priorities for local authority spending.

The mechanism we designed drew heavily on the experience of the women members of the group who had a background in the 'consciousness raising' approach of the feminist movement. Description of similar approaches and techniques can be found in references such as Ernst and Goodison (1981). Similar ideas are also found in the literature on 're-evaluation co-counselling' (see Jackins, 1968; Personal Counselors Inc., 1970), which concerns itself with community and social change along many of the same principles as we have discussed – something that is perhaps not immediately obvious from the name 're-evaluation co-counselling'. A similar mechanism is also found in the case study of the UK Open University's 'New Directions' programme described by Russell and Peters (1998), which included a series of workshops on 'making better mistakes – banishing the blame culture'.

Source: not previously documented in published form, notes kept in my (Ann Taket's) reflective diary of the time.

The fourth paradox, also pertinent to facilitation, can be viewed as providing an optimistic slant on the possibility of change (in a direction that our ethical values view as positive). The balance to be achieved is one which involves recognising the existence of oppression and the exercise of 'power over', but not slipping into a (fatalistic) view that nothing can change. Foucault expresses this well in his introduction to Deleuze and Guatarri's work (which we have already quoted in Chapter 8), when he says: 'do not think that one has to be sad in order to be militant, even though the thing one is fighting is abominable. It is the connection of desire to reality (and not its retreat into forms of representation) that possesses revolutionary force' (Foucault, in Deleuze and Guattari, 1984:xiii–xiv). Sawicki (1991) provides a further case study that illustrates this at work in a chapter on the new reproductive technologies and their impact on women. In this she analyses the activities of FINRRAGE (Feminist International Network on Resistance to Reproductive and Genetic Engineering) and shows how a Foucauldian understanding of power can provide a useful framework for criticism and for identifying possibilities for effective resistance. Or, as Shange expresses the closely related point in the context of talking about her activism: 'Yes we still have to have romance in the face of adversity, this is a fact' (Shange, 1992:19). The type of attitude conducive to maintaining an appropriate balance to 'manage' this paradox can be illustrated in Box 9.2 through the two Kiswahili phrases, *hakuna matata* (no problem) and *karibu tena* (welcome again).

**BOX 9.2   HAKUNA MATATA – KARIBU TENA:
EXPERIENCES FROM ZANZIBAR**

While holidaying in Zanzibar, I had the chance to learn a little Kiswahili and experience its use in everyday conversation. Two particular phrases and their use (often jointly) seemed to me to indicate (and foster) an extremely positive and optimistic attitude towards everyday negotiation, interaction and decision-making in social and work settings. The two phrases are *hakuna matata*, which translates literally I am told as 'no problem' and *karibu tena* ('welcome again' or 'welcome back'). The way in which I first experienced their use was when as a tourist I was approached and offered various services – a guide, a taxi, a tour, some good or other (this is a frequent occurrence). If I did not want to take up the offer, once I explained this, the response would be *hakuna matata* – no problem, usually this would be followed by a list of one or more alternatives that were offered in case I was interested, discussion would proceed and when all current possibilities seemed to have been exhausted or one or other party wished to end the interaction, the phrase *karibu tena* would form part of the ending. This I interpreted to mean, well that is it for now, but let's be positive about the future possibilities. Once I had got used to this as a pattern of interaction between tourist and local resident, and observed how it functioned to foster a very amicable joint exploration of possibilities, I also started to observe it in use between local residents as well.

Comment: This illustration should be recognised on one level for what it is – an observation based on a short period of time in one particular place, albeit with many instances of the sort of interaction described. I would not wish it to be seen as elevated to the level of a technique or 'magic mantra' to be repeated to guarantee getting to the point of balance or resolution of paradox. On the other hand it did function in those local circumstances to signal to all concerned that (a) the initial outcome desired by one of the parties had not been achieved; (b) there were other opportunities that would arise in the future; (c) interaction could continue (present and future) on a positive basis.

Source: Ann Taket's reflective diary.

STAGES IN THE APPLICATION OF PANDA

Figure 9.1 presents one conceptualisation of the stages in the application of PANDA. Within this we can identify a number of different tasks or focuses for activity, all of which require attention. As we have already mentioned, we will discuss these under our three Ds described in Chapter 4: deliberation; debate; and decision. There are two sections on deliberation, one at the beginning and one at

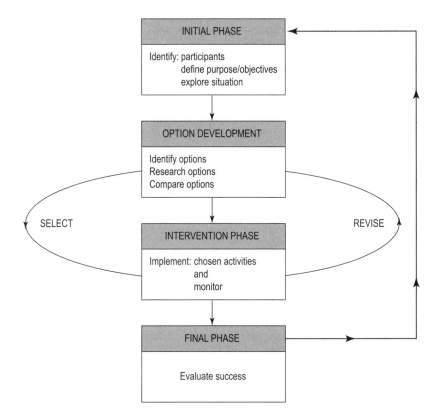

Figure 9.1 Stages in the PANDA Process

the end; this is intended firstly to remind the reader that what we discuss is a cyclical process, and secondly to provide an opportunity to focus on the deliberation that goes on to explore a situation/issue (deliberation I) separately from the deliberation that goes on to monitor or evaluate the effects of action taken on the situation/issue (deliberation II). Table 9.2 shows how our three Ds relate to our nine tasks or focuses. Note that the mapping displayed in Table 9.2 looks deceptively simple. Beware! Note that any task or focus may necessitate cycling through other tasks/ focuses to complete it. For example, the item titled monitoring/evaluating might require addressing the issue of participation and discussing different options for how to monitor/evaluate and so on. To put it another way, any instantiation of PANDA will involve moving through these phases (the three Ds) and the eight tasks/focuses in a unique fashion, progression will cycle back and forward, jumping at times with only a general overall movement through from beginning to end.

Other authors have presented different categorisations. De Reuck et al. (1999) suggest a simpler three-phase version when discussing decision conferencing (see Table 9.3). Given that they are concerned with a single event (a decision confer-

Table 9.2 Three Ds and Nine Tasks or Focuses

Deliberation I	Selecting participants Define purpose/objectives Exploring the situation
Debate	Identifying options Researching options (which could include consulting on options) Comparing options
Decision	Deciding action Recording decisions
Deliberation II	Monitoring/evaluating

Table 9.3 Three Phases of Decision Conferencing

Information focused phase	Including situation audit, review of desired future, stakeholder and competitor analyses
Decision focused phase	Formulation and description of possible courses of action, evaluation of options and choice between them
Action planning phase	Planning how the choice of strategy can be put into effect

Source: de Reuck et al. (1999).

ence), it is perhaps not surprising that the monitoring/evaluating phase is not found. When the purpose of the multiagency work is project planning, (or for any component where this is the objective), Friend and Hickling (1997) provide a useful division of activities into five different kinds, summarised in the acronym ISCRA (see Table 9.4). Again, we can note that there is no coverage of the action and monitoring/evaluation components.

We can also see similarities with Guba and Lincoln's fourth-generation evaluation (Guba and Lincoln, 1989), which distinguishes 12 steps (see Table 9.5). As we have done above, Guba and Lincoln also emphasise that a linear flow through their 12 steps should not be expected or adhered to rigidly, in their words there is 'progression only in a general way; it is the case that frequent back and forth movement, sometimes involving jumps over multiple steps is not only possible but desirable' (Guba and Lincoln, 1989:185). Here we note that although Guba and

Table 9.4 Project Planning: the ISCRA Delineation of Activities

I	Identifying the Issues
S	Setting the Structure
C	Confirming the Concept
R	Reviewing the Recommendations
A	Approving any Amendments

Table 9.5   The 12 Steps of Guba and Lincoln's Fourth-generation Evaluation

1. Initiate a contract with the client or sponsor commissioning the evaluation
2. Organise the evaluation
3. Identify stakeholders
4. Develop joint, collaborative, shared understandings (constructions), specifically focused on claims, concerns and issues
5. Test and enlarge understandings through use of new or additional information
6. Sort out resolved claims, concerns and issues (those where consensus exists)
7. Prioritise unresolved claims, concerns and issues
8. Collect further information bearing on unresolved claims, concerns and issues
9. Prepare agenda for negotiation
10. Carry out negotiation
11. Report outcomes
12. Recycle through steps as necessary

Comment: Aronoff and Gunter (1994) make the particularly useful suggestion that part of the negotiation for items for which there is no, or incomplete, consensus may involve the development of a loose consensus, or an agreement to disagree on certain issues; we have already discussed a similar notion – the concept of consent – in Chapter 5.

Source: adapted from Guba and Lincoln (1989).

Lincoln are specifically concerned with questions of evaluation, we can see their 12 steps as an appropriate categorisation for other participative group decision-making activities. Aronoff and Gunter (1994) present an example of just such a use in putting forward a seven-step variant as a recommended public involvement process for the resolution of technological disputes.

Finally, in the specific case of intersectoral action, Saan (1990) distinguishes three phases, depicted in Table 9.6. He goes on to provide a series of nine checklists that cover various different aspects of these phases.

Table 9.6   Saan's Three Phases of Intersectoral Action

Phase	Content
Pre-intersectoral action	Orientation: identification of potential partners
Intersectoral action	Three stages (not sharply distinct): approach – initial negotiation with potential partners planning – planning of specific of intersectoral action action – implementation of action
Post-intersectoral action	Some action may continue, further intersectoral action in different areas may result

Source: adapted from Saan (1990).

Before moving on to discuss the different stages, we note one final point we wish to make about the process of planning PANDA, which is the importance of being critically reflective throughout. We have already covered critical reflection in Chapter 8 in terms of its importance in facilitation; it is equally important in the planning stage, although the individuals involved may well be different. As for critical reflection on PANDA in action, critical reflection at the planning stage can benefit from the inclusion of different viewpoints, and from being performed as a group, as well as an individual, activity. The whole process of planning can be treated as an opportunity for participative debate and decision (without wanting to suggest ever-circling recursive loops into deciding about the planning stage, planning the deciding of the planning stage, deciding the planning of the deciding of the planning stage and so on *ad infinitum*).

DELIBERATION I – STARTING OFF

In this first section on deliberation we focus on the deliberation that goes on to explore a situation/issue. This might be at the very start of some multiagency engagement, or as an already established multiagency group turns its attention to some new situation or issue. Table 9.7 presents some ideas as starting points for

Table 9.7 Deliberation I – Some Favourites for Use

Selecting participants	• brainstorming • critical systems heuristics • stakeholder analysis • analysis using the categories contained in Table 1.2 and Figure 1.1 can also be helpful	• Delphi technique • hexadic reduction (from team syntegrity) • self-selection, as in open space technology for example
Define purpose/ objectives	• brainstorming • nominal group technique • early stages of RGA (selecting elements and constructs) • root definitions	• CATWOE • concept maps • analysis using the categories contained in Table 1.2 and Figure 1.1 can also be helpful
Exploring the situation	• rich pictures • cognitive mapping • concept mapping • influence diagrams • Venn diagrams • IDONS • SWOT • transects • SCA • nominal group technique • Delphi technique	• problem jostle (from team syntegrity) • critical systems heuristics • CATWOE • root definitions • RGA • deconstruction • action methods • participatory theatre • story-telling • pictures • photovoice

planning the first deliberation phase. The list given is not comprehensive, nor is it intended to be prescriptive, it merely illustrates our personal (tried and tested) favourites. We expect to add to this as time goes on, so that perhaps the table becomes superfluous and the statement to be made instead is to use your imagination and the feedback you get in critical reflection and try all sorts of things for all sorts of purposes.

Particular points to bear in mind for this first phase of deliberation are the need to:

- open a space for discussion
- acknowledge and respect diversity
- create necessary safety for participants
- enable access to participation
- multiply rather than close off options

DEBATE

Table 9.8, in a similar form to Table 9.7, presents some ideas as starting points for planning the debate phase. At this stage there is a focus on structuring and deepening the description of options under consideration. The number of options under discussion may need to be reduced. This might be done through eliminating the

Table 9.8 Debate – Some Favourites for Use

Identifying options	• brainstorming • nominal group technique • Delphi technique • SWOT • IDONS	• RGA • rich pictures, drawing • problem jostle (from team syntegrity) • hexadic reduction (from team syntegrity)
Researching options (which could include consulting on options)	• OST • SAST • SCA • concept maps • influence diagrams • cognitive mapping	• critical systems heuristics • RGA • AIDA, including option graphs • action methods to explore scenarios (playlets, small dramas, role-plays)
Comparing options	• SAST • deconstruction • decision trees	• AIDA • ranking • MCDA*

* MCDA = multi criteria decision analysis. Although this is certainly a possibility, we have not covered it in detail in this book, beyond a brief mention in Chapter 3; this is not something we have ever used in any formal sense.

unfeasible and/or unlikely, and/or combining or collapsing options. Whatever methods are chosen, there are a number of particular points to be borne in mind:

- the possible need for explicit negotiation over what is considered and why
- the need to enable the agreed ground (options for example) to be systematically covered and re-covered
- the need to enable similar interrogation of each option being considered
- continued attention to enabling access to participation

This phase may require rather more active and forceful facilitation to achieve than the first phase of deliberation.

DECISION

We notice that as we draw up Table 9.9, on the same basis, considerably fewer options are included, but we do not wish to make too much of this. We do notice that at this point, the method to be used for decision-making may need to be explicitly discussed and negotiated within the group. This may necessitate another loop through the entire process as different options for decision-making are identified, their pros and cons discussed and a decision made about which to use. We note that there is a danger of disappearing into an endless spiral of recursive loops of consideration, and sound a warning. A well-known delaying tactic is to repeatedly call for a re-examination of starting assumptions, and/or a revisiting of matters already well rehearsed. It is, however, particularly important that there is a clear understanding of the method(s) in use at this point. Consensus may be impossible to achieve and be may substituted by consent or accommodation in the sense discussed in Chapter 5.

Table 9.9 Decision – Some Favourites for Use

Deciding action	• ranking/voting • SAST • self-nomination • decision trees	• outcome resolve (from team syntegrity) • AIDA • MCDA*
Recording action	• diagrams • commitment package	• action points

* MCDA = multi criteria decision analysis. Although this is certainly a possibility, we have not covered it in detail in this book, beyond a brief mention in Chapter 3; this is not something we have ever used in any formal sense.

DELIBERATION II – MONITORING/EVALUATING – REFLECTION AND REACTION

This second section on deliberation focuses on the deliberation that goes on to monitor or evaluate the effects of action taken on the situation/issue. Table 9.10 concentrates on methods that can typically be used in a fairly informal fashion. Where more formal evaluation is required, for example to demonstrate that resources should continue to be provided to permit the activities concerned to continue, then there will usually be the need for careful consideration of evaluation design and often considerable data collection requirements. It is way beyond the scope of this book to present full details of this aspect, that will have to wait for a separate book.

Table 9.10   Deliberation II – Some Favourites for Use

Monitoring/evaluating	• cognitive mapping • story-telling • rich pictures/drawing • key informant report • critical reflection	• action methods • photos • formal measurement of various types* (not covered in detail anywhere in this book)

* By formal measurement we refer to rather larger-scale information collection, involving recourse to resources outside the group. This might involve quantitative or qualitative data collected through a variety of means such as surveys of various kinds, routine data collection, examination of documents, participant observation, etc.

The second deliberation stage leads naturally back into one of the earlier phases and the next pass through the cycle, that is of course assuming that the multiagency work concerned is not confined to a one-off event or a very strictly bounded interaction. Exactly which phase it leads back into will obviously depend on the nature of the work and the nature of the findings that emerge from the deliberation.

MOVING ON – CASE STUDIES OF PRACTICE

We have deliberately keep this chapter short, in keeping with the desire not to fool the reader into believing that we have a foolproof recipe for them to follow, we do not. To emphasise this, we remind you of the metaphors with which we started this chapter: those of cookery, and of jazz improvisation. Before we invite you to hasten on to the next chapter, which presents some case studies of PANDA in action, we just want to remind the reader of the importance of planning for fun in the process. In Chapter 8 we discussed the importance of beginnings and endings, of warming people up to work in a group, and of ending, wherever possible on a high. We also noted the importance of humour. Critical reflection, which we have suggested should be incorporated into the work of the group whenever possible, is not to be thought of as an unrelentingly solemn activity; fun and humour can be built in, without distracting from the seriousness of what may be at hand, and the literature on emotional intelligence (Goleman, 1995) points to a directly productive effect of laughing on flexible, complex and creative thinking.

Case studies using PANDA 10

10

INTRODUCTION

This chapter will describe five case studies demonstrating PANDA in action. We have already presented many examples drawn from case studies in our practice to illustrate various points in the book. What we do in this chapter is rather different. Here for each of the five case studies in turn, we first describe the whole case, briefly, pointing out the main features of what happened. We then discuss how the case study fits within the PANDA framework. Each case study illustrates how the PANDA framework was applied in practice and the results this had. In the discussion and commentary on each case study we also identify the particular type(s) of multiagency setting that is/are involved and contrast the findings with other similar case studies elsewhere in the literature.

We have selected these particular case studies for inclusion in this chapter for a number of reasons. They are case studies about which we know a great deal, either through direct involvement acting as facilitators, or through close contact with individuals involved, with whom we have debated the case study and its implications. In four of the case studies, we were directly involved in the facilitating role. In the other one, the material is used by permission of the facilitator involved, and at his request the case is presented anonymously. The case studies also illustrate a wide range of different settings: private sector, not-for-profit sector, and different parts of the public and voluntary sectors. They took place in a variety of different countries: North America, Central America, Europe, covering both developed and developing country settings. We have also picked these studies to describe in depth since they have not been presented elsewhere in any detail, unlike the other case studies that we have used elsewhere in the book, which we have published elsewhere in various forms.

The first case study is the oldest of those presented in this chapter, it describes work undertaken in the private sector to help a multinational company with the issue of supply chain management. The second describes the use of PANDA in a development context, where work was carried out with a network of NGOs who interacted with a variety of aid agencies and public and private sector organisations. This is an example where PANDA was used to help several development agencies plan and execute development strategies. The third centres on the use of PANDA with a voluntary organisation (NGO) concerned with urban regeneration in a particularly deprived part of London. The voluntary organisation was part of a regeneration consortium for the area, which involved all sectors. The fourth looks at how PANDA was used to help form a community development project which aimed to encourage multiagency working through the development of networks between voluntary agencies, statutory agencies and community groups. Finally, the fifth case study is an application of PANDA to the case of workplace democratisation in a university setting.

CASE A: SUPPLY CHAIN MANAGEMENT IN THE PRIVATE SECTOR

A.1 Background

The pharmaceutical industries are now faced with a new search for a sustainable competitive advantage. One response has been a move towards mergers or take-overs. Alternatively, it has been argued that a major source of competitive advantage may well come from a company's own supply chains, where it may be possible to substantially reduce costs and improve levels of service, including the reduction of time to market for many products. Opportunities exist outside of organisations, in that further cost reductions and improvements in service levels can be sought from their supply chains.

The concept of supply chain management (SCM) calls for a 'systemic' view of the supply chain, in that drives for improvements in parts of the supply chain must be viewed in terms of their overall impact on the supply chain as a whole. Such 'integrated' supply chain management offers potential synergetic benefits which are not possible when management of the supply chain is fragmented.

There are a number of hurdles to be overcome before these suggested synergetic benefits can be achieved. One of the major hurdles is the ever-changing business environment in which the supply chain exists. A related problem is that of 'demand amplification' whereby the actual process of exchanging information between adjacent organisations in the supply chain causes enormous swings in the levels of inventory being held by the organisations. This results in high inventory holding costs.

Another problem to be overcome is that organisations cannot simply implement local operational improvements (improving efficiency and effectiveness) and expect problems with the supply chain to cease. Any action taken will have an effect upon the supply chain as a whole. The supply chain must be viewed as a whole and solutions must be arrived at as such. Finally, the nature of the relationship between the supply chain organisations needs to be explored. These relationships need to become more co-operative and have mutual objectives, offer mutual benefits to both parties and evolve around a culture of openness and reciprocity between organisations. Organisations are beginning to realise that co-operative relationships are the way to obtain the potential benefits of the supply chain.

As part of an overall change management project the pharmaceutical company in this case study wanted to explore ways to improve the supplier relationship and improve productivity while at the same time reduce stockholding costs. The products produced have a development phase lasting many years and in the production phase quality is imperative. The name of the company has been withheld to respect confidentiality, and the models described are extracts and have been simplified for ease of presentation.

In order to explore these issues the company established the 'company excellence' team as part of its change management programme. The team consisted of representatives from the divisions within the organisation who were seconded from their duties for the change programme. They were mainly senior managers and came from diverse backgrounds.

The change programme followed Lewin's three-step process (Lewin, 1947) of *unfreezing, change* and *refreezing*. The 'company excellence' team was essentially a transformation team which has been given the authority for change, has been given power or clout, and had a remit to communicate with the whole organisation and suppliers. The objective for the change was to alter the working relationships with the supplier so that they adopted the supply-chain principles of co-operative working.

The problem for the team was that there was a wall of resistance to the change both within the organisation and without. The team had to devise a strategy to remove people's anxieties for change and to move the process on from unfreezing to change.

A.2   The case study

First meeting

The aspect of the work here relates to a short encounter with the team and some of the key stakeholders. The team had approached the university to explore how it could help them to encourage the stakeholders to accept the principles of the supply chain.

During the first meeting with the team, the discussion followed an agenda; first the team described the organisation and the problems and their change programme. This was followed by the university team discussing their expertise and experience in similar situations. An attempt was made by a number of individuals to see if they could describe the problem from their particular expertise. Even among this quite sophisticated group the problem of holding a range of complex concepts and sharing an understanding of them was very difficult. It was suggested that the problem could be represented as an influence diagram. One of the university team acted as facilitator and through a series of questions was able to draw up some causal relationships. Soon other members of the team amended the diagram. Although what emerged was messy, there was an improvement in appreciation of the problem situation. In particular, a very useful influence diagram of the company's supply chain was produced (Figure 10.1). One of the tasks set for the next meeting was to develop this model for the meeting with the team and other stakeholders, in particular the suppliers.

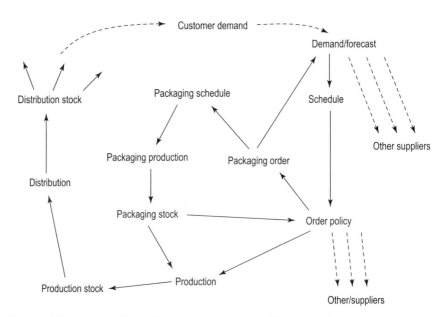

Figure 10.1   Causal Loop Diagram of Part of the Supply Chain

Second meeting

Before the second meeting, the influence diagram was converted to a systems dynamic model using the nomenclature of stocks and flows to represent the dynamics of the feedback loops. The model was different in that rather than show lines of arguments it showed the relationships between variables. Some data were collected and a working visual model was prepared. The model graphically described the changes in the environment that are echoed throughout the supply chain (see Figure 10.2 for extract).

The second meeting started with a description of the company and its supply chain strategy and a heated discussion took place in terms of the relationship with the supplier and what benefits the supply chain would have for them. Again, it was difficult to share perspectives and some of the participants were feeling frustrated. The model of the supply chain was presented and a few what-if scenarios were presented. Both the team and the other stakeholders began to interrogate and offer

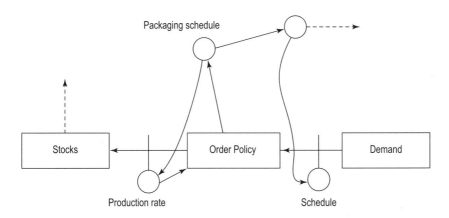

Figure 10.2   Flow Diagram for Part of the Supply Chain

different scenarios and what-ifs. The model was not sophisticated in that it could not handle most of the enquiries, but issues were beginning to be shared and particular difficulties each group had were being articulated and dealt with.

Following the meeting, the model was developed further and was the basis of 'unfreezing' the current situation within the organisation and suppliers. The model was distributed to a number of key people within the organisation and the additions and modifications were incorporated. Our engagement with the group ended here, but the team was able to start exploring some of the anxieties many of the senior managers had about the supply chain approach. They were also able to work with some of their suppliers to identify their needs and anxieties in relation to the change management programme.

One problem dealt with was that it was suggested that the increased usage and role of information technology as a means of enhancing competitiveness for the company may hold the key to integrating the supply chain as a whole. Information (even sensitive information) had to be shared with other organisations along the supply chain. If this could happen then many of the problems they faced might be overcome.

A.3   Commentary: PANDA in action

The work used a combination of influence diagrams – in the early stage of the work to negotiate the different perspectives and manage conflict, and system dynamics – to explore the difficulties of the supply chain and options. Using these modes of representation was vital in the sense that it made clear different perspectives, and the participants had the opportunity to interrogate the maps and diagrams rather than each other. The modes of representation were sufficiently transparent and transferable (i.e. the models were used in other meetings beside the two we were involved in). The transparency of the methods used meant that active participation of all the participants was possible. However, the transparency of the representations alone did not bring about participation. Sensitive facilitation was also needed to ensure that conflict within the group was minimised.

CASE B: PANDA IN DEVELOPMENT: AN NGO NETWORK IN BELIZE

B.1 Background

As with many other underdeveloped countries, the NGO or not-for-profit sector is involved in a range of activities from welfare and relief services to community development work through to large-scale development programmes undertaken by a partnership of several agencies. There are in general three types of NGO operating in Belize:

1. The international organisations and NGOs such as UNHCR, CAFOD and many donors come into this category.
2. The national NGOs – these are the main conduits for international NGOs and donors to exercise programmes for development. One or more international NGO or donor usually funds them.
3. Local or indigenous NGOs – these are usually community based and are run by local people, usually through the support of the national NGOs.

The effectiveness of the NGOs usually refers to things such as:

- record on integrating disadvantaged groups such as women
- scaling up activities
- extent to which NGOs reach the poorest
- role in maintaining a safety net for the poor

At the time of this study the international NGOs were reassessing their work globally and one of the regions where funding was being considered for a cut was Central America and the Caribbean. Due to a number of factors including governments reducing funds for international development, a change in priority for many funders away from the developing world towards redeveloping Eastern Europe, and the principle that past funding should lead to self-sustainability, many local NGOs are facing the threat of having their funds cut by international donors. Other major donors, such as USAID, Canada Fund and the Sweden International Development Fund, were also considering where to prioritise their work. With funding being cut, what are the priorities for the NGO sector? The potential shortage of funds would have a dramatic impact in that it would lead to the creation of competition between the NGOs which was seen as detrimental to co-operation. Also there would be effects on priorities, planning and institutional capacity. The national NGOs in Belize, in response to the impending cuts, formed a national network. The network was seen as important for two reasons: (a) as a collective they may be in a better position to negotiate with donors and international NGOs, and (b) internally, it may be possible for them to listen and learn from each other in dealing with the changes that may occur.

In Belize/Central America, at the time of this study, one or two agencies were already facing the prospect of having no funder, and other agencies were beginning to feel anxious that they would soon be facing the same problem or they were feeling under pressure to take up the work left by agencies that have folded, with few or already over-burdened resources.

B.2   The case study

This case study describes work with the network of NGOs in Belize. The Association of National Development Agencies (ANDA) represented most of the agencies in Belize. ANDA was formed to represent the interests of the NGOs to government and international donor agencies. It is a network of eight non-governmental development organisations in Belize and is concerned with rural development. It was set up to provide links with other networks in the Caribbean and Central America, to provide a focus for lobbying the Belize government on development issues and to undertake a programme of activities to support NGOs in Belize. The NGOs concerned take on a range of rural development projects, working with co-operatives, groups and individuals on agricultural, health and other development issues.

The work was seen as pressing in that a letter was circulated to most of the NGOs detailing that the main donor – Canada AID – was about to reduce its level of funding to the region. ANDA felt that the decision was fast approaching and a strategy which reflected the interests of all its members was needed. Involvement in this work came out of a piece of research sponsored by the Association of Commonwealth Universities. The methods of working were discussed and the work was carried out over a six-week period. Initially, it was decided that each NGO in ANDA would be interviewed and the results would be used to explore the issues in a couple of workshops.

Individual interviews and first workshop

After the initial meeting with the key ANDA representatives, it was agreed that each member of ANDA should be interviewed prior to any collective group strategy development. The NGOs in Belize were very different and some were better established and more influential than others. The interviews were to ensure that common themes were identified as well as individual concerns.

The key representatives of the NGOs were interviewed and each interview was converted into cognitive maps. The maps were fed back to the individuals. The maps clearly represented the interest of the NGOs and many common themes emerged. The maps were then combined into a composite map (see Figure 10.3),

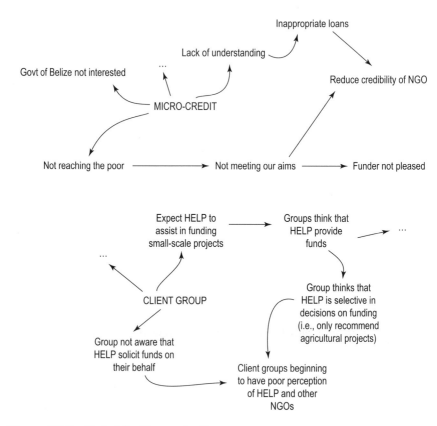

Figure 10.3   Part of the Composite Map

highlighting key issues and their consequences as well as different and alternative perspectives. A workshop was arranged to explore the issues, however, this was poorly attended.

At this stage the interviews confirmed the belief held that the donors were going to reduce funds in the region. Many of the informants claimed that the sector had been aware of this for some time now. In fact some of the NGOs were told that they had received their last grant. The donors expected the sector to become 'self-sustainable' and were encouraging projects to set up micro-credit schemes with rolling funds (these are programmes of loans given to the rural poor as a means of starting a project). This was seen as contentious to some of the NGOs because they felt that the clients would have to meet certain criteria for the loans, i.e. the ability to repay and this would mean that they would not be necessarily reaching the poorest people (see Figure 10.3). Other issues that were mapped were relationship with clients, future priorities and so on.

During the workshop, nominal group technique was used to enable individuals to comment on the map, explore alternative views and prioritise the issues to be addressed. During this session a number of obvious themes emerged and there was some agreement on the priorities. However the group was stuck in a mode where the more powerful organisations were setting the agenda and it was clear that the less powerful were being silenced. Given this the group held views which were rigid. In terms of facilitation a change of style was needed and in terms of process something more engaging was necessary. It did seem that NGT and the more verbal approaches were relevant to some but were closed to others. The session ended in a graph of issues drawn as a causal map; as this was drawn up the discussion became more animated. New ideas and themes emerged.

Second workshop

By word of mouth the news spread about the work of the first session. In the second session attendance was greater. Each attendee was sent the final map from the first session. During this session the participants discussed planning a larger workshop. The ANDA representative suggested joint facilitation and the use of role-play was discussed so that the smaller less powerful agencies could be brought in to participate (by less powerful it was meant that these groups had less staff and less resources). Participation between the groups was much better in this session. The more powerful groups were more open and the less powerful ones felt less suspicious. The situation was, however, tense; each time funding or resources were mentioned in that given that there were a number of groups chasing very few funds, the pressure to keep to oneself knowledge about donors was high. If ever there was a need for developing a collaborative environment, this was the time.

The session ended with the group discussing who to invite to the next workshop (i.e. representatives of donors, the government of Belize and so on). The group also found areas where collaboration would be fruitful, and this was around developing a country-wide system for micro-credits, although a number of the grass-roots organisations felt that the micro-credit route would be against their aims and objectives in that they could not see how loans would reach the poorest in the region if the loans are given based on the criterion of ability to pay it back.

Session three

This session had the following components. First, there was a series of sketches or role-plays followed by reflection. Second, the group was be broken down into small teams tackling particular issues using modes of representation they were comfortable with. This was followed by a facilitated plenary session. Finally the whole group would be broken down into small planning teams to produce an action plan.

The session had a range of agencies including representatives of the government of Belize and donors. Held in a large hall, the role-play was seen by the participants as fun but at the same time it engaged them into thinking about the issues of concern. Each of the subsequent small group work started with reflections on the sketches and then an exploration of the issues by the groups. Each group had its own facilitator(s), who used their own means of facilitating and representing. Some groups adopted a quite linear process while others used role-play and so on. Aggregating the outputs was always going to be difficult, but it was soon realised that most of the groups converged towards the same themes and issues.

B.3   Commentary: PANDA in action

One of the main issues to arise out of this study is the nature of network organisations. The idea of the network organisation (DiMaggio and Powell, 1983; Powell, 1990) stresses the need to focus on a level of analysis which transcends traditional organisational boundaries. Networking activity can be undertaken either informally, whereby individual members pick up new ideas through their relationships with individuals in other organisations (Macdonald, 1995), or formally when an organisation enters into an alliance and other forms of partnerships to form an inter-agency relationship. Especially when considering formal alliances the premise is that organisations, by coming together, can share different competencies and thereby generate new ideas.

ANDA is one particular type of network organisation. It was set up to represent the interests of the various NGOs in Belize. It was formed with the ethos that problems exceed the capacity of any single organisation to solve, and the premise that a diverse range of individuals can create, through synergy, ideas which go beyond what any single individual could have produced on his or her own. The organisation saw the main benefits of networking as the greater potential for knowledge sharing and diffusion through the network, and better prospects for funding being more likely since the network involved close linkages among multiple members who may not all be competing for the same funds.

ANDA is also a bureaucratic network which is underpinned by formal agreements and formally identified roles and co-ordination of mechanisms. Thus, the flexibility that can be achieved in networks may easily be swamped by the formality of the structure. Although structure can help the organisation identify complementary interests, the opportunities for learning and the overall effectiveness of the organisation may fall off the more structure is present. In the case of ANDA, problems arose because the bureaucratic structure was too formal and it was unable to handle the multiplicity of actors and institutions. Another problem, not unrelated, was that the network itself was dominated by a few powerful voices, who sometimes acted as gatekeepers for the network, i.e. deciding what information flowed through the network. The study implicitly showed that the connections between the players are an important consideration to deal with in network settings. The connections can vary in terms of content (type of connection) and form (strength of connection) (Smith and White, 1996). The position of the players is also an important consideration, it is important to identify who is central and how well linked people are within the network. These issues can be explored visually by using sociometric modes of representation. The use of sculpting (see chapter 7) to map the relations between participants has been found useful and non-threatening. Connections and relationships can easily be explored. Each node in the network can be explored to identify sources of conflict, difference and even reciprocity. Careful attention to the way the network is sculpted can help the players to develop trust.

CASE C: EAST LONDON REGENERATION CONSORTIUM

C.1 Background

The organisation described in this study is a voluntary organisation based in east London. The area in which it operates has very high levels of social deprivation, unemployment and poverty, and the employment opportunities available are often poorly paid and insecure. Much of the housing in the area is in need of major investment – this is crucial, particularly for the most vulnerable, i.e. the elderly. Here many live in dwellings without central heating, and of those who own private accommodation much of it lacks basic amenities. The area also has a substantial refugee community, who face considerable hardship while awaiting decisions on asylum applications (which can take up to four years). Often the whole family (sometimes more than one family) is forced to live in a hotel room. The adults have very few opportunities to gain employment, and a number of other problems are intensified by a lack of rights associated with their status and acute communication difficulties.

The organisation was set up over 20 years ago by the local churches who wanted to promote community development in the area. The local ministers recognised that the statutory agencies were unwilling or unable to provide services for many of the local communities, and so growing numbers were becoming socially excluded. The need for support so that the communities could become more actively involved in the wider community was blatantly obvious to the local community workers. The organisation was set up with a community development focus.

The organisation's ethos is to provide support and resources to a broad range of people throughout the district to help them to articulate and realise their needs, and also to help raise awareness of these issues in the wider population. It currently manages five diverse projects, ranging from projects working with homeless people, to the elderly living in substandard accommodation, to refugees and asylum seekers. Therefore it is an umbrella organisation for these projects. The advantage of an umbrella organisation is that it allows a number of complementary projects, each of which may not be viable on its own, to pool resources and ultimately enable a wider range of issues to be addressed.

The structure of the organisation is as follows: there is an executive committee who have ultimate responsibility for the organisation; a management team which is made up of project managers, the director and representatives from administration and finance; and each project has an advisory committee. The director also attends executive committee meetings and so is the link between the executive members and the projects.

To understand the current situation we need to delve a little into the past. The previous director was a key element in the organisation's history, having been there for 17 years. He had been involved in not only the organisation's growth and development, but he was also the driving force behind many other initiatives in the area. For many who knew of the organisation, he was its personification. When he left in 1994 a project manager filled his role until a new director was appointed in January 1995. There were changes in management of some of the projects at around this period, and also changes in membership of the executive committee. This led, understandably, to a certain amount of uncertainty at this time, particularly in the management team, which had five new members out of eight by the end of 1995. A period of change often results in an opportunity to take stock and for a time of consolidation. Consequently the executive committee was keen to take a more active role in the management of projects, which led to a degree of conflict between the executive committee and the project managers, who wished to retain their autonomy.

The projects are very different. Each has evolved in a different way. For example, they started at different times, they perform different functions, and they operate independently of each other. Hence, each seems to have a unique identity. This has led to there being very little interaction between them. Thus, each of the projects operates as a separate entity, and there are few areas of overlap leading to lack of cross-fertilisation between them; therefore it is unusual for any to, say, refer clients from one to another. Although the targeted client bases may differ, the project managers encounter a number of common issues, such as personnel, recruitment, etc., and the monthly management team meeting provides a forum for these issues to be discussed. However, the management team is essentially a committee with representational functions and subsequently identification of a common goal is often difficult. Additionally, the influx of new personnel led to uncertainty over specific focus. The new director was keen to develop more programme-wide cohesion, and was looking to the management team meetings to provide a base for this.

The year 1995 was a period of change and reflection for the organisation. The members of the management team and the executive committee felt that although they had good working relationships and all of the projects were doing well, they were a little unsure of what each expected of the other. Although many felt that the injection of new members of staff may provide new ideas and impetus, ways were needed of teasing these out and developing a team spirit. In particular it was thought that there was room for improvement in group meetings, with specific emphasis on uncovering differences in opinion and perception.

C.2   The study

The work described began in August 1995. The first contact was with the new director, with whom the aims of the study were drawn up. She was enthusiastic for what was proposed, particularly because she felt that the work might help the group work more effectively together, although she was a little unsure how it would be achieved. The organisation had used consultants/researchers in the past. But the studies were usually more quantitative studies. This meant that even though that sort of approach was not appropriate to address the current issues, the organisation had at least some idea of what they were getting involved in. It was agreed that the management team would be the main focus of the study because it was felt that because of all of the recent changes there was a lack of cohesion and overall sense of direction within it. It was thought important to stress that the research was not offering to provide a specific answer to all of the group's problems, but that the process would promote within-group interaction and so they would learn more about each other's views and opinions, which would hopefully enable them to determine what they wanted to achieve as a group.

C.3   The process

The process adopted for the work was as follows. The first stage involved data collection; this took the form of semi-structured interviews, a review of reports, minutes and so on, and observation of meetings. The interviews were used to capture each individual's perspectives of the organisation and the issues important to them. The secondary data review included various publications by the projects and the organisation, and also minutes of the executive committee meetings over a period of two years. This enabled a picture to be built up of the background of the organisation. Finally, this stage also involved attendance at management team, project and executive committee meetings in a non-participative role. From this it was hoped to observe the interaction of the group in addition to gleaning more information of the issues and problems, and areas of conflict. The data were arranged as cognitive maps (Eden et al., 1983). We felt this was an important and useful way to organise and analyse the vast quantity of information being collected. The analysis strategy was based on the use of cognitive mapping as a form of text analysis. It should be emphasised that this is very different from the more simple quantitative forms of text or content analysis that are based solely around numerical counts of the occurrence of key concepts or phrases; the analysis we used works with the structures of the text as well as their content.

Documents, interview transcripts and group discussion transcripts were examined to identify effects connected to the key questions identified above, which form the conceptual framework for the analysis. These were converted to maps similar to cognitive maps. For the interviews with the key stakeholders, we used the well-tested cognitive mapping approach (Eden et al., 1983), which we have found to be highly compatible with other forms of text analysis. Cognitive mapping allows the researcher to map the beliefs of the person being interviewed about the causal relationships between elements in a situation or issue. The map takes the form of a diagram with various elements linked by arrows. Where an arrow links two elements, the strength of the person's belief that there is a causal relationship can be represented by a numerical value assigned to the arrow. Maps from different individuals can be compared easily to identify similarities and differences.

The strength of the method is that it represents complex information in a visually accessible form, and is capable of exploring chains of reasoning. This was particularly important for the work because of the need to appreciate interrelations between many different factors. The method also allows one to work with individuals confidentially, representing their views in a manner that is not likely to identify them when they are made public. This was crucial to the work: people may discuss relationships within and between agencies, and they must be guaranteed confidentiality for the outputs to be meaningful. Different stakeholders have different roles in the project activities, for example: some collating information, others using what has been collated, etc. Cognitive mapping allows us to look at the shaping of the information at each point in this process, so we can see how the output from one individual becomes the input for the next.

The cognitive maps generated can be used in the group workshop sessions as a starting point for discussion, to enable negotiation over shared understandings of particular issues, and to identify areas of agreement and disagreement.

A concurrent piece of analysis was the investigation of group structure. The data were collected both from meetings, on a longitudinal basis, and from the interviews. This allowed both business–professional and social–expressive relationships to be uncovered. The data were then analysed using social network analysis technique, this is not explored any further here.

C.4 Representation of the issues

The project management team has a membership of eight. It was thought likely that there would be a rich diversity of perspectives among the group members, and hence cognitive mapping was chosen as a way of eliciting and handling the data. A semi-structured interviewing technique was used, which allowed the interviewee the freedom to mention those issues that they saw as important, and also enabled a picture to be built up of the organisation as they perceived it.

Many multiorganisational groups encounter problems of uncertainty and conflict. In this case the problems seemed intensified by the changes that had taken place over the preceding year, so that each member was very unsure of the thoughts and opinions of others. The consequences of this were that the management team members were reluctant to discuss with each other key ideas and opinions, because they were unsure of the reaction of others. This was causing them to feel that the team was not functioning properly.

Many of the issues raised seemed exacerbated by the problem of the value-led versus funding-led conundrum that many voluntary organisations face, see Figure 10.4 for part of the director's map. Funding has become outcome based; the results of this are twofold. Firstly, managers find that they have to tailor their services to fit in with the funding criteria, and this may force them in directions away from their ideals. Secondly, it is increasingly difficult to attract funding for areas such as

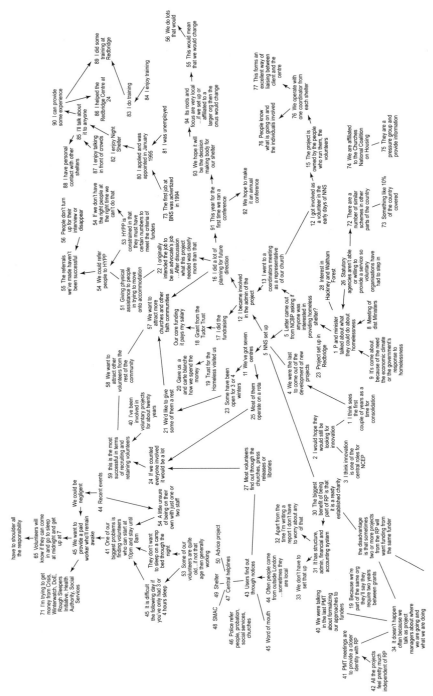

Figure 10.4 Part of Cognitive Map of the Director

administration. The resulting administration charge passed on to the projects by the
organisation was causing conflict between the organisation and the projects. Many
felt unsure about the future direction of the organisation and felt there had been an
unconscious shift away from the original ethos.

A recurring quandary was the role of the management team. Handy (1988)
observes that the difference between teams and committees is that members of a
team have a common goal whereas committee members have to attend as representatives of different functions. In the management team each member is there by
virtue of representing his/her project, but what is their common goal? This leads to
the conclusion that the management team may be better classified as a committee.
Furthermore, Handy (1988:51) claims that 'it is tempting to try to turn committees
into teams, with a common purpose, shared goal and individual contribution;
tempting but unrealistic...'. However, if this group was viewed from a multiorganisational perspective, we may find that the projects benefit from collaborative
advantage by being part of the organisation, in terms of money, support, etc., and
so the meta-strategy ought to be relevant to the management team. With this in
mind it was decided to merge the individual maps and an overall concept map was
produced; see Figure 10.5 for part of the concept map. The key points that emerged
from the maps were broken down into areas of conflict and areas of uncertainty.

One of the hopes of the management team was that through some outside
involvement they may find a way of 'gelling' as a team. A workshop seemed

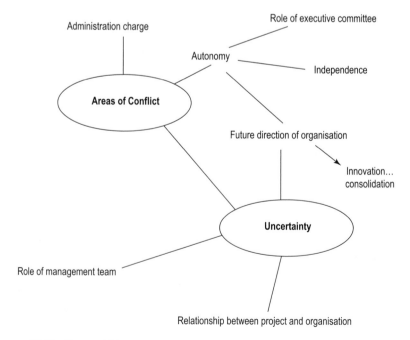

Figure 10.5   Concept Map

appropriate to provide an opportunity for discussion of some of the emerging issues, however, 'awaydays' had been unsuccessful in the past and so there was likely to be wariness. Therefore, it seemed crucial to establish commitment to the model/problem at an early stage.

C.5 First workshop

A number of issues were considered with regard to choice of methodology for the workshop. The lack of social–expressive relationships, coupled with a scarcity of links between projects seemed to be contributing to the difficulties faced by the management team. The need to encourage interaction within the group seemed paramount.

The technique adopted for the workshop was the Strategic Option Development and Analysis (SODA) methodology. This was chosen because of its ability to deal with complex, messy problems, and its focus on uncovering different perceptions as a tool to aid negotiation. Another benefit was that it was hoped it would help to develop high levels of ownership of the problem quickly.

The concept map was fed back to the group and the discussion quickly progressed. Often conversations around certain points would develop between the participants which were allowed to continue, increased interaction was one of the aims of the workshop, and these normally resulted in new suggestions for the map. The process inspired fresh thinking about the organisation's problems and also its strengths.

The map had enabled the management team to clarify their thoughts and it provided a model of the context of their problem. The next stage was for them to decide what they wanted to discuss in more detail at a later date. All participants seemed less reserved than at the start and each generated a number of ideas which were shared and put to a vote. It was decided that the design of a five-year plan for the organisation would be most useful, incorporating issues such as attitude towards independence and financial planning.

The group felt that it had been important in the reduction of potential conflict to have an outside facilitator involved who therefore had 'no axe to grind'. Also, they felt the model had promoted thinking about the issues and that they had not only learnt more about each others perceptions but had also uncovered a number of uncertainties they held personally. In addition they felt they had been given the space needed to share views. From an observer's point of view it seemed that the group had become more interactive, and discussion of points raised during the workshop continued immediately afterwards between individual members. The director suggested that in future management team meetings it may be useful to devote a section to discussing issues in a similar way to the workshop.

C.6   Commentary: PANDA in action

This case study illustrates a number of points. First, the umbrella organisation is an example of a multiagency setting typical in the voluntary sector/non-governmental sector. In many instances, umbrella organisations may be made up of a diversity of organisations that may have in common the fact that they share a building, or have grown out of small projects set up by the original organisation or group. Handy (1988) refers to these as 'tight-loose' organisations – they hold loosely on to a lot of things. Umbrella organisations usually form when an organisation, through its project work, grows, i.e. the projects themselves become organisations with some resources. However, in most cases the projects cannot sustain themselves without the help of the parent organisation, for example help with administration. Thus, the parent organisation takes care of the core functions. Tensions arise when the projects feel they should be independent, and the parent organisation feels it is losing control and is unable to co-ordinate activities.

A recent published case study on Nucleus Housing (Taket and White, 1994; Rosenhead and White, 1996) describes work with an umbrella organisation. The organisation had similar characteristics to case C. The organisation was growing and some of the projects under it wanted to be independent while at the same time the organisation felt that if some of the groups became independent, it would lose its collective strength which may undermine its ability to influence funders and policy. Crucial to the functioning of the umbrella is the way the committee representing the different projects operates. The dilemma faced is balancing two principles of diversity and uniformity. In case C here and the Nucleus study, the form of governance was via a multiagency committee that needed to operate as a collective but at the same time acknowledge the different needs each project had. In both studies, the other confounding factor was that the pattern of the committee occasionally changes, bringing with it a sense of disruption. When the organisation or umbrella keeps on altering there may not be a flexibility within the structure to handle it. In the early days of the east London consortium, a dominant player brought uniformity to the diversity, but in light of the change in personnel a period of uncertainty ensued. The aim of the work with the consortium was to help them find the balance between uniformity and diversity without the organisation losing its integrity *vis-à-vis* its clients and funders. The processes used in the study were an attempt to help the organisation find a diverse unity. This oxymoron was the conundrum the group was trying to solve.

Work was done with the team that undertook the core functions. The team felt it was being pulled in different directions and also that it was perceived as ineffective. Processes such as cognitive mapping and the strategic choice approach helped to highlight the tensions and share perspectives. This helped the team tremendously in being able to deal with the difficult situation.

Case C and the Nucleus Housing case study illustrate another problem. Both organisations were left in a vacuum when the originators of the projects left. This was, for both organisations, seen as an opportunity and a problem. It was an opportunity in the sense that it could attempt to steer a different course and redirect its efforts along different lines. However, it was a problem in that the organisation's image was forged in the shape of the originator and it was difficult to break with this.

The main issue dealt within case C is conflict. In the study we find that the management committee members were reluctant to discuss their ideas and opinions with each other because they felt unsure of the reaction of others. They felt that the committee was not functioning properly. This was also felt in the growing tension between the committee and the projects. Dealing with conflict is a major issue in multiagency working. When it comes to conflict much of the literature is concerned with the need to resolve it. However, conflict can be a positive force in that it can encourage the group to question group norms and consider alternatives. Its absence may lead a group to indulge in 'groupthink' (Janis, 1972). Alvesson (1987) suggests that conflict can stimulate new ideas, and improve cohesiveness within a group. Conflict can be harnessed and can contribute to attaining better decisions through the input of divergent opinions. This was seen in the Nucleus case study referred to earlier (Taket and White, 1994; Rosenhead and White, 1996). The divergent views and beliefs were harnessed and this resulted in decisions that were qualitatively better than otherwise possible if the conflict between the members of the group was not harnessed.

It is widely acknowledged that conflict is an integral element of organisational life (Kahn and Katz, 1966). Nicholson (1970) defines a conflict to exist when two people wish to carry out acts which are mutually inconsistent. This definition defines the simplest form of conflict. In a group setting, the participants may be representatives of different departments or increasingly, of different organisations. In a multiorganisation or multiagency setting, each organisation will have its own goals and its own values, and as Pettigrew (1971) observes, the more complex, heterogeneous and differentiated a political structure is, the more likely are disparate demands to be made. He claims that in the absence of a clearly set system of priorities conflict is likely to ensue. In addition to the accepted factors of different perceptions and objectives, Friend (1993) has observed a further source of uncertainty and conflict in his work with multiorganisational groups compared with traditional 'team-like' groups in that the individual group members may have varying levels of power to commit their organisation to action within the multiorganisational context. The uncertainties and conflicts that result are exacerbated by behavioural factors such as group history and personality traits, and the ability of the group to make decisions is strongly dependent on the ability of group members to interact.

In the Nucleus case study, it was suggested that conflict management rather than conflict resolution was needed. It was recognised that if you dealt with conflict by attempting to resolve it, at best the conflict is only partially dissolved, only to precipitate at a later date. If on the other hand, the members of the group can openly discuss their values and preferences the conflict can be managed and an agreement for action can be reached. The objective is to see conflict as being a creative and useful side of the barrier that divides opposing views. In order to manage conflict, an understanding of the different types may be useful. Pruzan (1991) offers three classes of conflict:

- Intra-personal conflict, where the individuals have difficulty in arriving at a decision because no single decision is optimal with respect to all of their values.
- Interpersonal conflict, where the members of a group have difficulty balancing their own values and aspiration with the other members of the group.
- Systemic conflict, where the individuals not only have to consider their own and the group's values but also those of all the stakeholders affected by the potential decision.

The intra-personal and systemic forms are most likely to be found in non-profit making, value-led organisations, and in those multiorganisations working for collaborative advantage (Huxham, 1996). In contrast, Paelinck and van Gastel (1992) define two aspects of conflict:

- Structural: issues involved, parties concerned, underlying values, overt objectives, the environment of the conflict system.
- Behavioural: i.e. strategies and tactics, patterns of interaction, direct or indirect efforts to bring pressure to bear on an adversary.

Case C exhibits both kinds, which act to reinforce each other. The issue for managing the conflict is to enable the participants to share in understanding issues giving rise to the conflicts. Cognitive mapping proved to be extremely helpful in that it displayed the varying perspectives and allowed the participants to interrogate the maps and not each other. They were able to address issues rather than personalities. Good facilitation proved invaluable in that it addressed issues relating to the individual characteristics of the group members, i.e. individual biases, and differences in power. This involved the ability to recognise and generate alternative options for dealing with conflict.

Finally, in the situation described in case C, it was difficult to expect the group to reach a consensus, even within a voluntary organisation where it is often assumed that democracy and participation are prime. In practice a system of consent is a sensible goal, however, it may feel as though it is not enough.

CASE D: NEEDS ASSESSMENT THROUGH MULTIAGENCY WORKING

D.1   Background

The Penge and Anerley Community Development Project was set up to address problems of inequality in health and to improve health and quality of life for people living in the area. From local data the following were identified as key issues:

- The needs of the high number of single-parent and low-income families in the area (6.5% compared to 2.8% in Bromley as a whole).
- The particular health issues of black and ethnic minority groups (12.8% compared to 4.7% in Bromley as a whole) including the needs of the refugee communities in the area (190 families registered with GPs).
- The high levels of stress, depression and mental health problems relating to high levels of unemployment (11.1% compared to Bromley), deprivation and associated social issues. (Anecdotal evidence indicates that on high stress estates, unemployment is around 15%).
- The needs of young families with children under five who are a group known to use health and other community-based services more often (the area has the second highest level of households with children under five; 13.4% compared to 11.3% for Bromley as a whole).

The project has a primary care focus and aims to complement the work of the wider primary care services. It uses a community development approach to identify local concerns and develop fresh approaches to tackle issues that affect people's health and quality of life on a daily basis. Its aim is to encourage multiagency working through the development of networks between voluntary and statutory agencies and community groups.

D.2 Context

At the beginning of 1996, Bromley Council decided to bid for central government funding through the Single Regeneration Budget Programme (SRB) for the Crystal Palace area which includes the wards of Penge and Anerley. Bordering on the London boroughs of Southwark, Lambeth, Lewisham and Croydon, Penge and Anerley has many of the characteristics and problems of inner-city areas and is generally considered to be the most deprived locality in the borough.

The chief executive of the health authority gave an organisational commitment to supporting the council bid. At a meeting of directors in April 1996 to discuss Bromley Health's input into the regeneration of the area it was agreed that:

- The council focus on the locality provided an opportunity for Bromley Health to look at Penge and Anerley and to set out a public perspective on the health needs of the locality.
- This was an opportunity to develop a co-ordinated approach with other agencies inputting into the locality to improve health and quality of life.
- Bromley Health would need to put resources in that would fit into primary care purchasing.

Against this backdrop, the shift that was starting towards purchasing and providing health services locally though primary care, along with the introduction of new arrangements for providing practice-based health promotion activity, opened up new opportunities for innovative projects involving local people and primary care teams together in identifying and addressing health and social needs of population groups.

This emphasis on new approaches was also reflected in Bromley Health's five year purchasing strategy which gave an organisational commitment to developing community involvement in the improvement of health in identified localities. In addition a pilot 'Healthy Bromley' partnership community development project in the Cray's area of Bromley, established two years previously, had demonstrated successes in:

• Establishing new partnerships between agencies and the voluntary sector.
• Identifying the concerns and tackling the issues affecting health and quality of life of local residents in the area.

Bromley Health was keen to replicate a community development model in Penge and Anerley. In the meantime, the council continued with their submission for SRB funding. Although the health authority were subsequently involved in drawing up proposals for the SRB bid, the attempt to get a clear 'health' component into the bid did not fit into the then central government criteria for regeneration.

As a result a decision was taken to establish a new Community Health project which would use a community development approach as a strategy for engaging local people to:

1. Establish a model for identifying and meeting their own health needs.
2. Influence the planning and provision of health and social care services according to local people's expressed needs affecting their health and quality of life.

It was also intended that the new initiative would both complement and support the regeneration work of the local authority and act as a catalyst for addressing problems of inequality in health in Penge and Anerley.

Funding was committed in May by the health authority to extend the Cray Community Development Co-ordinator's role to Penge and Anerley and to fund a community development post for the area.

The six-month period between Bromley Health's initial decision to 'do something in Penge and Anerley' and the advertising of the community development post in October 1996 gave the project important and much needed 'lead in' time to:

• Scope the possibilities and options for a new locality based community project.
• Facilitate and co-ordinate working up a project proposal and cross-organisational support and involvement in working up a project proposal and developing the project's aims and objectives.
• Collect baseline information on both the locality and activity that the project would undertake.
• Identify academic support for developing the project's action research base and assisting with its evaluation.

- Establish an initial multiagency project steering group.
- Engage the support of key agencies such as Ravensbourne NHS Community Trust, Joint Commissioning, Broomleigh Housing Association and Bromley Council for Voluntary Services.

This planning process, detailed below, clearly assisted in both giving the new project and its new worker a high profile and a firm base to start from. Work involved the following:

1. A cross-organisational Bromley Health Penge and Anerley Co-ordinating Group was initially established to collect, collate and share information on the area. Two meetings focused on (a) mapping of current activity, (b) reviewing past and current work and (c) identifying gaps and current priorities.
2. South Bank University expressed an interest in supporting the project via a Department of Health funded initiative to strengthen the research base in community and primary care. As a result the university was formally attached to the project in an advisory basis. This included assisting with the initial setting up of the project.

D.3   First workshop: setting the objectives for the project

The first workshop took place in November 1996 to develop the aims and expected outcomes for the project. The workshop used a combination of concept mapping and nominal group technique. With so many different interests represented, adopting a diagrammatic approach allowed the participants to listen and share views and information on the project. The workshop lasted four hours and the participants produced the aims shown in Table 10.1.

Throughout the workshop ideas on outcomes and benefits were collated and the items shown in Table 10.2 were prioritised by the participants.

D.4   Second workshop: tightening up the scope

As with most new project work there is a crucial early stage in which those who have generated the project are challenged to identify in more or less precise terms the objectives for the project. This stage was identified by the project as 'tightening up the objectives'. Since the initiators had already developed a set of objectives for the project it became apparent after the funding was awarded that they would need further clarification. Initially, the initiators planned a workshop with key stakeholders. The workshop had dual usage. From the point of view of the initiators it was to gain acceptance for the project and to involve the stakeholders in identifying the objectives. The second usage was to bring to the table community health development for the stakeholders to appreciate. The initiators felt that there was a

Table 10.1 Aims for the Project Produced at the First Workshop

1. To develop a model and a structured approach to involving local people / patients in identifying issues that affect their health and influencing the planning and provision of services to improve health.
2. To provide a locality based, primary care focus to the future commissioning of services by establishing an initial needs assessment project in a GP practice in the Penge and Anerley areas which will gather, co-ordinate and analyse information to provide more comprehensive future planning of services and develop a framework for preventative health initiatives.
3. To bring to the attention of statutory providers and the voluntary sector aspects of 'health' that are not being addressed effectively, i.e. isolation and poor mental health of single parents; homeless families, health and social needs and access to primary care; the health and social needs of black and ethnic minority groups and their use of services, etc.
4. To establish a community development health project attached to primary care with a view to developing different approaches to promoting health and self-help and a more holistic programme of interventions.

Table 10.2 Participants' Priorities for a Model for Involvement

Model for public/patient involvement which will provide:

1. People/patient-led identification of health and social care needs in the practice
2. Local input into the planning of health care services
3. Influence the provision of services from other agencies
4. Development of local people/practice-led initiatives aimed to promote health and quality of life
5. The start of locally based self-help community action
6. Mechanisms for monitoring and evaluating the effectiveness of the process of community involvement and development
7. Strengthening of relationships between primary care teams and voluntary and community sector

lot of scepticism about the approach that needed to be addressed and also in their early objectives it was stated that they wanted a wider appreciation of community health development by the health authority.

A workshop was then held in January 1997 for key people in the health authority and Joint Commissioning to:

- Provide an update on appointment of worker and plans for the management and funding of the project.
- To explore ideas for the community health development project and to develop a shared understanding of how the project fits with other health and quality of life initiatives in the locality.

- To consider the current structures and mechanisms which enable the statutory authorities and voluntary sector to gather information in order to prioritise, plan and provide services that improve health.
- To develop broad-based criteria for selecting a GP base for the project.

For the workshop the facilitator decided to use elements of soft systems methodology, mapping and strategic choice approach. Throughout the workshop the rich pictures and systems maps were used as the focus for debate and discussion. The group in the first instance focused on gaps and uncertainties. The following were identified as important to deal with through the project:

- In eliciting information from local people, there are gaps in understanding the different ways of collecting the data.
- There are gaps in knowledge on community groups – who are they? And where are they?
- There are gaps in knowledge on how different bodies/groups/organisations communicate with each other. Perhaps one could undertake an overall mapping exercise.
- There are gaps in knowledge on how primary care can be linked to the voluntary sector and local authority.
- There is a need to bridge the gaps in data.
- There is a need to understand the role of the project in relation to the primary care role.
- There are gaps in knowledge on where other primary care health professionals fit into the project (such as pharmacists and dentists).

From the discussion 'Where does the Community Health project fit in?' the following were identified:

- Needs assessment may lead to improved communication.
- Are there the requisite skills in GP team (e.g. health visitors can help provide needs information)? By using the skills within the practice for gathering information, the results might lead to better ways of deploying services. A good example of a local needs assessment project in Bromley is the Brook Lane Rapid Appraisal.
- If the aim is holistic health, how does one develop a means of collecting or eliciting good data on needs that can use both Bromley Health Needs Assessment statistics and data from community development needs assessment?
- How does one get voluntary groups to work more closely with primary care? Can the Community Health project facilitate this? There is an opportunity, from this project, to identify services and influence their developments.
- Will the Community Health project use the range of data (such as Bromley Health needs assessment, rapid appraisal, skill mix data)? How will they fit together? And how will the project play a role in enabling this to happen?

- There is an organisational issue here, in terms of making this happen, there is also a methodological problem in terms of working with the range of information. The project, since it is looking at one practice, can be a pilot to address these issues.
- Confidentiality may be an issue.

These issues provided the benchmark to further develop the scope for the project. It was clear that the project would be seen as a pilot to see whether there would be any benefits to the health authority in having this approach. It was also clear that there was a level of scepticism about whether the results emerging from the project would be valid and or add value to the current work on needs assessment already being carried out, and finally there was an interest in seeing whether a project can provide benefits to primary care by operating from a GP practice.

The outcomes from this early stage were clearer directions for the project and a clearer understanding of the role the project will or should have in relation to primary care and commissioning.

Following this meeting several other feedback meetings were held and clearer objectives for the project were identified. At the same time a multiagency steering group for the project began to take shape and public health and primary care were represented as well as Joint Commissioning, and the voluntary sector.

The workshop enabled participants to explore how a community health project could fit into the existing structures in the locality and resulted in identifying membership of the initial project steering group and involvement in the recruitment of the new community worker.

Subsequently, Jane Brown, a previous practice nurse with experience of cross-agency working with a Local Agenda 21 project in Sussex, was appointed to the post of the Penge and Anerley Community Health Development Project in February 1997. The Penge and Anerley Project was up and running.

D.5   Commentary: PANDA in action

The main issue that emerged from this case study was the need to develop a multiagency steering group. Steering groups have become an important form of governance for projects, but the development of such groups has often been neglected. It is often the case that a steering group usually brings together interested stakeholders and no attention is paid to the way this group works. Meetings are invariably run with an agenda and at the top of the agenda is a progress report for the project. Another issue is that the group may meet no more than monthly, and if the group is constantly changing its pattern of membership, this may lead to a lack of progress made in relation to steering the project. The dynamic pattern of diversity is important to deal with in this situation. The diversity of membership is important in order for a rich debate on the issues to be possible, and it also increases the opportunities for innovation. In the case study attention was paid to these issues and attempts at breaking with the traditional meeting and running participative workshops meant that the group can not only gel, but the changing patterns of diversity can also be accommodated.

A number of thinkers have claimed that meetings are too linear and not conducive to creativity (Beer, 1979; Emery, 1969; Friend and Hickling, 1987). As one of these commentators puts it:

> Then a technique is needed that recognises that if a meeting sets out with an agenda, it has structured the whole outcome in advance. Anything truly novel has two minutes as Any Other Business. Second, the meeting is merely a series of platforms for those who determine the agenda on which to ride their familiar hobby horse. Third the requirement to put the agenda in order says something about the priorities of the organiser rather than the exigencies of the problems (Beer, 1995:8).

Friend and Hickling (1987) discuss the problem when meetings are conducted where the communication is sequential. That is, 'an individual sits on a chair (symbolising a defined organisational role), with successive matters for decision arriving in an "in" tray on the table (symbolising the agenda). The matters are dealt with in sequence, agreed rules are applied and decisions are then transferred to the "out" tray one at a time' (Friend and Hickling, 1987:18). The process of working together means that this linear form of working operates with only one form of thinking. It is difficult in this circumstance to embrace verbal and non-verbal forms of communication together; most of the creative exchanges happen in the shadows of the meeting, i.e. during the coffee breaks or afterwards over a beer. But often these ideas fail to gel and end up drifting off or disappearing.

New ways of working in meetings are needed which can help to create an atmosphere of collaboration and creativity. We have outlined, in our earlier chapters, processes that can start the ball rolling.

CASE E: PARTICIPATIVE DEMOCRATISATION OF WORK IN A UNIVERSITY DEPARTMENT (IN A NON-DEMOCRATIC CONTEXT): WHAT ACTUALLY HAPPENED

This case study is drawn from an account provided to us by the initiator of the work described here, the Head of Department, and used with his permission. At his request, this is presented as an anonymised case study.

> 'Meetings are the lifeblood of a good university and the sewage of a bad one.'

E.1 Starting off

A smallish university, 5000 full-time student equivalents or 9000 warm bodies, multi-campus with the main campus located in a country town, population 60,000. The nearest universities are 700 km away. The Department is large, having one-sixth of the university's students, about the same size as some faculties. Staff number about 45: 33 academic and 12 general.

The Department expanded quite rapidly through the 1980s. Our rather informal organisation was getting a bit creaky by 1990. The problem as it appeared to the Head was what to do and how to do it, and since the 'what' was not completely obvious the 'how' took centre stage. During 1991 chewing things over with colleagues elsewhere, a participative design workshop was suggested. As the place was also in transition to becoming a university, I felt it wise to wait until the main new features were in position. Premature standardisation and then having to undo things can be rather painful. So in 1991 I started to sell these two ideas, got reasonably good acceptance. In 1993 we held our participative design workshop, now known as PDW1. I approached the workshop with two questions in mind. One was how to achieve parity of esteem between academic and general staff. The other was what to do about the two subject areas present in the Department: roughly speaking, one-third of academic staff thought of themselves as one, one-third the other, and one-third both. There was a strong body of opinion that we split into two and a strong body that we should not.

E.2 Participative design workshop 1 (PDW1)

The approach was based on Fred and Merrelyn Emery's *Participative Design* (1989, this is also described in Chapter 6), run as a three-day residential search conference. This produced:

- Scenarios of our environment
- Values
- Mission
- Outline plans to achieve goals

One extremely useful move was to construct a matrix wherein each member of staff expressed their job satisfaction. Overall we came across as a reasonably well satisfied lot, though everybody said they wanted more feedback on their performance. However one subgroup of the general staff came out as hemmed in and fairly unhappy.

As a social event the workshop was splendid.

We ran out of time but put into position the essence of the new organisation. This was:

1. The Department organise itself as three self-managed groups (SMGs), support staff, and two subject groups, with overlapping membership, each individual went to whichever groups he/she wished.
2. These groups were linked in the Whole of Department Meeting, WoD.
3. The WoD was likely to prove a little unwieldy so it had the Executive reporting to it. The Executive was a pre-existing body which met weekly and now had representatives from the SMGs.
4. the Head was the main interface with the university and the outside and left to sort out the role as best he could.
5. The Department's functional groups (Board of Studies, Equipment Committee and all the others) were to continue so that we stay in business, and to democratise themselves one by one.
6. We dispense with paper and do everything on e-mail.

It was agreed to hold a workshop annually.

E.3   What happened next

Initialisation was quite chaotic. The three groups were of size 10–15, a bit on the large side. The job of the Head might have been quite crucial for he had to be in there refusing to tell anyone what to do, maintaining the faith, occasionally asking questions and visibly not taking sides. Meetings, meetings, meetings, it took a lot of time, frustrating time.

Each group had to work out what to do and how to run itself. The academics were used to it but the support staff were not. Some very serious personality problems came to the fore. There were some very anxious times. All three groups had problems. The nadir, the pits, came in the middle of 1994 when a few key staff left. This was normal accident, indeed self-management, and realising what they were letting their colleagues in for made the departure particularly poignant. It was from this time that the quotation with which I started this case study comes.

Thus at PDW2, two months later, the news was not uniformly good. Quite a few members of the Department felt (a) they did not understand how decisions were made. Others knew very well. This lack of clarity was taken on board by a working party charged with delineating the structure and procedures and streamlining them. There was a feeling (b) that we had not sufficient identity, did not know where we are going. And (c) there was a lack of evaluation/review/feedback in 'everything we do'.

It is very important when running a PDW or Search Conference to make it as self-contained as possible. Work left to be done in a busy committed organisation takes far too long. Point (b), a lack of 'mission and objectives', is actually a task left over from PDW1. The person who took the job on after PDW1 never gained final agreement on the mission, and so he went off to pursue some less intractable tasks. It is now intended that this be the task of PDW3, though renamed 'aspirations' and 'plans'. Moreover a group of us will stay there after the PDW until our distillation of butcher's paper and writing is done.

E.4   Taking stock, after PDW2, approaching PDW3

The Support Self Managed Group is generally agreed to be the best thing which has happened to the Department since its creation. They are respected, liked, and chair some of the Department's key committees and working parties. Getting there was indeed a tale of valour and renown. Eight women and four men. That might have something to do with it. They are young, enthusiastic, took PDW1 at face value and were keen to get on with it. However there was a problem, initially around supervision, but also involving personal clashes. Eventually the support group took itself off for a workshop. One member did not attend. The support group did two things, restyled itself, and produced proposals for restructuring around the missing member's position. Meantime the missing member had secured a secondment to another part of the university.

Of the two subject groups, one just buckled down and set to work. One senior member of staff had not attended PDW1 and did not intend to participate, he has continued this way and become extremely isolated. There are also a few sceptics (possibly two). The group had a very major task to address in restructuring the degree. This task has been completed. The new course is quite radical. The combination of an exuberant Professor and an SMG has worked wonderfully well.

The second subject SMG is the biggest, the busiest, and in the early stages the least successful. It is difficult to pin down just why for they are true believers if anyone is. With hindsight it seems that they took on board too much. At any rate they appeared to be going in circles with the agenda getting longer and longer and in 1994 they took themselves off for a day and restructured themselves as a group with small staffing, research, teaching, and some other subgroups, since when it has worked very well. It might be that the group was just too big and diverse to work in any other way.

The Liaison Group, as the Executive is about to restyle itself, works nicely. It consists of two representatives from each group, the Head, Deputy, Chair of Board of Studies, Professors and Finance Officer. It meets weekly with a basic function to keep everyone up to date on what is happening, to be a source of cross-group advice, and to make decisions. The format is a quick report from the Head and each group, followed by any other matters which have to be dealt with. Importantly, the minutes are on e-mail for everyone (as are all minutes and agendas) and the SMG reps report back to the group what happened.

The WoD, Whole of Department Meeting meets once a month and does not seem to do anything, but nobody seems to mind. Perhaps it is too big and exists mainly as a safeguard and social function. The Liaison Group gets on with the real business, has to, and the PDWs deal with really significant stuff.

The functional groups, Board of Studies, Budget Committee, Equipment Committee, Overseas Operations Group and so on are where most of the decisions are finalised. Where appropriate they are democratised with structural group representation and an elected chair. Some groups, Overseas Operations for example, rely on specialised knowledge, have to work fast and very reliably, and so consist of the experts but report back on what they have done.

There is a back-up procedure. If a decision is needed and a functional group cannot meet to make it, the Liaison Group makes it, and if the time line is even shorter than that the Head makes it, reporting back to the group each time.

The foregoing bald account rather misses the flavour. The three SMGs meet weekly, and change their chair and deputy monthly or three-monthly. There is a great determination not to introduce hierarchy. The spin-off in energy, initiative and general understanding has been remarkable and continues.

As you can see it is a process, continually changing. This is no optimisation in pursuit of an objective. We just do the best we can in terms of what we can see and believe to be just over the horizon which itself is always changing, while being constrained in resources, mainly time.

A week before writing this, one subject group suggested that we not hold PDW3 on the grounds that PDW2 had not been implemented and we were all too busy anyway. (This is indeed for real. It has been a very tough year so far.) Since we had to make a decision fast yet sufficiently democratically I sent a side of A4 note to the groups putting their case against persuasively and accurately and the case in favour of PDW3 neutrally. The other SMGs were unanimously in favour and the dissenting group changed its mind. It is really exciting to be with a bunch who you might take to be unreconstructed positivists talking about process and interaction, and recognising that important though the work we do at a PDW may be, it is the *social* bit that makes the glue holding us together.

And a last observation. Do not even think about participative democracy unless your department is fairly open and enthusiastic. The common style of management is by fear and patronage (and it works quite well actually, people know what to expect). Get rid of fear and patronage first. Participative democracy is eliminating personal hierarchy. It needs a lot of trust which will be sorely tested in the early stages. And one does not know what to expect and has to be prepared to welcome that on a global faith the system will continue to be open and fair.

E.5 Afterword

The foregoing presents an abbreviated version of the Head of School's account. Views of staff as to the success of the process are not radically dissimilar, further workshops have solved some of the issues raised above and raised further ones for action. Perhaps the most telling outcome is that the structures set up continued to flourish, change and evolve, after the Head is no longer part of the Department.

E.6 Commentary: PANDA in action

There are a number of points we would like to make in relation to this case study. First of all we notice that it involves a programme of change, carried out over a number of years, from the beginning of the 1990s, up until the present day. To us, it seems obvious that the role of the facilitator, here the Head of Department, was crucial in several ways: in building support for starting the process of change; in modelling the new roles implied in the change sought; and in responding to the dynamics of what occurred in the light of new roles and responsibilities – in this case by letting things take their course. In terms used elsewhere in the literature, we can see the role of the Head as a product champion or as a change agent; Bain (1998), in discussing three action research/action learning projects (spanning private and public sectors), also identifies the importance of such a 'high-level' support in project success.

The case study demonstrates the possibilities of achieving participatory, democratic ways of working, in parts of an organisation, even when the rest of the organisation, in this case the university, was operating in a traditional, hierarchical model. Note, however, that accommodations, in terms of interfaces with the rest of the university, had to be made to achieve this. Again here the role of the Head of Department seems crucial as the changes were being established, and we note that change of Head has not affected this so far. We note also that not every member of the Department chose to participate. Some effectively exited from the process and the structures while remaining in their posts, something that while possible within this setting, might not be so achievable in others. Others exited entirely from the Department.

In terms of the processes used within the case study, overall planning and strategy making utilised the PDW and was carried out by the Department as a whole. The SMGs have evolved their own ways of working, as indeed has the whole of the department for the operational decision-making between PDWs. We have not discussed in detail the work in these groups, save to note that there is no requirement for uniformity, either between groups or within groups over time.

The multiagency features of this case study are several: firstly, in terms of the two different academic subject areas and the general staff; secondly, in terms of the different relationships of individuals to the university hierarchy outside the Department. The structures that were put in place were designed in order to accommodate both these features.

There are a number of case studies in the literature which it is interesting to contrast with case E. Chisholm (1996) reports a case study of a network organisation, the New Baldwin Corridor Coalition in Harrisberg, Pennsylvania, USA. This coalition was aimed to involve government, labour, community, business and education leaders and regional institutions in the creation of a prototypical twenty-first-century community that can compete globally and provide an advanced standard of living, focusing on business revival, educational integration, governmental restructuring, housing and human services among other things.

Network development work has involved an action research process, which included a strategic planning meeting based on (substantially) modified search conference design. The 96 participants in this meeting came from the business, government, education, labour and community sectors, with broadly similar representation from each. The guidelines/ground rules for this conference were presented in Table 8.3. The outcomes of the conference, detailed in Chisholm (1996), demonstrated the ability of a large diverse group of practitioners to work together on the detailed task of network design. The process used is similar to that in case E, yet here we see its effectiveness in a much broader multiagency setting. Chisholm also emphasises the importance of careful preparation, including exchange of background information on participants in this situation, which involved individuals who did not have uniform and detailed knowledge of each other prior to working together.

Working within the same setting as case E, although in a different country, Russell and Peters (1998) report on the 'New Directions' programme of the UK's Open University. This programme 'deliberately created a "chaotic" space for random communication across organizational boundaries – so that the organization can begin to learn as a whole and respond faster to change' (Russell and Peters, 1998:236). Initiatives included workshops for random cross-sections of staff, conferences, theme workshops, working groups, etc. One strand that deliberately set out to tackle the organisational learning process directly was a series of workshops on 'making better mistakes – banishing the blame culture'. Initiatives were set up to 'facilitate self-organization' (Russell and Peters, 1998:239). Russell and Peters (1998:245) report that: 'The pattern of events, of which the New Directions programme has been part, is complex. There is no simple cause–effect chain that we can follow to prove conclusively that the programme did what it set out to do.'

Actions did occur in communications, restructuring of units, etc. This provides an interesting contrast to case E, in its much broader scope, namely an entire university. The findings reported by Russell and Peters echo those of case E, in that people, given agreement on what they need to do and some simple guidelines/ directions, managed to organise themselves to take appropriate action without needing detailed structure or plans. They concluded that although there was no clear cause–effect link between the events in the New Directions programme and the changes that have taken place, they are clear indications that it encouraged organisational learning, and a direct link between individual learning/empowerment (their use of the term) and organisational learning. In these respects the findings are very similar to those in case E, although the scale and the wider context (in terms of the different countries involved, with marked differences in their higher education sectors) are markedly different.

Lest this paint too rosy a picture and leave the impression that all that is required is to let people get on with it, it is important to recognise that in other contexts, more is definitely required. This returns us to our point that generalisation is dangerous; specific responses, tailored to the specifics of the circumstances, are required. Elsewhere in this book, the work described in Boxes 8.3 and 8.7 illustrates examples of where such a hands-off approach would not have been productive. Another example is provided by Onyett et al. (1997) who examine the multiagency work involved in community mental health teams in the UK, and indicate that a more active facilitation role is required in order to avoid what Hackman (1990) has identified as trip wires to be avoided when establishing productive work groups:

1. Describing the performing unit as a team, but continuing to manage members as individuals.
2. Failing to exercise appropriate authority over the team, leaving it to clarify its own aims and objectives.
3. Providing inadequate internal structures for operational management — leaving the team to 'work out the details'.
4. Failing to provide organisational supports in the form of rewards, training, information and the material resources required to get the job done.
5. Assuming that team members already have all the competence they need to work well in teams.

Note that we would not elevate Hackman's trip wires to the status of a general law. We would argue that in some circumstances (for example case E above), the specific features of the context are such that these become not trip wires, but assumptions that can be made as describing the features of the situation, but do not prevent productive work groups occurring. We might of course enter into debate about how much more productive things might have been if they were not present, but here we would leave the reality of the case study and depart into speculation. A key feature here is the specific form of power and authority relations in existence (see also our discussion of a BPR case study that follows). A study based on participant observation of a community mental health team reported by Lang (1982) bears this out. Lang identified concealed power relations which were all the more oppressive by being implicit and difficult to challenge owing to supposed consensus operation of teams (re Hackman's trip wire number 2), and noted hierarchies based on gender and team members' facility with jokes based on psychoanalytical principles (re Hackman's trip wire number 3).

As a final contrast, of a different type, to case E, we consider the case study (a postmodern ethnography) of business process re-engineering (BPR) in a division (350 staff) of an Australian public sector organisation reported by Sayer (1998). Here BPR aimed to re-engineer communication processes, but succeeded only in automating existing processes. Middle management felt threatened (fearing change to their power and position through re-engineered communication), and success-fully resisted. They managed this through defining IT as a dangerous tool (using the metaphor of clinical infection, plus also pointing to downgrading of face-to-face communications and personal contact) unless controlled, and succeeded in winning imposition of protocols which effectively prevented re-engineering and resulted in mere automation, and reinforcement of the power of middle management. Sayer concludes: 'There can be no true empowerment until those who are to be empowered are able to participate in the re-engineering discourse. As it presently stands in the re-engineering literature, only those with the power will continue to be empowered. Until the implementation of empowerment is taken out of the hands of those that are to be disempowered (middle management) then the notion of BPR will remain a theoretical concept' (Sayer, 1998:256). In terms of contrast to case E, we might notice that the inability of other participants to counter the metaphor wielded by middle management, meant that the re-engineering that took place was reduced to only automation, with little change occurring. In case E it is difficult to identify such a class of 'middle management'.

SUMMING UP – SOME OBSERVATIONS

In this chapter we have presented five case studies demonstrating PANDA in action. We have already presented many examples drawn from case studies in our practice to illustrate various points in the book. What we have done in this chapter is rather different. Here for each of the five case studies in turn, first we described the whole case, briefly, pointing out the main features of what happened. We then discussed how the case study fits within the PANDA framework. Each case study illustrated how the PANDA framework was applied in practice and the results this had. In the discussion and commentary on each case study we also identified the particular type(s) of multiagency setting that is/are involved and contrasted the findings with other similar case studies elsewhere in the literature.

One important feature to note is the diversity of settings that have been covered in the five cases. One is completely located in the private sector, and one completely in the public sector. The rest are essentially a mixture, although centred on community, non-governmental or public sector organisations. The particular combination in each case varies. The diversity serves to demonstrate to us the widespread applicability of the PANDA framework with which we are concerned. We immediately remind the reader that, as we have emphasised elsewhere in this book, this framework is not prescriptive, offers no guarantees, is driven by a process of critical reflection and requires ongoing choice on the part of those who assume the task of facilitation. As we have indicated in this chapter and elsewhere in this book, we find the existence of many other case studies in the literature based on similar principles, and bearing a variety of labels, such as action research, action learning, participatory action research, organisational development, organisational learning, collaboration and co-operation.

Conclusion 11

'a ludibrium – a playful toying with ideas – more than anything else and contains hidden meanings of which I am not aware. You are invited not to treat it seriously but look for enjoyment and pain where you can find it within the back streets of this imagination'. Burrell (1997:28)

ludo: from the latin to play

PRE-LUDE

This chapter is not to express a finality or closure but a beginning. Thus, it will not offer much in the way of conclusions but opportunities for starting to work or engage in the multiagency setting.

We wish to apologise for the linear nature of the book and we take our cue from other writers such as Burrell (1997) who experimented with trying to break with a linear presentation by having his chapters flowing counter-current with each other. We feel that this is important in that an aspect of our book is to indicate that working in the multiagency setting requires one to break away from applying ideas and techniques sequentially or linearly. Thus, our book should be read as a cook-book, where favourite recipes can be tried and variation on themes encouraged.

We started this book with the view that organisational life is changing, that multiagency working is increasingly seen as important and that partnership has become the touchstone of social and public policy. We have also acknowledged that there are various forms of multiagency working operating in the different sectors and therefore there are a number of terms such as alliances, collaboration, trans-sectoral working to name a few, frequently used to describe this setting. Some commentators have felt that this has led to a quagmire of terminology (Leathard, 1994) where the terms are used interchangeably without having a specific defini-tion. However, whereas most may feel that this can only lead to confusion, to us the fact that there are so many domains grappling with the same notions in all but name is an indication that we are experiencing a sweeping change in organisational life – multiagency working is with us and is a rich source of issues on organisational life. The book is not aimed at explaining this change but to contribute to an understanding of how to manage the multiagency setting in order to gain maximum benefits from participation and partnership in decision-making and action.

We have stated that managing in the multiagency setting is not easy, no single theoretical perspective can serve as a foundation for explaining how to work in the multiagency setting. Most theories take as their focus a single organisation or single sector and ignore the domain dynamics. Most methodologies do not exhibit enough complexity to deal with the complexities of the multiagency setting. In this book we have claimed that a pluralist approach is appropriate. However, in order to deal with the issue of what is best to use and when, we have suggested this needs to be a pragmatic approach as well. We are not declaring that 'anything goes', but 'doing what feels good'. We are not suggesting that choice is unreflective, but that a sceptical rigour is applied, i.e. in a pluralist world we refuse to privilege one statement or view over another. The aim is to be deconstructive. This would mean:

- To find exception to generalisations and grand narratives
- To question rhetorical devices
- To challenge 'taken-for granted' statements
- To acknowledge, respect and work on difference
- To employ new and unusual terminology (following Rorty)

Finally in our prelude we would like to say that in working in the multiagency setting reason and rationality are not enough, confidence in the use of emotions, feelings, intuition, creativity, imagination and flexibility are also priorities. This way managing in the multiagency setting will be participative and involve the social body in all its heterogeneous forms. It will be non-exclusive and non-isolationist and the criteria of evaluation may be in the aesthetic or beauty as judged by the participants in the form of collaboration produced.

INTO THE LUDIBRIUM

Having decided that you are working in the multiagency setting, you may be faced with having to deal with a situation that requires immediate attention or be working in a more developmental fashion over a long period of time. The value of each is that it is recognised that by working with multiple perspectives, there are things that can be achieved that could not have been achieved by working individually. Some authors have called this searching for collaborative advantage (Huxham,

1996). In the multiagency setting advantage is one of the goals being sought, and Huxham views it as the 'focus on the distinctive value of collaboration' (p. 176). What is needed to achieve this is a space where a playful toying with ideas can be achieved and we wish to call this space the 'ludibrium'. It is a place where we can effectively work with different clients, different methods, different modes of facilitation and different modes of representation. It is a place where we can follow a strategy of mix and match, adopting a flexible and adaptive stance and operationalising 'doing what feels good'. It is a place of fun and creativity and also a place where reflection and judgement can take place. We hope it is also a place where constant theorising can happen and new ways of seeking advantage can occur.

We have suggested a whole series of ingredients and offered a number of our favourite recipes. In the ludibrium the recipes can be followed or variations can take place. Each new setting may mean a new set of ingredients, but you may find that only certain combinations work − that is fine too. Other uses of PANDA have seen new combinations and applications that are continuously being improvised and invented (Gibbon, 1999).

The use of PANDA in the multiagency setting has led to groups developing shared meanings which have been in the main iconic and open to all to interrogate and share. Issues are dealt with qualitatively, learning occurs within the group and between the organisations or agencies. Debate and dialogue are also enhanced and the possibility of agreement is enabled in the local situation, but these agreements are fragile. At times these local meanings are shared across the agencies, and at other times concepts emerge through the groups theorising and/or constructing meaning with each other. We have seen that partnerships develop and evolve, however, there needs to be a capacity and willingness to work in partnerships and in a participative way. There needs to be a willingness for agencies to challenge the dynamics of the partnerships and the rules under which they operate. Methods and techniques must evolve to manage the development or evolution of joint working.

Representation is key in working in the multiagency setting; however, a paradox occurs in that the demand for wider representation and inclusiveness in the multiagency setting leads to greater dynamics and difficulties encountered to maintain the arrangement. The roles and structures would have to be different the larger the group becomes.

POST-LUDE

In the book we have talked about the ways you can work in the multiagency setting and the question which will be asked is 'does it work?' and 'how do we know if it works?' Given that the multiagency setting is complex, work in this arena is not simple. Our framework provides a start to work in this setting and from our experience we have found that the participants have enjoyed themselves and found it fun as well as being able to work across boundaries and make decisions.

There is an aesthetic value in working in the multiagency setting which does not preclude having an ethical position (note 'aesthetic' has the word 'ethic' within it). Our aim in managing in the multiagency setting is to produce something qualitatively different that could not have been produced otherwise. This can only be judged to be a success (or not) locally and for that moment – and whatever the verdict, it serves as a stimulus for further work and action.

References

Ackermann, F., Eden, C., Nunamaker, J. and Vogel, D. (1992). Approaches to group-problem solving. *IFIP Transactions — a computer science and technology*, **9**: 323.

Ackoff, R. (1974a). *Redesigning the future*, Wiley, Chichester.

Ackoff, R. (1974b). The social responsibility of operational research. *Operational Research Quarterly*, **25**: 361–371.

Ackoff, R. (1979a). The future of OR is past. *Journal of the Operational Research Society*, **30**: 93–104.

Ackoff, R. (1979b). Resurrecting the future of operational research. *Journal of the Operational Research Society*, **30**: 189–199.

Alvesson, W. (1987). *Consensus, control and critique*. Gower Avebury, Aldershot.

Amason, A.C. (1996). Distinguishing the effects of functional and dysfunctional conflict on strategic decision making: resolving a paradox for top management teams. *Academy of Management Journal*, **39**: 123–148.

Andersen, D.F., Maxwell, T.A., Richardson, G.P. and Stewart, T.R. (1994). Mental models and dynamic decision making in a simulation of welfare reform. *Proceedings of International System Dynamics Conference 1994, Systems Dynamics: exploring the boundaries: social and public policy*, pp. 11–18.

Andersen, D.F. and Richardson, G.P. (1997). Scripts for group model building. *System Dynamics Review*, **13**(2): 107–129.

Argyris, C. (1990). *Overcoming organisation defenses: facilitating organisational learning*. Allen and Bacon, Boston, Mass.

Argyris, C. (1993). *Knowledge for action: a guide to overcoming barriers to organizational change*. Jossey-Bass, San Francisco.

Argyris, C. and Schon, D. (1974). *Theory in practice: increasing professional effectiveness*. Jossey-Bass, San Francisco.

Aronoff, M. and Gunter, V. (1994). A pound of cure — facilitating participatory processes in technological hazard disputes. *Society and Natural Resources*, **7**(3): 235–252.

Ashby, W.R. (1965). *Introduction to cybernetics*. Chapman & Hall, London.

Bachrach, P. and Baratz, M.S. (1970). *Power and poverty: theory and practice*. Oxford University Press, London.

Bain, A. (1998). Social defenses against organizational learning. *Human Relations*, **51**(3): 413–429.

Balbo, L. (1995). Social structure and demography. Paper presented at the World Health Organization third consultation on future trends and the European HFA strategy, Bratislava, 25–27 October 1995, document ICP/HSC 024 (EHFA 01/MT 01)/6.

Bales, R.F. (1950). *Interaction process analysis*. Addison-Wesley, Reading, Mass.

Barker, D. (1980). *TA and training*. Gower, London.

Barnett, E. (1991). *Pictures as discussion starters*. Learning for Health No. 1, Liverpool School of Tropical Medicine.

Baron, R.S., Kerr, N. L. and Miller (1992). *Group process, group decision, group action*. Open University Press, Buckingham.

Baudrillard, J. (1983). *Simulacra and simulations*. Semiotext(e), New York.

Baudrillard, J. (1990). *Fatal strategies*, Pluto, London.

Beath, C.M. and Orlikowski, W.J. (1994). The contradictory nature of system development methodologies: deconstructing the IS–user relationship in information engineering. *Information Systems Research*, **5**(4): 350–377.

Becker, H. (1967). Whose side are we on? *Social Problems*, **14**: 239–247.

Beer, S. (1979). *Heart of the enterprise*. Wiley, Chichester.

Beer, S. (1981). *Brain of the firm*. Wiley, Chichester.

Beer, S. (1985). *Diagnosing the system for organisation*. Wiley, Chichester.

Beer, S. (1995). *Beyond dispute*. Wiley, Chichester.

Belbin, R.M. (1981). *Management teams: why they succeed or fail*. Butterworth Heinemann, Oxford.

Bell, D. (1973). *The coming of post industrial society*. Basic Books, New York.

Bell, S. (1990). If . . . *fatarse the vulture*. Guardian, Saturday 14 July.

Belton, V. (1990). Multi criteria decision analysis. In: Hendry, L.C. and Eglese, R.W. (eds), *Operational research tutorial papers 1990*, Operational Research Society, Birmingham.

Bennett, P.G. and Cropper, S.A. (1986). Helping people choose: conflict and other perspectives. In Belton, V. and O'Keefe, R.M. (eds), *Recent developments in operational research*. Pergamon, Oxford, pp. 13–25.

Berg, B.L. (1984). Inmates as clinical sociologists – the use of sociodrama in a non-traditional delinquency prevention program. *International Journal of Offender Therapy and Comparative Criminology*, **28**(2): 117–124.

Berger, J. (1972). *Ways of seeing*. BBC/Penguin, London.

Berger, P.L. and Luckman, T. (1966). *The social construction of reality*. Penguin, Harmondsworth.

Bhaskar, R. (1989). *Reclaiming reality: a critical introduction to contemporary philosophy*. Verso, London.

Boal, A. (1979). *The Theatre of the Oppressed*. Pluto Press, London.

Bohm, D. (1984). *Thought as a system*. Routledge, London.

Bohm, D. (1985). *Unfolding meaning*. Routledge, London.

Boonekamp, G.M.M., Gutiérrez-Sigler, M.D., Colomer, C. and Vaandrager, H.W. (1996). Opportunities for health promotion. the knowledge and information system of the Valencian food sector, Spain. *Health Promotion International*, **11**(4): 309–319.

Bourdieu, P. (1991). *Language and symbolic power*. Tr. G. Raymond and M. Adamson. Polity, Cambridge.

Bradley, S. (1994). *How people use pictures*. IIED/British Council, London.

Branthwaite, A. and Lunn, T. (1985). Projective techniques in social and market research. In: Walker, R. (ed.), *Applied qualitative research*, Gower, Aldershot.

Brockner, J. (1992). Managing the effects of layoffs on survivors. *California Management Review*, **34** (Winter): 9–27.

Brown, A.D. (1998). Narrative, politics and legitimacy in an IT implementation. *Journal of Management Studies*, **35**(1): 35–58.

Brunsson, N. (1982). The irrationality of action and action rationality: decision, ideologies and organizational actions. *Journal of Management Studies*, **19**: 29–44.

Brunsson, N. (1985). *The irrational organisation*. Wiley, New York.

Bryant, J. (1989). *Problem management: a guide for producers and players*. Wiley, Chichester.

Bryant, J. (1993a). Computer-supported cooperative work: supporting management teams. In: Norman, J.M. (ed.), *Developments in Operational Research*, Operational Research Society, Birmingham.

Bryant, J. (1993b). OR enactment: the theatrical metaphor as an analytic framework. *Journal of the Operational Research Society*, **44**(6): 551–561.

Buckminster Fuller, R. (1979). *Synergetics: the geometry of thinking*. Macmillan, New York.

Burrell, G. (1992). Back to the future: time and organization. In: Reed, M. and Hughes, M. (eds), *Rethinking organization: new directions in organizational theory and analysis*, Sage, London, pp. 165–183.

Burrell, G. (1993). Eco and the bunnymen. In: Hassard, J. and Parker, M. (eds), *Postmodernism and organizations*. Sage, London, pp. 71–82.

Burrell, G. (1997). *Pandemonium: towards a retro-organisation theory*. Sage, London.

Burrell, G. and Morgan, G. (1979). *Sociological paradigms and organisational analysis*. Heinemann, London.

Butler, J.P. (1990). *Gender trouble: feminism and the subversion of identity*. Routledge, New York.

Cacioppe, R. (1997). Leadership moment by moment. *Leadership and Organization Development Journal*, **18**(7) : 335−345.

Cadbury, R. (1993). The partnership challenge: the need for public partnership in urban regeneration. *Public Policy Review*, **1**(3) : 11−12.

Calnan, M. (1987). *Health and illness: the lay perspective*. Tavistock, London.

Chambers, R. (1981). RRA: rationale and repertoire. IDS Discussion Paper 115, Institute of Development Studies, University of Sussex.

Chambers, R. (1994a). The origins and practice of PRA. *World Development*, **22**(7) : 953−965.

Chambers, R. (1994b). Participating rural appraisal: analysis of experience. *World Development*, **22**(9) : 1253−1268.

Chambers, R. (1994c). Participating rural appraisal: challenges, potentials and paradigms. *World Development*, **22**(10) : 1437−1454.

Chavis, D.M. (1995). Building community capacity to prevent violence through coalitions and partnerships. *Journal of Health Care for the Poor and Underserved*, **6**(2) : 234−245.

Checkland, P. (1981). *Systems thinking, systems practice*. Wiley, Chichester.

Checkland, P. (1998). Review of: R.L. Flood, 1995, Solving Problem Solving. *Journal of the Operational Research Society*, **49**(9) : 1014−1015.

Checkland, P. and Holwell, S. (1998). *Information, systems and information systems − making sense of the field*. Wiley, Chichester.

Checkland, P. and Scholes, J. (1990). *Soft systems methodology in action*. Wiley, Chichester.

Chisholm, R.F. (1996). On the meaning of networks. *Group and Organization Management*, **21**(2) : 216−235.

Christiansen, T. (1997). Tensions of European governance: politicized bureaucracy and multiple accountability in the European Commission. *Journal of European Public Policy*, **4**(1) : 73−90.

Church man, C.W. (1968). *The systems approach*. Dell Publishing, New York.

Clegg, S.R. (1990). *Frameworks of power*. Sage, London.

Cooper, R. (1992). Formal organisation as representation. In: Reed, M. and Hughes, M. (eds), *Rethinking organisation*, Sage, London.

Cooper, R. and Burrell, G. (1988). Modernism, postmodernism and organisational analysis: an introduction. *Organisational Studies*, **21**(4) : 391−404.

Coover, V., Deacon, E., Esser, C. and Moore, C. (1985). *Resource manual for a living revolution*. New Society Publishers.

Costongs, C. and Springett, J. (1997). Joint working and the production of a City Health Plan: the Liverpool experience. *Health Promotion International*, **12**(1) : 9−19.

Cropper, S. and Huxham, C. (1994). From many to one and back. *OMEGA*, **22**(1) : 1−11.

Cullen, J. (1998). The needle and the damage done: research, action research, and the organizational and social construction of health in the 'Information society'. *Human Relations*, **51**(12) : 1543−1564.

Cummings, E. (1994). Celebrating change and achievement. *Communicare*, **2** : 6, Social Services Inspectorate/NHS Management Executive.

Dando, M. and Bennett, P. (1981). A Kuhnian crisis in management science? *Journal of the Operational Research Society*, **32** : 91−103.

Davies, M., Stankov, L. and Roberts, R.D. (1998). Emotional intelligence: in search of an elusive construct. *Journal of Personality and Social Psychology*, **75**(4) : 989−1015.

De Geus, A. (1988). Planning as learning. *Harvard Business Review*, March−April: 70−74.

Delbecq, A.L., van de Ven, A.H. and Gustafson, D.H. (1975). *Group techniques for program planning: a guide to nominal group and Delphi processes*. Scott Foresman, Glenview, Ill.

Deleuze, G. and Guattari, F. (1980). *A thousand plateaus: capitalism and schizophrenia*. Tr. B. Massumi, Athlone, London, 1988.

Deleuze, G. and Guattari, F. (1984). *Anti-Oedipus: capitalism and schizophrenia*. Tr. R. Hurley, M. Steem and H.R. Lane, Athlone, London.

De Reuck, J., Schmidenberg, O. and Klass, D. (1999). A reconceptualisation of decision conferencing: towards a command methodology. *International Journal of Technology Management*, **17**(1−2) : 195−207.

DiMaggio, P. and Powell, W. (1983). The iron cage revisited. *American Sociological Review*, **48**(2) : 147−160.

Drucker, P.F. (1993). *Managing for the future*. Butterworth-Heinemann, Oxford.

Duncan, S. and Edwards, R. (eds) (1997). *Single mothers in an international context: mothers or workers?* UCL, London.

Duncan, S. and Edwards, R. (1999). *Lone mothers, paid work and gendered moral rationalities*. Basingstoke, Macmillan.

Easterby-Smith, M. and Malina, D. (1999). Cross-cultural collaborative research: toward reflexivity. *Academy of Management Journal*, **42**(1).

Eco, U. (1984). *The name of the rose*. Picador, London.

Eden, C. (1979). Images into models, *Futures*, 11.

Eden, C. (1986). Problem solving or problem finishing. In Jackson, M.C. and Keys, P. (eds), *New directions in management science*. Gower, Aldershot.

Eden, C. (1989). Using cognitive mapping for strategic options development and analysis. In: Rosenhead, J. (ed.), *Rational analysis of problematic world*. Wiley, Chichester.

Eden, C. (1990). The unfolding nature of group decision support — two dimensions of skill. In: Eden, C. and Radford, J. (eds), Tackling strategic problems: the role of group decision support. Sage, London, pp. 48–52.

Eden, C. and Ackermann, F. (1998). *Making strategy: the journey of strategic management*. Sage, London.

Eden, C., Jones, S. and Sims, D. (1979). *Thinking in organisations*. Sage, London.

Eden, C., Jones, S. and Sims, D. (1983). *Messing about in problems*. Pergamon, Oxford.

Eden, C. and Radford, J. (1990). *Tackling strategic problems: the role of group decision support*. Sage, London.

Effken, J.A. and Stetler, C.B. (1997). Impact of organizational redesign. *Journal of Nursing Administration*, **27**(7–8) : 23–32.

Elder, M.D. (1991). Visual interactive modelling. In: Mumford, A.G. and Bailey, T.C. (eds), *Operational research tutorial papers 1991*, Operational Research Society, Birmingham.

Elg, U. and Johansson, U. (1997). Decision making in inter-firm networks as a political process. *Organization Studies*, **18**(3) : 361–384.

Emergy, F. (1969). *Systems thinking*. Penguin, Hermondsworth

Emery, F. and Trist, E. (1965). The causal texture of organisational environments. *Human Relations*, **4** : 21–32.

Emery, F. and Trist, E. (1973). *Towards a social ecology*. Plenum, New York.

Emery, F. and Emery, M. (1989). Participative design: work and community life. In: Emery, M. (ed.), *Participative design for participative democracy*. Centre for Continuing Education, Australian National University, pp. 94–113.

Emery, M. (1993). *Participative design for participative democracy*. ANU, Centre for Continuous Education, Canberra, Australia.

Ernst, S. and Goodison, L. (1981). *In our own hands*. The Women's Press, London.

Fargason, C.A., Barnes, D., Schneider, D. and Galloway, B.W. (1994). Enhancing multiagency collaboration in the management of child sexual abuse. *Child Abuse and Neglect*, **18**(10) : 859–869.

Feighery, E. and Rodgers, T. (1992). *Building and maintaining effective coalitions*. How to Guides in Community Health Promotion No. 12. Stanford Health Promotion Resource Center, Palo Alto, Calif.

Fisher, R. and Ury, W. (1981). *Getting to yes*. Hutchinson, London.

Flax, J. (1987). Postmodernism and gender relations in feminist theory. In: Nicholson, L.J. (ed.), *Feminism/postmodernism*. Routledge, New York, pp. 39–62.

Flood, R.L. (1995). *Solving problem solving*. Wiley, Chichester.

Flood, R.L. (1996). *Total systems intervention: local systemic intervention*. Research Memorandum No. 13. Centre for Systems Studies, University of Hull.

Flood, R.L. and Jackson, M.C. (1991). *Creative problem solving: total systems intervention*. Wiley, Chichester.

Flood, R.L. and Romm, N.R.A. (1996). *Diversity management: triple loop learning*. Wiley, Chichester.

Floyer-Acland, A. (1992). *Consensus building*. The Environment Council.

Ford-Smith, H. (1986). Sistren: exploring women's problems through drama. *Jamaica Journal*, **19**(1).

Foster-Fishman, P.G., Salem, D.A., Chibnall, S., Legler, R. and Yapchai, C. (1998). Empirical support for the critical assumptions of empowerment theory. *American Journal of Community Psychology*, **26**(4): 507–536.

Foucault, M. (1976). *The history of sexuality*. Volume 1: *An introduction*. Tr. R. Hurley. Penguin, London.

Foucault, M. (1982). The subject and power. In: Dreyfus, H.L. and Rabinow, P. (eds), *Michel Foucault: beyond structuralism and hermeneutics*. Harvester, Brighton, pp. 208–226.

Fox, J. (1987). *The essential Moreno: writings on psychodrama, group method and spontaneity*. Springer.

Freire, P. (1972). *Pedagogy of the oppressed*. Sheed and Ward, London.

French, J.R.P. and Raven, B. (1968). The bases of social power. In: Cartwright, D. and Zander, A. (eds), *Group dynamics: research and theory*, 3rd edn. Harper & Row, New York, pp. 259–269.

Friedman, M. and Friedman, R. (1985). *The tyranny of the status quo*, Penguin, London.

Friend, J. (1990). Handling organisational complexity in group decision support. In: Eden, C. and Radford, J. (eds), *Tackling strategic problems*. Sage, London, pp. 18–28.

Friend, J. (1993). Searching for appropriate theory and practice in multiorganisational fields. *Journal of the Operational Research Society*, **44**(6): 585–598.

Friend, J. and Hickling, A. (1987). *Planning under pressure: the strategic choice approach*. Pergamon, Oxford.

Friend, J. and Hickling, A. (1997). *Planning under pressure: the strategic choice approach*, 2nd edn. Butterworth-Heinemann, Oxford.

Friend, J.K. and Jessop, W.N. (1969). *Local government and strategic choice: an operational research approach to the processes of public planning*. Tavistock Publications, London. Second edition published in 1977 by Pergamon, Oxford.

Fuglesang, A. (1982). *About understanding*. Dag Hammarskjold Foundation, Uppsala.

Gibbon, M. (1999). Meetings with meaning. Unpublished Ph.D. thesis, South Bank University, London.

Giddens, A. (1990). *The consequences of modernity*. Stanford University Press, Stanford.

Giddens, A. (1994). *Beyond left and right: the future of radical politics*. Polity, London.

Gleick, J. (1987). *Chaos*. Abacus, London.

Goble, J. (1990). Didactic psychodrama and sociodrama. *Nurse Education Today*. Dec., **10**(6): 457–463.

Goleman, D. (1995). *Emotional intelligence*. Bantam Books, New York.

Gordon, C. (1980). *Power/Knowledge*. Pantheon Books, New York.

Graetz, F. (1996). Leading strategic change at Ericsson. *Long Range Planning*, **29**(3): 304–313.

Graver, L.D. (2000). The evaluation of the local multidisciplinary facilitation teams in primary health care, in Liverpool. Unpublished PhD thesis, Liverpool, John Moores University.

Gray, B. (1985). Conditions facilitating interorganizational collaboration. *Human Relations*, **38**(10): 911–936.

Gray, B. (1989). *Collaborating: finding common ground for multiparty problems*. Jossey-Bass, San Francisco.

Gray, B. (1996). Cross-sectoral partners: collaborative alliances among business, government and communities. In: Huxham, C. (ed.), *Creating collaborative advantage*. Sage, London, pp. 57–79.

Gregory, W. (1999). OR practitioners as facilitators – a health case study. Paper given at the AGM of the Operational Research Society Health and Social Services Study Group, March 1999.

Gregory, W. and Romm, N. (1994). Developing multi-agency dialogue: the role(s) of facilitation. Working Paper No. 6, Centre for Systems Studies, University of Hull.

Gregory, W. and Romm, N. (forthcoming). *Critical facilitation: learning through intervention in group processes: Management Learning*.

Griffiths, V. (1984). Feminist research and the use of drama. *Women's Studies International Forum*, **7**(6): 511–519.

Gronstedt, A. (1996). Integrated communications at America's leading total quality management coroporations. *Public Relations Review*, **22**(1): 25–42.

Guba, E.G. and Lincoln, Y.S. (1989). *Fourth generation evaluation*. Sage, Newbury Park.

Habermas, J. (1985). *Theory of communicative action*. Translated by T. McCarthy. Beacon Press, Boston.

Hacking, I. (1983). *Representing and intervening: introductory topics in the philosophy of natural science.* Cambridge University Press, Massachusetts.

Hackman, J.R. (1990). *Groups that work (and those that don't).* Jossey-Bass, San Francisco.

Hall, S. and Jacques, M. (1990). *The changing face of politics in the 1990s.* Lawrence & Wishart, London.

Handy, C. (1988). *Understanding voluntary organisations.* Penguin, London.

Handyside, T. and Light, J. (1998). An experiment in organization for innovation. *International Journal of Technology Management,* 15(1–2) : 160–172.

Haraway, D.J. (1991). *Simians, cyborgs and women: the reinvention of nature.* Free Association Books, London.

Harden, I. (1992). *The contracting state.* Open University Press, Buckingham.

Hardy, C. (1996). Understanding power: bringing about strategic change. *British Journal of Management,* 7 : S3–S16.

Harrington, B., McLoughlin, K. and Riddell, D. (1998). Business process re-engineering in the public sector: a case study of the Contributions Agency. *New Technology, Work and Employment,* 13(1) : 43–50.

Harvey, D. (1989) *The condition of postmodernity.* Blackwell, Oxford.

Hassard, J. (1993). Postmodernism and organizational analysis: an overview. In: Hassard, J. and Parker, M., (eds), *Postmodernism and organizations.* Sage, London, pp. 1–23.

Hatch, M.J. (1997). *Organization theory: modern, symbolic and postmodern perspectives.* Oxford University Press, Oxford.

Hayek, F. (1952). *The counter revolution of science.* Liberty Press, Indianapolis.

Heller, F., Pusic, E., Strauss, G. and Wilpert, B. (1998). *Organizational participation: myth and reality.* Oxford University Press, Oxford.

Heracleous, L. and Langham, B. (1996). Strategic change and organizational culture at Hay Management Consultants. *Long Range Planning,* 29(4) : 485–494.

Heron, J. (1996). *Co-operative inquiry: research into the human condition.* Sage, London.

Hickling, A. (1990). Decision spaces: a scenario about designing appropriate rooms for group decision management. In: Eden, C. and Radford, J. (eds), *Tackling group problems: the role of group decision support.* Sage, London, pp. 169–177.

Higgins, R., Oldman, C., and Hunter, D. (1994). Working together: lessons for collaboration between health and social services. *Health & Social Care in the Community,* 2 : 269–277.

Hodgson, T. (1992). Hexegons for systems thinking. *European Journal of OR,* 59(1) : 220–230.

Hoggett, P. (1990). *Modernisation, political strategy and the welfare state: an organisational perspective.* Studies in Decentralisation and Quasi-Markets No. 2. SAUS publications, Bristol.

Hooks, B. (1990). Postmodern blackness. *Postmodern Culture,* 1(1).

Huff, A.S. (1990). *Mapping strategic thought.* Wiley, Chichester.

Huxham, C. (1991). Facilitating collaboration: issues in multi-organisational group decision support in voluntary, informal collaborative settings. *Journal of the Operational Research Society,* 42 : 1037–1045.

Huxham, C. (1993). Pursuing collaborative advantage. *Journal of the Operational Research Society,* 44(6) : 599–611.

Huxham, C. (1996). The search for collaborative advantage. In: Huxham, C. (ed.), *Creating collaborative advantage,* Sage, London, pp. 176–180.

Huy, N.Q. (1999). Emotional capability, emotional intelligence, and radical change. *The Academy of Management Review,* 24(2) : 325–345.

Jackins, H. (1968). *The human side of human beings.* Rational Island Publishers, Seattle.

Jackson, M.C. (1987). Preset positions and future prospects in management science. *Omega,* 15 : 455–466.

Jackson, M.C. (1990). Beyond a system of systems methodologies. *Journal of the Operational Research Society,* 41(8) : 657–668.

Jackson, M.C. (1993). Social theory and operational research practice. *Journal of the Operational Research Society,* 44 : 563–577.

Jackson, M.C. and Keys, P. (1984). Towards a system of systems methodologies. *Journal of the Operational Research Society,* 33 : 473–486.

Jacques, R. (1989). Post-industrialism, postmodernity and OR: toward a 'custom and practice' of responsibility and possibility. In: Jackson, M.C., Keys, P. and Cropper, S.A. (eds), *Operational Research and the Social Sciences*, Plenum, New York, pp. 703–708.

Jameson, F. (1984). The cultured logic of capital. *New Left Review*, July/August, 146.

Janis, I.L. (1972). *Victims of groupthink*. Houghton Mifflin, Boston.

Johnson, H. and Mayoux, L. (1998). Investigation as empowerment: using participatory methods. In: Thomas, A., Chataway, J. and Wuyts, M. (eds), *Finding out fast: investigative skills for policy and development*. Sage, in association with the Open University, London, pp. 147–171.

Johnson-Laird, P.N. (1987). *Mental models*. Cambridge University Press, Cambridge.

Judge, A. (1993). *Traps and opportunities of dialogue*. Union of International Associations, http://www.uia.org/uiadocs/confran/xsptrap3.htm

Judge, A. (1994). *Time-sharing in meetings: centralized planning versus free-market economy?* Union of International Associations, http://www.uia.org/uiadocs/time.htm

Kahn, K. and Katz, J. (1966). *The social psychology of organisations*. Wiley, Chichester.

Kanter, R.B. (1994). Collaborative advantage: the art of alliances. *Harvard Business Review*, July–August : 96–108.

Kanter, R.M. and Corn, R.I. (1994). Do cultural differences make a business difference? *Journal of Management Development*, **13** : 5–23.

Kelly, G.A. (1958). *The psychology of personal constructs: a theory of personality*. Norton, New York.

Kelly, K.J. and van Vlaenderen, H. (1996). Dynamics of participation in a community health project. *Social Science and Medicine*, **42**(9) : 1235–1246.

Keys, P. (1994). *Studies in the process of operational research*. Wiley, London.

Kickert, W.J.M., Klijn, E-H. and Koppenjan, J.F.M. (1997). *Managing complex networks: strategies for the public sector*. Sage, London.

Kohlberg, L. (1981). *The philosophy of moral development*. Harper & Row, San Francisco.

Kuhn, T.S. (1970). *The structure of scientific revolutions*, 2nd edn. University of Chicago Press, Chicago.

Lang, C.L. (1982). The resolution of status and ideological conflicts in a community mental health setting. *Psychiatry*, **45** : 159–171.

Lash, S. and Urry, J. (1987). *The end of organised capitalism*. Polity, Cambridge.

Latour, B. and Woolgar, S. (1979). *Laboratory life: the social construction of scientific facts*. Sage, Beverly Hills, Calif.

Lawrence, J. (ed.) (1966). *OR and the social sciences*. Tavistock, London.

Leathard, A. (1994). *Going inter-professional: working together for health and welfare*. Routledge, London.

Ledford, G.E. and Mohrman, S.A. (1993). Self-design for high involvement: a large scale organisational change. *Human Relations*, **46**(1) : 143–173.

Levenson, R. et al. (1999). Multidisciplinary and inter agency work in public health. In: Griffiths, S. and Hunter, D. (eds), *Perspectives in public health*. Radcliffe Medical Press, Oxford.

Lewin, K. (1947). Frontiers in group dynamics. *Human Relations*, **1** : 5–41.

Lewis, H.R. and Streitfield, H.S. (1972). *Growth games*. Souvenir Press, London.

Linney, B. (1994). Pictures, people and power. *Learning for Health* No. 4, Liverpool School of Tropical Medicine, pp. 3–7.

Lober, D.J. (1997). Explaining the formation of business–environmentalist collaborations: collaborative windows and the Paper Task Force. *Policy Sciences*, **30** : 1–24.

Loveman, G. and Sengenberger, W. (1991). The re-emergence of small-scale production: an international comparison. *Small Business Economics*, **1** : 1–38.

Luhmann, N. (1995). The control of intransparency. Plenary address, ISSS conference, July 1995, Amsterdam.

Lukes, S. (1974). *Power. A radical view*. Macmillan, New York.

Lyotard, (1984). *The postmodern condition: a report on knowledge*. Manchester University Press, Manchester.

Macdonald, S. (1995). Learning to change. *Organization Science*, **6**(5) : 557–568.

Maclagan, P. (1998). *Management and morality*. Sage, London.

Mason, R.O. and Mitroff, I.I. (1981). *Challenging strategic planning assumptions*, Wiley, New York.

Mayer, J.D. and Salovey, P. (1997). What is emotional intelligence? In: Salovey, P. and Slayter, D.J. (eds), *Emotional development and emotional intelligence: implications for educators*. Basic Books, New York, pp. 3–31.

Mead, G.H. (1934). *Mind, self and society*. University of Chicago Press, Chicago.

Meyer, A. (1991). Visual data in organisational research. *Organisation Science*, **2**(2): 218–236.

Miller, G. (1956). The magic number 7 ± 2. *Psychological Review*, **63**: 81–96.

Miller, H., Rynders, J.E. and Schleien, S.J. (1993). Drama: a medium to enhance social interaction between students with and without mental retardation. *Mental Retardation*, **31**(4): 228–233.

Mingers, J. (1997). Towards critical pluralism. In: Mingers, J. and Gill, A. (eds), *Multimethodology*. Wiley, Chichester, pp. 407–440.

Mingers, J. and Gill, A. (eds) (1997). *Multimethodology*. Wiley, Chichester.

Moran-Ellis, J. and Fielding, N. (1996). A national survey of the investigation of child sexual abuse. *British Journal of Social Work*, **26**(3): 337–356.

Morecroft, J. (1988). System dynamics and microworlds for policymakers. *European Journal of Operational Research*, **35**(3): 301–329.

Morecroft, J. (1994). Executive knowledge models and learning. In: Morecroft, J. and Sterman, J. (eds), *Modeling for learning organisations*. Productivity Press, Portland.

Morecroft, J. and Sterman, J. (eds) (1994). *Modeling for learning organisations*. Productivity Press, Portland.

Nicholson, M. (1970). *Conflict analysis*. University of Liverpool, Liverpool Press.

Nietzsche, F. (1986). *Human, all too human*. Cambridge University Press, Cambridge.

Nonaka, I. and Takeuchi, H. (1995). *The knowledge-creating company: how Japanese companies create the dynamics of innovation*. Oxford University Press, New York.

Offner, A.K., Kramer, T.J. and Winter, J.P. (1996). The effects of facilitation, recording and group brainstorming. *Small Group Research*, **27**(2): 283–298.

Oliga, C. (1996). *Power, ideology and control*. Plenum, New York.

O'Neill, M., Lemieux, V., Groleau, G., Fortin, J.P. and Lamarche, P.A. (1997). Coalition theory as a framework for understanding and implementing intersectoral health-related interventions. *Health Promotion International*, **12**(1): 79–87.

Onyett, S., Standen, R. and Peck, E. (1997). The challenge of managing community mental health teams. *Health & Social Care in the Community*, **5**(1): 40–47.

Opie, A. (1997). Teams as author: narrative and knowledge creation in case discussions in multidisciplinary health teams. *Sociological Research Online*, **2**(3).

Osborne, D. and Gaebler, T. (1992). *Reinventing government*. Addison, Wesley, Reading, Mass.

Owen, H. (1992). *Open space technology: a user's guide*. Abbott, Potomac, Md.

Paelinck, J. and van Gastel, M. (1992). Generalization of solution concepts in conflict and negotiation analysis. *Theory and Decision*, **32**(1): 65.

Pahl, R.E. (1988). *On work*. Blackwell, Oxford.

Papert, S. (1980). *Mindstorm*. Basic Books, New York.

Parston, G. (1994). Brave new word. *Health Service Journal*, **104**(5385): 19.

Personal Counselors Inc. (1970). *Fundamentals of co-counseling manual*. Rational Island Publishers, Seattle.

Pettigrew, T. (1971). *Racially separate or together*. McGraw Hill, London.

Phillips, L.D. (1984). A theory of requisite decision models. *Acta Psychologica*, **56**: 29–48.

Phillips, L.D. (1988). People-centred group decision support. In: Doukidis, G.I., Land, F. and Miller, G. (eds), *Knowledge-based management support systems*. Ellis Horwood Ltd, Chichester, pp. 205–224.

Phillips, L.D. (1989). Decision analysis in the 1990s. In: Shahani, A. and Stainton, R. (eds), *Tutorial papers in operational research 1989*. Operational Research Society, Birmingham.

Phillips, L.D. and Phillips, M.C. (1993). Facilitated work groups: theory and practice. *Journal of the Operational Research Society*, **44**(6): 533–549.

Pidd, M. (1984). *Computer simulation in management science*. Wiley, Chichester.

Pidd, M. and Woolley, R. (1980). A pilot study of problem structuring. *Journal of the Operational Research Society*, **31**: 1063–1068.

Pindar, S. (1994). Planning a network response to racial harassment. In: Ritchie, C., Taket, A.R. and Bryant, J. (eds), *Community works*. Pavic, Sheffield, pp. 167–172.

Piore, M.J. and Sabel, C.F. (1984). *The second industrial divide*. Basic Books, New York.

Pizey, H. and Huxham, C. (1991). 1990 and beyond: developing a process for group decision support in large scale event planning. *European Journal of Operational Research,* **55**(3): 409–422.

Powell, W. (1990). Neither market nor hierarchy – network forms of organisation. *Research in Organizational Behavior,* **12**: 295–336.

Pruzan, P. (1991). *Planning with multiple criteria: investigation, communication, choice*. Elsevier, Amsterdam.

Prystupa, M.V. (1998). Barriers and strategies to the development of co-management regimes in New Zealand: the case of Te Waihora. *Human Organization,* **57**(2): 134–144.

Rapley, K. (1993). Operational research is alive and well. *Journal of the Operational Research Society,* **44**: 634.

Reed, M. (1992). Introduction. In: Reed, M. and Hughes, M. (eds), *Rethinking organizations: new directions in organizational theory and analysis*. Sage, London, pp. 1–16.

Reed, M. and Hughes, M. (eds) (1992). *Rethinking organization: new directions in organizational theory and analysis*. Sage, London.

Reger, R., Gustafson, L., DeMarie, S. and Mullane, J. (1994). Reframing the organization: why implementing total quality is easier said than done. *Academy of Management Review,* **19**: 565–584.

Revans, R.W. (1982). *The origins and growth of action learning*. Chartwell Bratt, Bromley.

Riseborough, R. (1993). The use of drama in health education. *Nursing Standard,* Jan. 6–12; **7**(15–16): 30–2.

Ritchie, C. (1994). Community OR – five years of organised activities and beyond. *International Transaction of Operational Research,* **1**: 41–49.

Ritchie, C. Taket, A.R. and Bryant, J. (eds) (1994). *Community works: how community operational research can help community organisations*. Community Operational Research Unit/Operational Research Society, Barnsley/Birmingham.

Rorty, R. (1989). *Contingency, irony and solidarity*. Cambridge University Press, Cambridge.

Rosenau, P.M. (1992). *Postmodernism and the social sciences*. Princeton University Press, Princeton, NJ.

Rosenhead, J. (1986). Custom and practice. *Journal of the Operational Research Society,* **37**: 335–345.

Rosenhead, J. (ed.) (1989). *Rational analysis for a problematic world*. Wiley, Chichester.

Rosenhead, J. and White, L.A. (1994). Conflict resolution at Nucleus. In: Ritchie, C., Taket, A.R. and Bryant, J. (eds), *Community Works*. Pavic, Sheffield, pp. 39–42.

Rosenhead, J. and White, L. (1996). Nuclear fusion: some linked care studies in community operational research. *Journal of the Operational Research Society,* **47**(4): 479–489.

Ross, F. and Tissier, J. (1997). The care management interface with general practice: a case study. *Health & Social Care in the Community,* **5**(3): 153–161.

Russell, C. and Peters, G. (1998). Chaos has no plural – trying out a holistic approach to organizational learning. *Systems Research and Behavioral Science,* **15**(3): 235–248.

Saan, H. (1990). A checklist to assist the planning of intersectoral action. In: Taket, A.R. (ed.), *Making partners: intersectoral action for health*. World Health Organisation/Ministry for Welfare, Health and Cultural Affairs, The Netherlands, pp. 91–104.

Safer, L.A. and Harding, C.G. (1993). Under pressure program: using live theatre to investigate adolescents' attitudes and behavior related to drug and alcohol abuse education and prevention. *Adolescence,* **28**(109): 135–148.

Salovey, P. and Mayer, J.D. (1990). Emotional intelligence. *Imagination, Cognition and Personality,* **9**(3): 185–211.

Salovey, P. and Sluyter, D.J. (1997). *Emotional development and emotional intelligence: implications for educators*. Basic Books, New York.

Sawicki, J. (1991). *Disciplining Foucault: feminism, power and the body*. Routledge, New York.

Sayer, K. (1998). Denying the technology: middle management resistance in business process re-engineering. *Journal of Information Technology,* **13**(4): 247–257.

Schein, E.H. (1992). *Organizational culture and leadership,* 2nd edn. Jossey-Bass, San Francisco.

Schön, D. (1987). *Educating the reflective practitioner,* Jossey-Bass, San Francisco.

Scott, J. (1991). *Social network analysis,* Sage, London.

Senge, P.M. (1990). *The fifth discipline: the art and practice of the learning organisation*. Random House, Sydney.

Senge, P. and Sterman, J.D. (1992). Systems thinking and organisational learning. *European Journal of Operational Research*, **59**(1) : 137–150.

Shange, N. (1992). The love space demands – an interview. *Spare Rib*, **238** : 17–19.

Shotter, J. (1993). *Conversational realities: constructing life through language*. Sage, London.

Silva, E.B. and Smart, C. (eds) (1999). *The new family?* Sage, London.

Simon, H. (1976). *Administrative behaviour*. Free Press, New York.

Sistren, with Ford-Smith, H. (1986). *Lionheart Gal: life stories of Jamaican women*. The Women's Press, London.

Smith, G. and White, L. (1996). Making the connection. *Proceedings of the 'Researching the UK Voluntary Sector' Conference*, NCVO, Birmingham, Sept.

Stacey, R. (1993). *Strategic thinking and the management of change*. Kogan Page, London.

Starhawk (Simos, M.) (1982). *Dreaming the dark: magic, sex and politics*. Beacon Press, Boston.

Stasser, G. *et al.* (1989). Influence processes and consensus models in decision-making groups. In: Paulus, P. (ed.), *Psychology of group influence*, 2nd edn. Erlbaum, Hillsdale, NJ.

Stein, S.L. *et al.* (1992). A study of multiagency collaborative strategies: did juvenile deliquents change? *Journal of Community Psychology*. OSAP special issues: 88–105.

Sternberg, P. and Garcia, A. (1989). *Sociodrama: who's in your shoes?* Praeger, New York.

Stewart, J. (1998). Advance or retreat: from the traditions of public administration to the new public management and beyond. *Public Policy and Administration*, **13** : 12–27.

Strauss, G. (1998). Participation works – if the conditions are appropriate. In: Heller, F., Pusic, E., Strauss, G. and Wilpert, B. (eds), *Organizational participation: myth and reality*. Oxford University Press, Oxford, pp. 190–219.

Swan, J. (1997). Using cognitive mapping in management research: decisions about technical innovation. *British Journal of Management*, **8** : 183–198.

Taket, A.R. (ed.) (1990). *Making partners: intersectoral action for health*. World Health Organisation/ Ministry for Welfare, Health and Cultural Affairs, The Netherlands.

Taket, A.R. (1992). Review of: *Creative problem solving: total systems intervention* by R.L. Flood and M.C. Jackson (Wiley, Chichester, 1991). *Journal of Operational Research Society*, **43**(10) : 1013–1016.

Taket, A.R. (1993) Mixing and matching: OR and innovatory health promotion projects. *OR Insight*, **6**(4) : 18–23.

Taket, A.R. (1994a). Undercover agency? – ethics, responsibility and the practice of OR. *Journal of the Operational Research Society*, **45**(2) : 123–132.

Taket, A.R. (1994b). Starting from where I was working in a feminist collective. In: Ritchie, C., Taket, A.R. and Bryant J. (eds), *Community works*. Pavic, Sheffield, pp. 47–51.

Taket, A.R. (1997). Creating the future: responding to diversity with diversity. In: Bush, R. and Macdonald, J.J. (eds), *Designing the future . . . strategic directions for primary health care in economically advanced countries*. (in press).

Taket, A.R. (1998a). Review of: *Diversity management: triple loop learning*, R.L. Flood and N.R.A. Romm (Wiley, Chichester, 1996). *Journal of the Operational Research Society*, **49**(3) : 293–296.

Taket, A.R. (1998b). Designing future primary health care systems – research into the role of partnerships – what have we learnt? Proceedings of the fourth FICOSSER (Federation for International Cooperation of Health Services and Systems Research Centres) General Conference, Cuernavaca, Morelos, Mexico, 28–30 July 1998. National Institute of Public Health, Mexico. Health Education Authority, London (in press).

Taket, A.R. (1999). Review of: *Information, systems and information systems: making sense of the field*, Peter Checkland and Sue Holwell (Wiley, Chichester, 1998). *Journal of the Operational Research Society*, **50**(5) : 554–557.

Taket, A.R. (forthcoming). Institutional development and capacity building in Pakistan. In: Friend, J., Taket, A. and White, L. (eds), *Entangled or empowered? Applying participatory decision support tools in international development*. Intermediate Technology Press, London.

Taket, A.R. and White, L.A. (1993). After OR: an agenda for postmodernism and poststructuralism in OR. *Journal of the Operational Research Society*, **44**(9) : 867–881.

Taket, A.R. and White, L.A. (1994). Doing community operational research with multicultural groups. *Omega: International Journal of Management Science*, **22**(6) : 579–588.

Taket, A.R. and White, L.A. (1996a). Pragmatic pluralism – an explication. *Systems Practice*, **9**(6): 571–586.

Taket, A.R. and White, L.A. (1996b). Creating common cause. In: Gregor, S. and Oliver, D. (eds), *Proceedings Processes of Community Change: A Colloquium Inspired by Professor John D. Smith*, October 1996, Central Queensland University Publishing Unit, Rockhampton, 1997, pp. 17–36.

Taket, A.R. and White, L.A. (1997) Wanted: dead OR alive – ways of using problem-structuring methods in community OR. *International Transactions in Operational Research*, **4**(2): 99–108.

Taket, A.R. and White, L.A. (1998). Experience in the practice of one tradition of multimethodology. *Systemic Practice and Action Research*, **11**(2): 153–168.

Taket, A.R. and White, L.A. (1999). Strengthening health service research capacity. *International Transactions in Operational Research* (forthcoming).

Thomas, A. Chataway, J. and Wuyts, M. (eds) (1998). *Finding out fast: investigative skills for policy and development*. Sage, in association with the Open University, London.

Toffler, A. (1980). *The third wave*. Collins, London.

Tuckman, B.W. (1965). Developmental sequences in small groups. *Psychological Bulletin*, **63**: 384–399.

Tuckman, B.W. and Jensen, M.A.C. (1972). Stages of small group development revisited. *Group and Organisational Studies*, **2**: 419–427.

Ulrich, W. (1983). *Critical heuristics of social planning*. Haupt, Berne.

Ulrich, W. (1987). Critical heuristics of social system design. *European Journal of Operational Research*, **31**: 276–283.

Union of International Associations (1993). *Towards a new order of meeting participation*. Union of International Associations, http://www.uia.org/uiadocs/contract.htm#reminder

Vaandrager, H.W. and Koelen, M.A. (1997). Consumer involvement in nutritional issues: the role of information. *American Journal of Clinical Nutrition*, **65**(6 Suppl.): 1980S–1984S.

Van der Vorm, J. (1990). Intersectoral action: the case of accidents. In: Taket, A.R. (ed.), *Making partners: intersectoral action for health*. World Health Organisation/Ministry for Welfare, Health and Cultural Affairs, The Netherlands, pp. 39–53.

Vennix, J.A.M. (1995). Building consensus in strategic decision-making. Systems dynamics as a group support system. *Group Decision and Negotiation*, **4**(4): 335–355.

Vennix, J.A.M. (1996). *Group model-building*. Kluwer Academic Publishers, London.

Vennix, J.A.M., Akkermans, H.A. and Rouwette, E.A.J.A. (1996). Group model-building to facilitate organizational change: an exploratory study. *System Dynamics Review*, **12**(1): 39–58.

Vickers, G. (1965). *The art of judgement*. Chapman & Hall, London.

Vince, R. and Broussine, M. (1996). Paradox, defense and attachment: accessing and working with emotions and relations underlying organizational change. *Organization Studies*, **17**(1): 1–21.

Wack, P. (1985). Scenarios: gentle art of re-perceiving, *Harvard Business Review*. September–October: 72–89.

Waldrop, M.M. (1992). *Complexity: the emerging science at the edge of order and chaos*. Simon & Schuster, New York.

Walsh, J.P. (1995). Managerial and organizational cognition: notes from a trip down memory lane. *Organization Science*, **6**: 280–321.

Walsh, K. (1991). *Competitive tendering for local authority services: initial experiences*. HMSO, London.

Walsh, K., Deakin, N., Smith, P., Spurgeon, P. and Thomas, N. (1997). *Contracting for change: contracts in health, social care and other local government services*. Oxford University Press, Oxford.

Wang, C.C., Yi, W.K., Tao, Z.W. and Carovano, K. (1998). Photovoice as a participatory health promotion strategy. *Health Promotion International*, **13**(1): 75–86.

Warihay, F.D. (1992). Are good facilitators born or can they be developed? *Journal for Quality and Participation*, January/February: 60–63.

Weeks, J. (1999). Families of choice: autonomy and mutuality in non-heterosexual relationships. In: McRae, S. (ed), *Changing Britain*. Oxford University Press, Oxford.

Weick, K. and Westley, F. (1996). Organizational learning: affirming an oxymoron. In: Clegg, S.R., Hardy, C. and Nord, W. (eds), *Handbook of organization studies*. Sage, London, pp. 440–458.

Weisinger, H. (1998). *Emotional intelligence at work*. Jossey Bass, San Francisco.

West, M.A. (1997). *Developing creativity in organisations*. BPS Books, Leicester.

Westen, D. (1985). *Self and society: narcissism, collectivism and the development of morals.* Cambridge University Press, Cambridge, Mass.

White, L.A. (1994a). Development options for a rural community in Belize. *International Transactions for Operational Research,* **1**(4) : 453–462.

White, L.A. (1994b). Enabling the Migrant Resource Centre to make their own decisions. In: Ritchie, C., Taken, A.R. and Bryant J. (eds), *Community works.* Pavic, Sheffield, pp. 52–56.

White, L.A. (1997). Tinker, tailor, soldier sailor, a syntegrity to explore London's diverse needs. *OR Insight,* **11**(3) : 12–17.

White, L.A. (1999). Changing the 'whole system'. *International Journal of Organisational Change* (forthcoming).

White, L. A. and Taket, A.R. (1993). Community OR – doing what feels good. *OR Insight,* **6**(2) : 20–23.

White, L.A. and Taket, A.R. (1994a). The death of the expert. *Journal of the Operational Research Society,* **45**(7) : 733–748.

White, L.A. and Taket, A.R. (1994b). Facilitating an organisational review. In: Ritchie, C, Taket, A.R. and Bryant, J. (eds). *Community works.* Pavic, Sheffield, pp. 32–38.

White, L.A. and Taket, A.R. (1995a). Changing faces: an investigation of guises for intervention. In: *Proceedings of the 39th Annual Meeting of the ISSS: Systems thinking, government policy and decision making,* Amsterdam, July, pp. 1088–1097.

White, L.A. and Taket, A.R. (1995b). Paradigm lost? Paper presented at Second International Workshop on multiorganisational partnerships: Working together across organisational boundaries, Strathclyde, Scotland, June, unpublished, available from authors.

White, L.A. and Taket, A.R. (1997a). Critiquing multimethodology as metamethodology: working towards pragmatic pluralism. In: Mingers, J. and Gill, A. (eds), *Multimethodology.* Wiley, London, pp. 379–405.

White, L.A. and Taket, A.R. (1997b). Beyond appraisal: participatory appraisal of needs and the development of action (PANDA). *Omega: International Journal of Management Science,* **25**(5) : 523–534.

Whiteley, A.M. and Garcia, J.E. (1996). The facilitator and the chauffeur in GSS: explorations in the forging of a relationship. *Group Decision and Negotiation,* **5**(1) : 31–50.

Whittington, R. (1992). Putting Giddens into action: social systems and managerial agency. *Journal of Management Studies,* **29**(6) : 693–712.

Whittington, R., McNulty, T. and Whipp, R. (1994). Market-driven change in professional services – problems and processes. *Journal of Management Studies,* **31**(6) : 829–845.

Whyte, W.F. (1991). Introduction. In: Whyte, W.F. (ed.), *Participatory Action Research.* Sage, London.

Willcocks, L.P. and Kern, T. (1998). IT outsourcing as strategic partnering: the case of the UK Inland Revenue. *European Journal of Information Systems,* **7** : 29–45.

Wilcox, D. (1994). *The guide to effective participation.* Joseph Rowntree Foundation/Partnership Books, Brighton.

Wilpert, B. (1998). A view from psychology. In: Heller, F., Pusic, E., Strauss, G. and Wilpert, B., *Organizational participation: myth and reality.* Oxford University Press, Oxford, pp. 40–64.

Wittgenstein, L. (1969). *Blue and brown books.* Blackwell, Oxford.

Wolstenholme, E.F. (1999). Qualitative vs quantitative modelling: the evolving balance. *Journal of the Operational Research Society,* **50**(4) : 422–428.

Yerbury, M. (1997). Issues in multidisciplinary teamwork for children with disabilities. *Child Care Health and Development,* **23**(1) : 77–86.

Young, K. (1996). Reinventing local government? Some evidence assessed. *Public Administration,* **74**(3) : 347–367.

Young, M. (1989). On the naming of the rose: interests and multiple meanings as elements in organisational culture. *Organisational Studies,* **10** : 187–206.

Zuboff, S. (1988). *In the age of the smart machine.* Basic Books, New York.

Index